PLOTINUS

ENNEAD IV.7

THE *ENNEADS* OF PLOTINUS

With Philosophical Commentaries

Series Editors: John M. Dillon, Trinity College, Dublin and Andrew Smith, University College, Dublin

Also Available in the Series:

Ennead I.6: *On Beauty* by Andrew Smith

Ennead II.5: *On What Is Potentially and What Actually* by Cinzia Arruzza

Ennead IV.3–4.29: *Problems Concerning the Soul* by John M. Dillon and H. J. Blumenthal

Ennead IV.4.30–45 & IV.5: *Problems Concerning the Soul* by Gary Gurtler

Ennead IV.8: *On the Descent of the Soul Into Bodies* by Barrie Fleet

Ennead V.1: *On the Three Primary Levels of Reality* by Eric D. Perl

Ennead V.5: *That the Intelligibles are not External to Intellect, and on the Good* by Lloyd P. Gerson

Ennead VI.4 & VI.5: *On the Presence of Being, One and the Same, Everywhere as a Whole* by Eyjólfur Emilsson and Steven Strange

Forthcoming Titles in the Series include:

Ennead I.1: *What Is the Living Being, and What Is Man?* by Gerard O'Daly

Ennead I.2: *On Virtues* by Suzanne Stern-Gillet

Ennead I.3: *On Dialectic* by Pauliina Remes

Ennead I.4: *On Well-Being* by Kieran McGroarty

Ennead II.4: *On Matter* by Anthony A. Long

Ennead II.9: *Against the Gnostics* by Sebastian Ramon Philipp Gertz

Ennead III.4: *On Our Allotted Guardian Spirit* by Wiebke-Marie Stock

Ennead III.5: *On Love* by Sara Magrin

Ennead III.7: *On Eternity and Time* by László Bene

Ennead III.8: *On Nature and Contemplation* by George Karamanolis

Ennead V.3: *On the Knowing Hypostases* by Marie-Élise Zovko

Ennead V.8: *On Intelligible Beauty* by Andrew Smith

Ennead V.9: *On Intellect, Ideas, and Being* by Matthias Vorwerk

Ennead VI.7: *The Forms and the Good* by Nicholas Banner

Ennead VI.8: *On Free Will and the Will of the One* by Kevin Corrigan and John D. Turner

Ennead VI.9: *On the Good or the One* by Stephen R. L. Clark

PLOTINUS
ENNEAD IV.7

On the Immortality of the Soul

Translation with an Introduction and Commentary

BARRIE FLEET

PARMENIDES
PUBLISHING

Las Vegas | Zurich | Athens

PARMENIDES PUBLISHING
Las Vegas | Zurich | Athens

This edition published in 2016 by Parmenides Publishing
in the United States of America

ISBN soft cover: 978–1–930972–95–7
ISBN e-Book: 978–1–930972–96–4

Library of Congress Cataloging-in-Publication Data

Names: Plotinus, author. | Fleet, Barrie, translator, commentator.
Title: Ennead IV.7 : on the immortality of the soul / Plotinus ; translation with an introduction and commentary, Barrie Fleet.
Other titles: Ennead. IV, 7. English | On the immortality of the soul
Description: First edition. | Las Vegas, Nevada : Parmenides Publishing, 2016. | Series: The Enneads of Plotinus with philosophical commentaries | Includes bibliographical references and index.
Identifiers: LCCN 2015045320 (print) | LCCN 2015051010 (ebook) | ISBN 9781930972957 (pbk. : alk. paper) | ISBN 9781930972964 (ebook)
Subjects: LCSH: Plotinus. Ennead. IV, 7. | Soul--Early works to 1800.
Classification: LCC B693.E52 E5 2016b (print) | LCC B693.E52 (ebook) | DDC 186/.4--dc23
LC record available at http://lccn.loc.gov/2015045320

Cover image "Soul Shards" © 2016 Arnold Hermann
and Light & Night Studios – www.lightandnight.com

Author photo by Jet Photographic, Cambridge, United Kingdom

Typeset in Warnock and Futura by Parmenides Publishing
Printed and lay-flat bound by Edwards Brothers Malloy
www.edwardsbrothersmalloy.com

www.parmenides.com

For my wife and daughters

Contents

Introduction to the Series With a Brief Outline of the Life and Thought of Plotinus (205–270 CE)

PLOTINUS WAS BORN IN 205 CE in Egypt of Greek-speaking parents. He attended the philosophical schools in Alexandria where he would have studied Plato (427–347 BCE), Aristotle (384–322 BCE), the Stoics and Epicureans as well as other Greek philosophical traditions. He began his serious philosophical education, however, relatively late in life, at the age of twenty-seven and was deeply impressed by the Platonist Ammonius Saccas about whom we, unfortunately, know very little, but with whom Plotinus studied for some eleven years. Even our knowledge of Plotinus' life is limited to what we can glean from Porphyry's introduction to his edition of his philosophical treatises, an account colored by Porphyry's own concerns. After completing his studies in Alexandria Plotinus attempted, by joining a military expedition of the Roman emperor Gordian III, to make contact with the

Brahmins in order to learn something of Indian thought. Unfortunately Gordian was defeated and killed (244). Plotinus somehow managed to extract himself and we next hear of him in Rome where he was able to set up a school of philosophy in the house of a high-ranking Roman lady by the name of Gemina. It is, perhaps, surprising that he had no formal contacts with the Platonic Academy in Athens, which was headed at the time by Longinus, but Longinus was familiar with his work, partly at least through Porphyry who had studied in Athens. The fact that it was Rome where Plotinus set up his school may be due to the originality of his philosophical activity and to his patrons. He clearly had some influential contacts, not least with the philhellenic emperor Gallienus (253–268), who may also have encouraged his later failed attempt to set up a civic community based on Platonic principles in a ruined city in Campania.

Plotinus' school was, like most ancient schools of philosophy, relatively small in scale, but did attract distinguished students from abroad and from the Roman upper classes. It included not only philosophers but also politicians and members of the medical profession who wished to lead the philosophical life. His most famous student was Porphyry (233–305) who, as a relative latecomer to the school, persuaded him to put into writing the results of his seminars. It is almost certain that we possess most, if not all, of his written output, which represents his mature thought, since he didn't commence writing until the age of forty-eight. The school seemingly had inner and outer circles, and Plotinus himself was clearly an inspiring and sympathetic teacher who took a deep interest in the philosophical and spiritual progress of his students. Porphyry tells us that when he was suffering from severe depression Plotinus straight away visited him in his lodgings to help him. His concern for others is also illustrated by the fact that he was entrusted with the personal education of many orphans and the care of their property and careers. The reconciliation of this worldly involvement with the encouragement to lead a life of contemplation is encapsulated in Porphyry's comment that "he was present to himself and others at the same time."

The *Enneads* of Plotinus is the edition of his treatises arranged by his pupil Porphyry who tried to put shape to the collection he had inherited by organizing it into six sets of nine treatises (hence the name *"Enneads")* that led the reader through the levels of Plotinus' universe, from the physical world to Soul, Intellect and, finally, to the highest principle, the One. Although Plotinus undoubtedly had a clearly structured metaphysical system by the time he began committing himself to expressing his thought in written form, the treatises themselves are not systematic expositions, but rather explorations of particular themes and issues raised in interpreting Plato and other philosophical texts read in the School. In fact, to achieve his neat arrangement Porphyry was sometimes driven even to dividing certain treatises (e.g., III.2–3; IV.3–5, and VI.4–5).

Although Plotinus' writings are not transcripts of his seminars, but are directed to the reader, they do, nevertheless, convey the sort of lively debate that he encouraged in his school. Frequently he takes for granted that a particular set of ideas is already familiar as having been treated in an earlier seminar that may or may not be found in the written text. For this reason it is useful for the reader to have some idea of the main philosophical principles of his system as they can be extracted from the *Enneads* as a whole.

Plotinus regarded himself as a faithful interpreter of Plato whose thought lies at the core of his entire project. But Plato's thought, whilst definitive, does according to Plotinus require careful exposition and clarification, often in the light of other thinkers such as Aristotle and the Stoics. It is because of this creative application of different traditions of ancient thought to the interpretation of Plato that Plotinus' version of Platonism became, partly through the medium of later Platonists such as Porphyry, Iamblichus (245–325), and Proclus (412–485), an influential source and way of reading both Plato and Aristotle in the Middle Ages, the Renaissance, and up to the early 19th century, when scholars first began to differentiate Plato and "Neoplatonism." His thought, too, provided early Christian theologians of the Latin and particularly of the Byzantine tradition, with a rich variety of metaphysical concepts with which to explore and express difficult doctrinal ideas. His fashioning of Plato's ideas into a consistent metaphysical structure, though no longer accepted as a uniquely valid way of approaching Plato, was influential in promoting the notion of metaphysical systems in early modern philosophy. More recently increasing interest has centered on his exploration of the self, levels of consciousness, and his expansion of discourse beyond the levels of normal ontology to the examination of what lies both above and beneath being. His thought continues to challenge us when confronted with the issue of man's nature and role in the universe and of the extent and limitations of human knowledge.

Whilst much of Plotinus' metaphysical structure is recognizably an interpretation of Plato it is an interpretation that is not always immediately obvious just because it is filtered through several centuries of developing Platonic thought, itself already overlaid with important concepts drawn from other schools. It is, nevertheless, useful as a starting point to see how Plotinus attempts to bring coherence to what he believed to be a comprehensive worldview expressed in the Platonic dialogues. The Platonic Forms are central. They become for him an intelligible universe that is the source and model of the physical universe. But aware of Aristotle's criticism of the Platonic Forms as lifeless causes he takes on board Aristotle's concept of god as a self-thinker to enable him to identify this intelligible universe as a divine Intellect that thinks itself as the Forms or Intelligibles. The doctrine of the Forms as the thoughts of god had already entered Platonism, but not as the rigorously argued identity that Plotinus proposed. Moreover the Intelligibles, since they are identical with Intellect, are themselves actively intellectual; they are intellects. Thus Plato's world of Forms has become a complex and dynamic intelligible universe in which unity and plurality, stability, and activity are reconciled.

Now although the divine Intellect is one it also embraces plurality, both because its thoughts, the Intelligibles, are many and because it may itself be analyzed into thinker and thought. Its unity demands a further principle, which is the cause of its unity. This principle, which is the cause of all unity and being but does not possess unity or being in itself, he calls the One, an interpretation of the Idea of the Good in Plato's *Republic* that is "beyond being" and that may be seen as the simple (hence "one") source of all reality. We thus have the first two of what subsequently became known as the three Hypostases, the One, Intellect, and Soul, the last of which acts as an intermediary between the intelligible and physical universes. This last Hypostasis takes on all the functions of transmitting form and life that may be found in Plato, although Plato himself does not always make such a clear distinction between soul and intellect. Thus the One is the ultimate source of all, including this universe, which is then prefigured in Intellect and transmitted through Soul to become manifest as our physical universe. Matter, which receives imperfectly this expression, is conceived not as an independently existing counter-principle, a dangerously dualist notion, but is in a sense itself a product of the One, a kind of non-being that, while being nothing specific in itself, nevertheless is not simply not there.

But this procession from an ultimate principle is balanced by a return movement at each level of reality that fully constitutes itself only when it turns back in contemplation of its producer. And so the whole of reality is a dynamic movement of procession and return, except for matter, which has no life of its own to make this return; it is inert. This movement of return, which may be traced back to the force of "love" in Plato or Aristotle's final cause, is characterized by Plotinus as a cognitive activity, a form of contemplation, weaker at each successive level, from Intellect through discursive reasoning to the merest image of rational order as expressed in the objects of the physical universe.

The human individual mirrors this structure to which we are all related at each level. For each of us has a body and soul, an intellect, and even something within us that relates to the One. While it is the nature of soul to give life to body, the higher aspect of our soul also has aspirations toward intellect, the true self, and even beyond. This urge to return corresponds to the cosmic movement of return. But the tension between soul's natural duty to body and its origins in the intelligible can be, for the individual, a source of fracture and alienation in which the soul becomes over-involved and overwhelmed by the body and so estranged from its true self. Plotinus encourages us to make the return or ascent, but at the same time attempts to resolve the conflict of duties by reconciling the two-fold nature of soul as life-giving and contemplative.

This is the general framework within which important traditional philosophical issues are encountered, discussed and resolved, but always in a spirit of inquiry and ongoing debate. Issues are frequently encountered in several different contexts, each angle providing a different insight. The nature of the soul and its relationship to the body is examined at length (IV) using the Aristotelian distinctions of levels of soul (vegetative, growth, sensitive, rational) whilst maintaining the immortal nature of the transcendent soul in Platonic terms. The active nature of the soul in sense-perception is maintained to preserve the principle that incorporeals cannot be affected by corporeal reality. A vigorous discussion (VI.4 and 5) on the general nature of the relationship of incorporeals to body explores in every detail and in great depth the way in which incorporeals act on body. A universe that is the product of design is reconciled with the freedom of the individual. And, not least, the time-bound nature of the physical universe and human reason is grounded in the life of Intellect, which subsists in eternity. Sometimes, however, Plotinus seems to break outside the framework of traditional metaphysics: the nature of matter and the One, each as non-being, though in a different sense, strains the terminology and structure of traditional ontology; and the attempt to reconcile the role of the individual soul within the traditional Platonic distinction of transcendent and immanent reality leads to a novel exploration of the nature of the self, the "I."

It is this restless urge for exploration and inquiry that lends to the treatises of Plotinus their philosophical vitality. Whilst presenting us with a rich and complexly coherent system, he constantly engages us in philosophical inquiry. In this way each treatise presents us with new ideas and fresh challenges. And, for Plotinus, every philosophical engagement is not just a mental exercise but also contributes to the rediscovery of the self and our reintegration with the source of all being, the Platonic aim of "becoming like god."

While Plotinus, like Plato, always wishes to engage his audience to reflect for themselves, his treatises are not easy reading, partly no doubt because his own audience was already familiar with many of his basic ideas and, more importantly, had been exposed in his seminars to critical readings of philosophical texts that have not survived to our day. Another problem is that the treatises do not lay out his thought in a systematic way but take up specific issues, although always the whole system may be discerned in the background. Sometimes, too, the exact flow of thought is difficult to follow because of an often condensed mode of expression.

Because we are convinced that Plotinus has something to say to us today, we have launched this series of translations and commentaries as a means of opening up the text to readers with an interest in grappling with the philosophical issues revealed by an encounter with Plotinus' own words and arguments. Each volume will contain a new translation, careful summaries of the arguments and structure of the treatise, and a philosophical commentary that will aim to throw light on the philosophical meaning and import of the text.

John M. Dillon
Andrew Smith

Abbreviations

BP	Brisson, L. and Pradeau, J.-F. *Plotin Traités*. Vol. 1. Paris: Garnier Flammarion, 2002.
DK	Diels-Kranz. *Die Fragmente der Vorsokratiker*. 6th ed. Berlin: Weidmann, 1961.
HS_1	Henry, P. and Schwyzer, H.-R., eds. *Plotini Opera*. Paris: Desclée de Brouwer et Cie, 1959 (editio major).
HS_2	Henry, P. and Schwyzer, H.-R., eds. *Plotini Opera*. Oxford: Clarendon Press, 1977 (editio minor) = OCT.
KRS	Kirk, G., Raven J., and Schofield, M., eds. *The Presocratic Philosophers*. 2nd ed. Cambridge: Cambridge University Press, 1983.
Loeb	Armstrong, H., ed. *Plotinus*. 7 vols. Cambridge, MA, and London: Harvard University Press, 1966–1988.

Lex. Plot. Sleeman, J. and Pollet, R. *Lexicon Plotinianum*. Leiden: E. J. Brill, 1980.

LS Long, A. and Sedley, D., eds. *The Hellenistic Philosophers*. Vol. 1: Translation of the Principal Sources with Philosophical Commentary. Cambridge: Cambridge University Press, 1987.

LSJ Liddell, H. and Scott, R. *A Greek-English Lexicon*. 9th ed. revised by H. Jones. Oxford: Oxford University Press, 1940.

MacK MacKenna, S., trans. Plotinus: *The Enneads*. 2nd ed. London: The Medici Society, 1930.

OCT Oxford Classical Text.

SVF Van Arnim, H. ed. *Stoicorum Veterum Fragmenta*. Leipzig: Teubner, 1905–1924.

VP *Vita Plotini* = Porphyry's Life of Plotinus printed at start of HS_1, HS_2, MacK, and Loeb.

Acknowledgments

THE AUTHOR WISHES TO EXPRESS his gratitude to John Dillon and Andrew Smith for their valuable advice on the substance of the introduction, translation and commentary, and to Eliza Tutellier and the editorial team at Parmenides Press for their excellent work on producing the final version of the book.

Introduction to the Treatise

It was an immutable tenet of Platonism that soul is immortal. So although the title given to this treatise might lead us to expect a reworking of Plato's *Phaedo*, Plotinus is not here concerned to *prove* the immortality of soul.[1]

The Platonist's position is well summarized by Alcinous (a Platonist of the mid-second century CE) at *The Handbook of Platonism* (ch. 25, 177, 16ff.): "That the soul is immortal [Plato] demonstrates by proceeding in the following way. To whatever it attaches itself, soul brings life, as naturally associated with itself. But that which brings life to something is itself non-receptive of death, and such a thing is immortal. But if the soul is immortal, it would also be imperishable; for it is an incorporeal essence, unchanging in its substance and intelligible, and invisible, and uniform. So therefore it is incomposite, indissoluble, indispersible. Body, on the other hand, is quite the contrary—sense-perceptible, visible, dispersible,

1 Although some, for example Bostock (1986), have questioned whether this was in fact Plato's intention.

composite, multiform. Further, when the soul, through the intermediacy of the body, comes to exist in the sensible realm, it becomes dizzy and is thrown into confusion and becomes, as it were, drunk, while when it comes to be on its own in the intelligible realm it comes to stability and enjoys calm. Now if it is thrown into confusion by contact with something, it is not akin to that thing. So it is akin rather to the intelligible, and the intelligible is by nature indispersible and indestructible."[2]

The distinction proclaimed by Alcinous between immortal soul and mortal body, was fundamental to Platonism, and the main thrust of IV.7 is to reiterate Plato's belief that the soul is an immaterial essence "which has being from within itself" (Ch. 9, 1), and cannot be body, which is subject to destruction, or an affection of body, which is subject to the destruction of the body of which it is an affection. Accordingly much of the treatise is taken up with a demonstration of the weakness of the materialists' position.

Alcinous makes a further distinction between soul "on its own in the intelligible realm" and soul "through the intermediacy of the body . . . in the sensible world." This is a distinction which Plotinus is careful to observe in

---

2 Tr. Dillon (1993), who points out (151–160) that Alcinous' arguments are largely taken from Plato *Phaedo*. They are under the surface of this treatise of Plotinus throughout, as readers familiar with *Phaedo* will quickly recognize. True Platonists show a united front.

this treatise, and which he explores at length throughout *Ennead* IV and elsewhere, for example in III.6.1–5 *On the Impassivity of the Bodiless.*

As IV.7 unfolds it becomes apparent that Plotinus' main focus is on the individual soul,[3] although much of the argument applies equally to the soul of the cosmos. The title given to the treatise by Porphyry in both the chronological list (*Life of Plotinus* 4–6) and the thematic list (*Life of Plotinus* 20) is non-committal: *On Soul's Immortality* (*peri psykhês athanasias*), without definite articles. Most commentators and translators insert definite articles, and most take it to be largely directed against the Stoics. Eusebius, a younger Christian contemporary of Plotinus, in his *Preparation for the Gospel*, mentions the treatise under the title *On soul's immortality and that it cannot be bodily* which is reflected in two 15th century manuscripts, C and M, or *On soul's immortality . . . and its eternality; against the Stoics that it cannot be bodily.*

Plotinus complains at IV.8.1, 23ff. that Plato does not always make himself clear, particularly on issues relating to the soul. One of the questions that Plato leaves unresolved concerns the divisions within the individual soul; Are there two—rational and irrational? Or three—rational, spirited, and appetitive? Or no individual parts—so that

3 The first 3 lines of Chapter 1 make a strong assertion in favor of this.

soul is unitary?[4] In the context of this treatise it is perhaps appropriate to see the soul as unitary, but manifesting itself in different phases according to circumstances. It is only when it is in the body that we can talk of the irrational part(s),[5] which ceases to be an applicable term when the soul is "on its own in the intelligible realm"—a situation that can occur in two different ways, either (a) after the death of the individual human and before his rebirth, or (b) on those occasions during the life of the individual when (s)he becomes "assimilated to the divine."[6] By contrast the embodied phase of the soul is temporary and intermittent in successive incarnations. But unlike the body, for which a change from life to death means destruction, the soul's involvement in body does not entail destruction, but rather "a different type of alteration," to use Aristotle's words at *On the Soul* 417b7 though in a different context, a change to actuality from potentiality and *vice versa.* Plotinus is able to maintain that (a) no part or phase of the soul is itself corporeal, and (b) its immortality is guaranteed by the permanent presence of its "true self" in the intelligible world. So although it could be argued that the irrational parts of

4 See Blumenthal (1971, 135) for Plotinus' rejection of Plato's tripartition.

5 Although the souls of the dead in Book 10 of Plato's *Republic* do manifest appetites and passions.

6 The subject of *Ennead* IV.8. In Chapter 8 Plotinus goes as far as to say that there is a part of the soul, "the true self" which "is always in the intelligible world."

the soul are in a way affections of the body, it would be a wrong way for a Platonist to think. Soul is prior to body, a question that Plotinus deals with in Chapter 8[3].

So a large part of the treatise is devoted to countering the suggestion that the soul, or any part of it, is corporeal. Against whom, then, is Plotinus directing his arguments? He rarely names his opponents in any of his treatises. For example Epicurus is mentioned by name only once, the Pythagoreans and Aristotle on a handful of occasions, and the Stoics and Gnostics never. This may be a convention, or else reflect the practice of the seminars where works by Platonists and Peripatetics were read aloud (Porphyry *Life of Plotinus* 14) and then went unacknowledged in the subsequent discussions. But this seems unlikely and does not account for Porphyry's failure to name authors of other persuasions. On the other hand Porphyry tells us (*Life of Plotinus* 14) that "in Plotinus' works both Stoic and Peripatetic doctrines are interwoven, although they lie under the surface," and at *Life of Plotinus* 20 he adds in the Pythagoreans: "Plotinus, as it appears, set forth the principles of Pythagoras and Plato more clearly than any of his predecessors." Certainly there are numerous indications in the *Enneads* of terminology and doctrine from philosophical sources other than Plato.[7] It must be said

7 The fullest exploration of this topic can be found in *Entretiens Hardt*: *Les Sources de Plotin* (Geneva, 1960), available in English translation.

that neither ancient nor modern commentators find any apparent difficulty in identifying particular philosophical schools as the supporters or targets of Plotinus' arguments, for example Eusebius' subtitling mentioned above.

However, the explanation for Plotinus' unwillingness to name names may lie in the complex nature of the philosophical world of Rome in the third century CE. On the one hand there was an increasing erosion of the boundaries between different schools and a corresponding syncretic approach, so that it is possible to talk, for example, of "stoicizing Platonists" and "platonizing Stoics."[8] Platonism was the school that had been most subject to such influences and it had passed through various stages[9] which have been fully documented and discussed in Dillon (1977).[10] The Academy as an institution seems to have lost its identity by the time of Augustus, and thereafter Platonism lost its earlier cohesion. It was just that cohesion that Plotinus was seeking to re-establish. The authority to whom he appeals is Plato himself, as evidenced by Chapters 9–11 of this treatise, where he expounds what he sees as Platonic doctrine pure and simple.

---

8 See Dillon (1977, 83–84) for an example of Antiochus of Ascalon in a stoicizing mood.

9 See Sorabji and Sharples (eds., 2007, vol. 2, 311n30) for the "five Academies" mentioned by Eusebius and Sextus Empiricus.

10 But see Barnes in Griffin and Barnes (eds., 1989), who takes a more sceptical view of the role played by Antiochus of Ascalon.

Of other philosophical schools the Stoics retained a greater degree of doctrinal integrity, particularly because of their willingness to embrace different perspectives, especially on ethical questions, with a continuing tradition of writers such as Panaetius (2nd century BCE), Posidonius (2nd–1st centuries BCE), Seneca (1st century CE), Epictetus (1st–2nd centuries CE), and the emperor Marcus Aurelius (2nd century CE). Graeser (1972) points to the impossibility of tracing Plotinus' Stoic sources. All we can say is that on the question of the material composition of the soul he appears to look to earlier Stoics, Chrysippus in particular. But, as Graeser points out, he may be offering us parallel passages rather than sources (*loci paralleli* rather than *fontes*). However, there is general agreement that Plotinus took careful note of the writings of the Peripatetic Alexander of Aphrodisias (2nd–3rd century CE),[11] especially his *On the Soul*, of which book 1 survives together with what is probably an abbreviated version of book 2 known as *Supplement*,[12] and his work *On Mixtures*. Alexander follows Aristotle in saying that the soul is not composed of matter distinct from the matter of the body, and he rehearses arguments against the Stoic position that the soul is just that—breath (*pneuma*), an active mixture of air and fire which pervades the passive earthy and watery matter of the body. Plotinus is happy to use Alexander's

11 Henry in Dodds (ed., 1960, 429–449).

12 Sharples in Adamson (2004, 51–69).

arguments against the Stoics and any who adopt a materialist position on this point in Chapters 1–8^{3}, although he later turns on the Peripatetics, when they claim that the soul is an affection of the body, in Chapter 8^{5}.

For Stoic testimony I have drawn mainly on two collections: (a) *Fragments of the Early Stoics* (*Stoicorum Veterum Fragmenta*) vol. 2 (SVF), and (b) Long and Sedley *The Hellenistic Philosophers* (LS). In the latter case I have used the translations given by Long and Sedley to allow interested readers easier access to the material. I am grateful to Professors Long and Sedley and the Syndics of the Cambridge University Press for permission to print these translations.

In Chapter 3, 1–6 there seems to be a brief argument directed against the Epicureans, who likewise claimed that the soul was made up of matter, in the form of fine atomic particles, distinct from the matter of the rest of the body. Little is known about the Epicureans after the age of Augustus (with the possible exception of Diogenes of Oenoanda, whose dates remain uncertain). Plotinus refers to the Epicureans in veiled terms at V.9.1 as "overweight birds who have taken in too much from the earth and are too heavy to be able to fly high." Unless there was a group of contemporary Epicureans who have gone undetected, Plotinus here in IV.7 is either referring to them as an historical curiosity, or including any philosophers who embraced a form of atomism.

In Chapters 8^{4-5} Plotinus turns first to attack the Pythagoreans and then the Peripatetics, both of whose psychic materialism was not that of the Stoics and Epicureans, for whom, as we have seen, the soul was composed of matter distinct from that of the body, but rather an affection of the material body. Pythagorean ideas were being promulgated in Plotinus' day—by Plotinus himself if we are to believe Porphyry as quoted above—and the corpus of Pythagorean writings was certainly available to Plotinus, although they are now generally agreed to be largely spurious compilation of the 3rd–1st centuries BCE.[13] Although in general Plotinus would have little quarrel with the Pythagoreans, he differs sharply on the nature of the soul.[14]

That Peripatetic doctrine was current in and before Plotinus' time is evidenced by the work of Alexander of Aphrodisias and by the vigorous and extensive corpus of writings of the commentators on Aristotle's works, starting with Aspasius in the 2nd century CE and continuing into the 6th century. Some 100 of these commentaries are now available in English in the *Ancient Commentators on Aristotle* series, ed. Sorabji; Cornell/Duckworth.

This is not, however, the place for a detailed survey of the philosophical schools and their aftermath in the later Greco-Roman world. That task has been adequately

13 Thesleff, *The Pythagorean Texts of the Hellenistic Period* (Åbo: 1965, 30–40).

14 Dillon (1977, 196) and Fleet (1995, 88–89).

performed by others, amongst whom should be singled out Dillon (1977); Mansfeld in Algra *et al* (2005, chapter 1); Frede (*ibid.*, Epilogue); Merlan in Armstrong (ed., 1970, part 1); and Griffin in Griffin and Barnes (1989, chapter 1).

Chapters 8^{1-5} somehow fell out of the manuscript tradition at some point after the time of Proclus (5th century CE) and were not included in the text used by Marsilio Ficino (15th century), who gave us the numbering of the chapters. But the chapters were preserved in Eusebius' *Preparation for the Gospel*, and first printed by Creuzer in his 1835 edition of the works of Plotinus, hence the rather curious numbering. For a full explanation see HS_1 (vol. 1, xviii–xxii). Alternatively John Dillon suggests that Chapters 8^{1-5} might be a later addition brought in from some other attack on materialist and supervenient theories of the soul; he points to the fact that although these five chapters do not contradict anything in the rest of the treatise, there is a more natural transition from the end of Chapter 8 to the start of Chapter 9 with the contrast between the two "natures."

In Chapters 9–10 Plotinus turns finally to expounding the Platonic doctrine on "the other nature which has its being from within itself," which comprises the contents of the intelligible world—Intellect and Soul, before turning to consider more precisely the human soul in its "kinship to the divine and eternal."

Chapters 11–14 are devoted to answering objections that might be raised by opponents, returning to some of the points made earlier in the treatise, addressing in particular the question of the different parts of the soul. The final chapter is an appendix in which Plotinus speaks to those seeking support for Platonic doctrine from religion, especially the oracles of the dead.

This is a very early treatise, number 2 according to Porphyry's chronological list at *Life of Plotinus* 4. It summarizes the findings of a seminar held soon after Plotinus' arrival in Rome in 245 CE when he was forty years old. Porphyry did not come to Rome for some years after this, so was not himself present at the seminar. He tells at *Life of Plotinus* 3 that Plotinus committed nothing to writing until his fiftieth year; Porphyry edited these writings after Plotinus' death, and it was Porphyry who added the titles to each treatise, with sometimes a discrepancy between those in the chronological and those in the thematic list, although not in the case of IV.7.

So we are offered Plotinus' considered summary of one of the seminars led by himself, at which texts such as those mentioned by Porphyry at *Life of Plotinus* 14 were read, with Plotinus' own interpretation of the findings of this early seminar. The treatise is the work of a mature philosophical mind. In keeping with the historical context of the original seminar there is little sign of the later systematization of Plotinus' Platonism. Hence I have put my main emphasis on interpreting Plotinus' text in the light of what I consider to have been the discussions in the seminar, leaving it to others to put them in the broader context of Plotinus' achievement. We are invited to share in the penetrating insights he brings to bear on an issue of major human concern. I hope that the text will speak for itself.

Note on the Text

Line numbers in the translation are approximate and do not always match the original Greek text. Since the commentary follows the sequence of the English translation, there may sometimes be a slight discrepancy in the ordering.

The Greek text adopted is that of the Oxford edition (taking into account the Addenda ad Textum in vol. 3, 304–325). Deviations from the text are noted in the commentary. Each *Ennead* is referred to by Roman numerals, followed by the number of the treatise, the chapter of the treatise, and, finally, separated by a comma, the line number or numbers, e.g, V.1.3, 24–27.

It is customary to add the chronological number given by Porphyry in his *Life of Plotinus* (*Vita Plotini*), so that, for example, V.1 is designated V.1 [10]. In this series the chronological number is given only where it is of significance for Plotinus' philosophical stance. The following chart indicates the chronological order.

Chronological Order of the ***Enneads***

Enn.		*Enn.*		*Enn.*		*Enn.*		*Enn.*		*Enn.*	
I.1	**53**	II.1	**40**	III.1	**3**	IV.1	**21**	V.1	**10**	VI.1	**42**
I.2	**19**	II.2	**14**	III.2	**47**	IV.2	**4**	V.2	**11**	VI.2	**43**
I.3	**20**	II.3	**52**	III.3	**48**	IV.3	**27**	V.3	**49**	VI.3	**44**
I.4	**46**	II.4	**12**	III.4	**15**	IV.4	**28**	V.4	**7**	VI.4	**22**
I.5	**36**	II.5	**25**	III.5	**50**	IV.5	**29**	V.5	**32**	VI.5	**23**
I.6	**1**	II.6	**17**	III.6	**26**	IV.6	**41**	V.6	**24**	VI.6	**34**
I.7	**54**	II.7	**37**	III.7	**45**	IV.7	**2**	V.7	**18**	VI.7	**38**
I.8	**51**	II.8	**35**	III.8	**30**	IV.8	**6**	V.8	**31**	VI.8	**39**
I.9	**16**	II.9	**33**	III.9	**13**	IV.9	**8**	V.9	**5**	VI.9	**9**

	Enn.		*Enn.*		*Enn.*		*Enn.*		*Enn.*		*Enn.*
1	I.6	**10**	V.1	**19**	I.2	**28**	IV.4	**37**	II.7	**46**	I.4
2	IV.7	**11**	V.2	**20**	I.3	**29**	IV.5	**38**	VI.7	**47**	III.2
3	III.1	**12**	II.4	**21**	IV.1	**30**	III.8	**39**	VI.8	**48**	III.3
4	IV.2	**13**	III.9	**22**	VI.4	**31**	V.8	**40**	II.1	**49**	V.3
5	V.9	**14**	II.2	**23**	VI.5	**32**	V.5	**41**	IV.6	**50**	III.5
6	IV.8	**15**	III.4	**24**	V.6	**33**	II.9	**42**	VI.1	**51**	I.8
7	V.4	**16**	I.9	**25**	II.5	**34**	VI.6	**43**	VI.2	**52**	II.3
8	IV.9	**17**	II.6	**26**	III.6	**35**	II.8	**44**	VI.3	**53**	I.1
9	VI.9	**18**	V.7	**27**	IV.3	**36**	I.5	**45**	III.7	**54**	I.7

Synopsis

Chapter 1

1–4 An enquiry according to nature will establish whether the human is immortal, entirely mortal, or part immortal, part mortal.

4–7 Man is a complex of soul and body. His body is either an instrument or an adjunct. Body and soul are different in nature and in essence.

7–17 Body is composite and cannot endure. We can see it undergoing all sorts of decomposition due to the nature of its constituents. Its cohesion depends on the presence of soul. Even if one element can be isolated, it is still a compound—of form and matter.

17–20 Since bodies have size they are divisible into smaller parts.

20–22 So whether the body is part of us or an instrument we are not entirely immortal.

22–25 But the soul is the true self and stands to body as form to matter (or as user to tool).

Chapter 2

1 What is the nature of soul?

1–4 Whether it is body or something else, it must still be investigated.

4–5 We should first analyze what is said to be the material soul.

5–10 Life is of necessity present to soul. So if the soul is a compound body, then life must be present in one or more of the constituent bodies.

10–14 If in one, that part would be soul. But that is impossible. Even the simplest bodies are lifeless in themselves.

14–15 Even those positing elementary bodies other than the traditional four do not claim that any of these are more than body.

16–19 A combination of lifeless elements cannot produce life.

19–25 There must be an organizing immaterial cause, soul, which is the source of the *logoi* bringing form to matter.

Chapter 3

1–6 Critique of the Epicurean doctrine that soul is the result of the coming together of atoms or things without parts.

6–12 Reversion to criticism of the Stoics, who claim that living creatures are the conjoint of (a sort of) form and matter; the soul must be the form and not the matter.

12–16 They cannot claim that soul is an affection of matter; they need to give the source of such an affection.

16–28 Any such source must be incorporeal, transcending matter or body; where there is no psychic power there can be no body, which otherwise would perish or not even exist. Soul is the unifying and organizing power in the cosmos.

28–35 Futhermore, soul gives body the very power of being.

Chapter 4

1–11 The Stoics must admit that there is a part of the soul prior and superior to body, since they make fire intelligent and breath intellective, as if the higher part of the soul needed somewhere to exist. But they should be doing the opposite—looking for a place for body to exist. They fall back on the formula "body so disposed."

11–21 But this disposition is (a) a non-entity, and their soul and god are just matter, or (b) if it is a reality, it will be other than matter—in matter but immaterial—a *logos.*

21–35 Body can produce only one effect in another body according to its own quality; but soul can produce many effects in living creatures.

Chapter 5

1–8 How do the Stoics account for the variety of movements, since each body has a single motion? Choice and *logos* account for such variety, but they do not belong to body *qua* body.

8–12 And how do they account for growth?

12–24 If it is a bodily soul that causes growth, it would need to grow *pari passu* with the body. What is added to the growing soul is either soul, or body lacking soul—both impossibilities; if the former, where will it come from and how will it join the soul already there? If the latter, how will what is lacking soul become soul? If, like our bodies, our soul is in constant flux, how will there be any constancy in our memories? And how can we judge what is appropriate to us?

24–32 The soul as a magnitude cannot retain the same qualities in its divided parts as in the whole.

32–51 Implications for the Stoics of positing a divisible soul. What about parts of the soul in the same body? If they say that each part is lacking in soul, then the soul will be made up of parts lacking soul. The facts of twin or multiple births show that where parts are identical to the whole, then the similarity transcends magnitude. The soul and *logoi* are like this.

Chapter 6

1–15 If soul is body, then there can be no mental or moral activity. A percipient must be single and perceive everything by the same faculty central to all our organs of perception, like the hub at the center of a wheel, with our perceptions converging like spokes.

15–26 This cannot be extended; if it were we would still need a point of convergence, or else our perceptions will lack cohesion. It is clear that our various perceptions are unified by the ruling part of the soul, and, like it, are partless.

26–37 How could the ruling part be divided as a magnitude? Since magnitudes are infinitely divisible, a soul as a magnitude would be too.

37–48 If perceptions are imprints on a material soul, they are either fluid—in which case they are obliterated—or solid—in which case they inhibit any new impressions; so there could be no memory. But there is memory; therefore soul is not body.

Chapter 7

1–7 Pain occurs in one part of the body, for example the toe, but awareness of the pain takes place in the ruling part of the soul, which is affected in its entirety.

7–22 The Stoics say that awareness is in the psychic breath in the toe, or that it passes on this awareness to the next portion of psychic breath, and so on until it reaches the ruling part "by transference." But each of these will be different perceptions, so that at the end of the chain the ruling principle will be aware only of pain in its vicinity.

22–28 But if the ruling principle is to be aware of the pain in the toe, then it cannot be "by transference," and must be by some other medium than body.

Chapter 8

1–7 If soul were body, it could not even think. Sense perception is the soul's apprehension through the body; thinking must be different, and not through the body; so the soul is not body.

7–12 Thinking is of non-sensory intelligibles, which lack magnitude and parts; so what thinks them must also be partless and lacking in magnitude.

12–23 Primary thoughts are of bodiless Forms, so the thinker must also be bodiless; even if the Forms are enmattered, they are abstracted from body; they lack magnitude and parts, and so does thinking about them.

24–26 Forms such as beauty and justice have no magnitude, and are not perceived by a soul having magnitude.

26–38 The virtues can hardly be body, even in the form of breath, which would have other needs than those of the soul.

38–45 Virtue is one of the eternal entities; its seat must be eternal too, and not bodily.

Chapter 8[1]

1–17 The Stoics are wrong to equate material effects such as warming and cooling to soul; these are produced by bodiless powers within bodies, and are not like psychic powers such as thought and perception. Quality is not the same as quantity; every body has quantity, but not all body has quality, for example matter. So quality is not the same as body.

17–35 Body loses its previous identity when divided, but quality does not; each drop of honey is as sweet as the whole pot. If powers were bodies, the powers of a body would be proportionate to its magnitude. This is not so; such powers must be lacking in magnitude; they are *logoi*, free of matter and body. The Stoics cannot rest on the fact that withdrawal of blood and breath cause death, since there are many other things necessary to life, and these are not soul. Neither breath nor blood pervade the body as soul does.

Chapter 8[2]

1–7 Soul does not blend as body blends with body; if it did it would lose its actuality.

7–22 If it were blended throughout as body with body, then like body it would be divided. Division would be into infinite number of points, and all points would exist both potentially and actually. So it is impossible for body to blend throughout; but soul does, and so is not body.

Chapter 8[3]

1–6 It is absurd to say that the soul is chilled, hardened breath. Many living creatures are born in heat and have a soul that has not been cooled.

6–25 By claiming that nature is prior to soul they give priority to what is inferior. But Intellect is prior to soul, and soul prior to nature. By reversing this order they do away with souls, God and Intellect. The potential is posterior to the actual and could not come into actuality without something actual prior to it—or if it looks to itself, then that self will exist in actuality. Intellect and soul, in that they are different from and better than body, exist in actuality and are prior to body.

Chapter 8[4]

1–9 What is the nature of soul—is it a property of body like an attunement, rather as Pythagoras claimed? Or is it a supervening affection arising when bodies are blended?

9–23 There are many arguments against this viewpoint.

(i) Soul is prior to body, but an attunement is posterior.

(ii) The soul rules the body, unlike an attunement.

(iii) The soul is substance.

(iv) Attunement is better seen as health.

(v) The soul would vary according to the blend of each part.

(vi) There would need to be another prior soul to produce the attunement.

23–28 They make the soul out of what is unensouled and random.

Chapter 8[5]

1–5 What do the Peripatetics mean when they call the soul "the form of a natural body with organs having life potentially"?

5–40 There are nine arguments against this view.

(i) If it is assimilated to body as form to matter, then it would be divided along with the division of matter.

(ii) The withdrawal of soul during sleep would be impossible.

(iii) There would be no opposition of reason to desire.

(iv) There could be no intellection—for which they import another soul, intellect.

(v) Perceptual impressions can be independent of the body as memories.

(vi) Similarly with non-material desires.

(vii) The vegetative phase of the soul cannot be an inseparable actualization.

(viii) How could something partless be an actualization of body with parts?

(ix) How could transmigration take place?

40–46 So the soul is substance, not form, and is independent of and prior to body.

46–50 It is true being, unlike the contents of the material world, which come to be and pass away.

Chapter 9

1–5 True being is eternal and is the guarantee of the qualified being of the cosmos.

6–16 Soul is the self-moving principle of motion in other things, and bestows life on the ensouled body; it has life without qualification.

16–26 It is the seat of all that is divine, existing and living without qualification, unchanging and free of coming-to-be and passing-away. It cannot be dead, but has pure life eternally.

26–29 Even if the individual soul is mixed in with something inferior, its access to the best is impeded only temporarily, until it returns to its former state.

Chapter 10

1–6 The soul is akin to the divine and the eternal, lacking shape, color and tangibility.

6–26 Let us enquire further what the nature of the soul is.

> 8–14 A consideration of the purified soul shows that evils are acquired from outside, while virtue is intrinsic.
>
> 14–20 Wisdom and virtue are divine, and need a host of a similar nature.
>
> 20–22 A virtuous person would only be inferior in that he is in a body.
>
> 22–26 Most men's souls are mutilated, and so do not seem to be divine.

26–37 We should consider what is pure, with all accretions stripped away. We will see an intelligible cosmos, apprehending the eternal by the eternal, flooded by the light of truth from the Good.

37–52 He will have knowledge of the true understanding which is inside him as an intelligible cosmos. He will see and compare his present and former self, like a statue cleaned of all rust, or like gold that has been refined.

Chapter 11

1–11 Soul is immortal in that it possesses inextinguishable life of itself, and not acquired as the heat is acquired by fire or what underlies fire.

11–18 Or else it may be said by our opponents that it is a compound with one element which is immortal, or else it is an acquired affection whose source is immortal. Either way there is a single underlying nature which is immortal.

Chapter 12

1–11 They cannot claim that only some souls are immortal. All souls are principles of movement, live, have intellection, and remember in the same way, and are prior to body.

12–20 Composites are broken up into their constituent parts; but soul is a simplex. If it has parts it cannot be quantitatively broken up in the same way as mass. It is not liable to quantitative change.

Chapter 13

1–4 The intellective part of soul remains entirely in the intelligible world.

4–11 The spirited part proceeds into the cosmos and helps the soul of the cosmos to organize the whole.

11–19 When it desires to organize a part it becomes isolated in that part, but still retains a toehold in the intelligible world. Intellect remains entirely aloof, but directs the cosmos through soul.

Chapter 14

1–8 Souls of animals and plants are immortal, since their common origin is living nature; they have some of the properties of human soul.

8–13 The tripartite human soul either sheds its lower parts when it is purified, or else retains them; these parts survive as long as the originating soul survives.

Chapter 15

1–8 The evidence of the senses provides further proof, especially divine oracles which require appeasement and respect for the deceased as being aware of them.

8–12 Souls of the deceased continue to benefit the living, especially by establishing oracles to show that their own souls and those of others have not died.

Translation of
Plotinus Ennead *IV.7*

On the Immortality of the Soul

1. Is each one of us immortal? Or do we perish entirely? Or do some parts of us perish through dispersal and decay, while others—the true self—survive forever? We might be able to discover the answers to these questions by examining them according to nature in the following manner.

A human could not be described as something simple; not only is there a soul present in him, | but he also possesses a body. This may either be an instrument for our use, or be attached to us in some other way. Whatever the case, let us accept this broad division and consider the nature and essence of each of the two parts.

Body is, of course, itself a composite. Not only does reason tell us that it cannot endure, but even our senses perceive | that it breaks up, decays, and undergoes all sorts of destruction. Each of its constituents is either carried away to its proper place, or one causes the destruction of another, or changes into another and so destroys itself. This happens particularly when soul is not present in the material masses to create a harmony. And even if each constituent in isolation | is something single, it is not truly so, since it can be broken down into form and matter, from which even the simplest bodies are of necessity composed. Furthermore, since bodies have magnitude, they can be divided into smaller fragments, and in this sense they undergo dissolution.

So if the body is a part of us, | we are not entirely immortal. But if it is an instrument, it is given to us for a certain time and must naturally be something temporary.

But the soul is the supreme part of us, the true self, and as such stands to the body as form to matter, or as user to instrument. In either case the soul is the true self.

2. So what nature does this part have?

Well, if it is body it must be wholly subject to dissolution. For all body, at least, is composite. And if it is not body but of a different nature, then that nature too must be investigated, either by the same method or by another.

But first we must consider into what constituents this body, which they call soul, must be broken down. | Life is of necessity present to soul. So if it were composed of two (or more) bodies, then of necessity either (or all) of them will have life inborn, or else one will have it and the other not, or else neither (or none) of them will have it. If in fact life were present to one of them, this very thing would be soul. |

So what body could have life of itself?

For fire, air, water and earth are of themselves lacking in soul. Any one of them which has soul present to it has come to enjoy life as something brought in from outside; and there are no bodies other than these.

Even those who thought that there are elements other than these said that they were bodies, not souls, and they did not | claim that even these have life. It would be absurd if none of them has life, but if their combination has produced life. (And if each of them could have life, just one of them would be sufficient.) Rather it is impossible for a collection of bodies to produce life, and for things lacking intellect to produce intellect. What is more, they will not claim that this happens when the elements are randomly mixed together. | There must, then, be something to order and cause the mixture, and this would hold the rank of soul. For there could not even be a simple body—let alone a compound—in existence in the cosmos unless soul existed, since it is the approach of a rational principle (*logos*) to matter that creates body, and a rational principle could not make its approach from any other source than soul.

3. If anyone were to say that this is not the case, but that atoms or things without parts come together to produce soul by unification and empathy, he would be refuted, because they are juxtaposed and not totally admixed. For nothing comes into being by unification or common affections from bodies that have no affections and cannot be united. | But soul does have a communality of affection with itself. Moreover, no body or magnitude could come from what is lacking in parts.

Further, if body is simple and they are going to deny that its material aspect of itself has life—for matter is something lacking in quality—and that that which holds the rank of form is what comports this life, then, if they are going to claim that this form is a substance, | the soul will not be the conjoint, but one of its two constituents. This could not be body since it cannot be material, since if it were we should have to analyze it in the same manner.

And if they are going to say that it is an affection of matter but not a substance, they need to tell us the source from which the affection and the life have come into matter. For matter, of course, | does not give itself shape or itself implant soul. So there must be something to bestow life, whether it bestows it on the matter or on any one of the bodies; it must be outside but transcending all bodily nature. For where there is no psychic power there could be no body. For body is in flux and its nature is swept away | and would perish in an instant if all things were bodies—even if someone were to name one of them "soul." For this would suffer the same fate as other bodies since it would have the same matter as them. Rather, it would not even come into existence, and all things would remain static in matter if there were nothing to give it shape. And perhaps there would not even be any matter at all, and this cosmos too would be dissolved | if one were to entrust it to a cohesive power of body, granting the nominal title of soul to it—to air and breath, which is most easily dispersed and does not have of itself unity. For since all bodies are subject to dissolution, anyone who attributes this cosmos to any one of them will surely be making it something lacking in intellect, swept along in random motion. | For what order would there be in breath, which needs the ordering of soul, or what rationality or intellect could there be? But when soul exists all these bodies assist it in bringing coherence to the cosmos and to each living creature, with different powers from different sources contributing to the constitution of the whole. But if soul were not present in the whole, these bodies would be nothing, let alone in any sort of order.

4. Even they, constrained by the truth, testify that there must be some phase of soul prior to bodies and superior to them. For they make breath intelligent and fire intellectual, as if the superior portion could not exist among real beings | without fire and breath and was seeking somewhere to become based. On the contrary, they should be seeking somewhere to base bodies, since, of course, bodies need to be based in psychic powers. But if they posit that life and soul are nothing more than breath, what do they mean by this much vaunted phrase of theirs "so disposed," which they fall back on when they are required | to provide some active principle other than bodies?

If, then, not all breath is soul (for there are countless forms of breath that lack soul) and if they are going to talk about "breath so disposed," then they will be saying that this disposition or state is either something real, or is nothing real. If it is nothing at all, | there would be just breath, and "disposition" would be nothing more than a word. So in this case the outcome for them will be the admission that soul and god are nothing but matter—just words—and that only matter exists. But if disposition is a reality and something other than its substrate and the matter, in matter but itself immaterial, then it would be a different nature, | a rational principle and not body, since it is, of course, not composed from matter.

Furthermore, the following argument makes it no less clear that soul cannot be any sort of body. For if it were it would be hot *or* cold, hard *or* soft, fluid *or* solid, black *or* white, or any of the different qualities found in different bodies. | If it is only hot, it heats; if it is only cold, it will cool; the addition and presence of light lightens, while the heavy makes things heavy; black will be the cause of blackness and white will be the cause of whiteness. For it is not the character of fire to cool, nor the character of cold to heat. But the soul produces | different effects in different living creatures, or opposite effects in the same creature, making some solid, others fluid, some dense, others rare, some black, others white, some light, others heavy. Yet if soul were body it could produce only one effect in keeping with the quality of the body—color as well. As it is, its effects are manifold.

5. How will they explain the fact that there are different movements, and not just one, since the motion of every body is single?

If they make choices the cause of some movements, and rational principles the causes of others, they are right. But neither choice nor even rational principles, which are certainly varied, | are intrinsic to body, which is one and simplex and has no share in at least this kind of rational principle, except what is granted to it by what caused it to be hot or cold, for example. And where would body get its power to grow over time and up to a certain point? It is right that it should grow, but it must be without the principle of growth itself | other than what might be received in the bulk of its matter to help that which causes growth by means of it.

Moreover, if the soul were to cause growth while itself being body, it too would have to grow, obviously by the addition of similar body, if it were to keep up with what it is causing to grow—and what is added will be either soul or body without soul. |

If it is soul, where will it come from? How will it enter? How will it be added? If the addition is without soul, how will this become ensouled? How will it come to be of the same mind and be one with what is already there and share the same opinions; will it not be like some alien soul, ignorant of what the other knows |?

And if, as is the case with the rest of our bodily mass, something will always be ebbing away, something always being added, and none of it remaining the same, then how can we account for our memories? How will we get to know what is appropriate to us if we never have the same soul?

Moreover, *if* soul is body, and the nature of body is such that when it is divided | into a plurality each part is different from the whole, and *if* soul is a particular magnitude and will not be soul if it is any smaller (just as all magnitudes cease by subtraction to be what they were), but *if* anything that has magnitude is made less in bulk but remains qualitatively the same, it is different *qua* body and *qua* magnitude, but is able to keep its identity in respect of its quality, which is not the same as its quantity. | What then will those who claim that the soul is body have to say in reply?

Will they admit first that in respect of each part of the soul which is in the same body, each part is soul of the same kind as the whole soul? Again, will they say that this is true of the part of the part? If so, then the magnitude contributes nothing to the being of the soul. | Yet it should do, at least if the soul is a certain magnitude. It is present as a whole in many places in the way that the body cannot be the same whole in many places, and the part cannot be what the whole is. And if they deny that each of the parts is soul then soul for them will be made up from parts lacking soul. Furthermore, the magnitude of each soul will be limited, | and there will be no soul in either direction beyond either the upper or the lower limit. So when from a single act of intercourse and from a single seed twin offspring result (or as is the case with other living creatures multiple births take place when the seed is widely distributed) | and each is undoubtedly a whole, this surely tells those whose minds are open that where the part is the same as the whole it transcends magnitude in its essence, and is necessarily not a thing of magnitude. For in this way it would retain its identity when its magnitude is stripped off it, since it would have no concern for magnitude and mass because its essence would be something different. | Therefore soul is not a thing of magnitude, nor are rational principles.

6. It is clear from what follows that if the soul is a body there will be no perceiving, thinking, understanding, virtue—or any noble activity. The following argument makes this clear: if anything is to perceive something, then it must itself be something single and must grasp what it perceives as a whole by what is the same element, whether a number of perceptions | enter through several organs of sense, or whether several qualities are perceived in a single object, or whether something complex is perceived through a single organ of sense, for example a face; for there is not one perception of the nose and another of the eyes, but it is the same perception of all these features together. And if one perception comes through the eyes and another through our hearing, there still must be something single to which both perceptions come. Otherwise how could we say | that the perceptions are different if they did not arrive together to the same point? So this must be a sort of hub, with our perceptions reaching it from all sides like radii converging from the circumference of a circle. This is the nature of what grasps the perceptions, something truly one.

But if this center point were extended | and the perceptions impacted at each end of it as if it were a line, then either the ends will meet again at one and the same point (the middle, for example) or each will have a perception of something different, just as I might perceive one thing and you something different. And if the object perceived were something single | such as a face, *either* it will be drawn together as a unity—which is clearly what happens, for it is drawn together in the very pupils of our eyes; otherwise how could very large things be seen by means of them? So that when the perceptions reach the ruling element of the soul they are all the more like thoughts which lack parts—and the ruling element will be lacking parts. *Or else,* if this center point were a magnitude the perception would be fragmented along with it, | so that each fragment would perceive something different, and none of us would have apprehension of the object of perception as a whole.

But in fact the whole is something single; for how could it be divided? For of course it will not be a case of equal matching equal, since the ruling element is not equal to any object of perception.

So into how many parts will the division be? Well, it will be divided into the number of parts | needed to match the complexity of the incoming perception. And of course each of those parts of the soul will correspondingly perceive with its own parts. Or will the parts of the parts lack perception? That is impossible. And if every part whatsoever perceives the whole, since magnitude is by its nature infinitely divisible, | the result will be that there will also be an infinity of perceptions of each object for each perceiver, like an infinite number of images of the same thing in our ruling element.

Moreover, since the object perceived is body, perceptions would have to be just like the impressions of signet rings in wax, whether the objects of sense are supposedly imprinted in blood or in air. | If the impressions are in fluid bodies, it is reasonable to suppose that they will be washed away as if imprinted on water, and there will be no memory. But if the impressions do endure, either it will be impossible for others to be made because the original impressions will inhibit them so that there will be no new impressions, | or else, if there are new impressions, the original impressions will be obliterated and there will be nothing to remember. But if it is possible to have memories and to perceive things in succession without the earlier perceptions standing in the way, it is impossible for soul to be body.

7. This same feature is evident in pain and the perception of pain. When a person's toe is said to be hurting, the pain is doubtless in the toe, but [the Stoics] will clearly agree that the awareness of the pain is in the ruling element. Although the ruling element | is aware of the painful area as something different, even so the whole soul suffers the same affection.

So how does this occur?

They will claim that it is by transference. In the first instance the psychic breath in the toe is affected; this passes the affection on to the breath adjacent to it, which passes it on a third portion, and so on until it reaches the ruling element. | Therefore, if the first portion of breath to suffer pain became aware of it, the perception in the second portion must be different if the perception is by transference. Similarly with the third portion, so that there will be a large or even infinite number of perceptions about a single pain, and the ruling element will be aware of it after all of these, and its own perception will be in addition to them. | In truth none of these later perceptions would be of the pain in the toe, but the perception in the breath adjacent to the toe would be that the sole of the foot was hurting, and the third perception would be that of pain somewhere further up the leg. So there would be many pains, and the ruling element would not be aware of the pain in the toe, | but of the pain in the part next to itself, and would recognize this alone and ignore the rest, not realizing that it was the toe that was hurting.

So if it is impossible for the awareness of something like this to come about by transference, or for any body, in that it is a mass, to recognize an affection in another body—for every part | of a magnitude is different—then we must assume that anything which has perception is identical to itself throughout. And this activity is proper to another kind of reality than body.

8. The following arguments should demonstrate that if the soul is body of any kind, then thought is an impossibility.

If sense perception consists in the soul's apprehending the objects of sense by making use of the body, then thinking could not be apprehension by means of the body, or else it would be the same as sense perception. | So if thinking is apprehension free of bodily involvement, that which is to do the thinking is even less likely to be body.

Furthermore, if sense perception is of sensibles and thinking is of intelligibles (even if they would be reluctant to admit it there will at least be thoughts of some intelligibles, and apprehension of some things without magnitude) | how will a magnitude think of something without magnitude, or of something without parts by means of something that has parts?

Well, with some partless part of itself.

But if this is so, then that which is to do the thinking will not be a body. For there is no need for the whole to be in contact, since there only needs to be contact at one point. So if they are going to admit the truth, that primary thoughts | are of things entirely pure and free of body, the Forms, then that which thinks must come to know them when it is free, or becomes free, of the body. And if they claim that thoughts are of enmattered forms, even so these thoughts occur when body is separated off, and it is the intellect which does the separating. For the separation of circle, triangle, line, and point has no need of flesh | or of matter in general. So the soul too must separate itself from body in such circumstances. So the soul is not body.

The beautiful and the just, in my opinion, have no magnitude; so neither does thought about them. So when they approach our soul, | it will receive them in its undivided state, and they will remain there in its undivided state.

And how could there be virtues of the soul—temperance, justice, bravery and the rest—if it were body. For temperance, justice and bravery would be some sort of breath or blood—perhaps bravery is impassivity of the breath, and temperance | a good intermixture of it, and beauty some kind of shapeliness in the impressions on it according to which we say that people are of a vigorous and beautiful physique when we see them. Of course it would be appropriate for breath to be strong and beautiful where impressions are concerned; but what need does breath have of wisdom? On the contrary, would it not take delight in embraces and touch, | where it will either be warmed or have a desire to be moderately cooled, or will it not tend toward soft, tender, and smooth things? Why should it be concerned about fair distribution?

Does the soul attain to the contemplation of virtue and of other intelligibles as eternal entities, or does virtue come to be in someone, benefit them and then pass away? | But in that case what causes it, and from what source?

For such an agent would in turn endure. So the virtues must be among eternal and enduring entities, like the principles of geometry. And if they belong among enduring and eternal entities, they cannot belong among bodies. Accordingly that in which they are to exist must also be of this nature, and so it cannot be body. | For the entire nature of body does not endure, but is in flux.

8^{1}. If, when they see the activities that bodies have in warming, cooling, exerting force and weighing down, they locate the soul in this world as if stationing it in the field of action, they show their ignorance. They fail to realize first that bodies produce these effects themselves | through the bodiless powers in them; secondly, that we do not consider these powers to belong to the soul, but rather thinking, perceiving, calculating, desiring and taking wise and good care, all of which require some other kind of existence. So by transferring the powers of the bodiless to bodies | they leave nothing for the bodiless. It is evident from what follows that it is by bodiless powers that even bodies are empowered to do what is in their power to do. They will agree that quality and quantity are different, and that all body is quantitative, but not all body is qualitative—for example matter; and in agreeing | to this they will also agree that quality, being different from quantity, is also different from body. For if it is not quantity, how can it be body?

Furthermore, as was stated earlier somewhere, if all body and all mass loses its previous identity when divided, but if the same quality endures in its entirety | in each part of a body which has been split up, then sweetness, for example, could not be a body since the sweetness of honey is no less sweetness in each individual portion of honey. This is true of all other qualities.

Again, if powers were bodies, strong powers would have to be large masses, and weak powers | small masses. But if large masses can have small powers, while a few very small masses have very great powers, then we have to ascribe their effectiveness to something other than magnitude, and this must therefore be something without magnitude.

And the fact that matter, being body, remains the same, according to them, but achieves different effects when it acquires qualities | proves that what it acquires are rational principles without matter and without body.

Nor must they base their claim on the grounds that when breath or blood is withdrawn, living creatures die. For while it is not possible to exist without these, that is true of a host of other things, and none of these could be soul. Moreover, neither breath nor blood pervades the whole living creature, but soul does.

8[2]. Again, if soul were body and pervaded the whole, it would also be blended with it in the same way that other bodies are blended. And if the blending of bodies prevents any of the bodies in the blend from existing in actuality, then not even the soul would be present in the body in actuality, but would lose its being | as soul and exist only in potentiality—just as the sweet does not exist when sweet and sour are blended. In which case we have no soul.

As for its being body mixed throughout with body, so that wherever the one is there too the other is, with both masses occupying an equal space and no increase taking place | when one is inserted into the other, then the admixture will leave nothing undivided. For it is not a blend when large portions alternate side by side (for this will be what he calls juxtaposition), but when what has been inserted pervades the whole even if it is quite a small quantity, which is impossible—for the lesser to become equal to the larger. | Even so, granted that in pervading it divides the whole up throughout, the necessary consequence is that, if it divides it up at every point and there is no intervening body which is not divided, the division of the body must be into points, which is impossible. If it were possible, since division is infinite (for whatever body you take is divisible) the infinity will exist not only in potentiality but also in actuality. | So it is not possible for body to pervade body throughout. But soul does pervade whole bodies; therefore it is bodiless.

8[3]. They say that this same breath was originally a natural principle of growth, but that when it got into the cold and was hardened it became soul, since it became refined in the cold. But this is absurd. For many living creatures are born in heat and have souls that are not cooled; | even so, they say that nature is prior to soul, which comes into being because of external circumstances. So the result is that they first create something inferior, and prior to this something still worse, which they call "state," while intellect is last, obviously because it derives from soul. Now if intellect is prior to all things, they should have made soul next, then nature, | with what is posterior always being inferior—which is what is natural. So if god as the equivalent of Intellect, in their view, is posterior, created and having intellection added to it from outside, then it would not be possible for soul or intellect or god even to exist. If the potential were to come into being without the prior existence of what is in activity and of intellect, then it could not come into activity. | For what will there be to bring it to actuality if there is nothing else prior to it in existence? And if it is to bring itself into actuality—which is absurd—it will do so at least by looking at something else which will exist in actuality, not potentiality. Yet if what is in potentiality is always going to remain the same in itself, it can bring about an actuality, and even this will be better than the potential, being, so to speak, its object of desire. | So the superior is prior, having a nature different from body and always existing in actuality. Therefore intellect and soul are prior to nature. So in that case soul is not like breath or body.

Other arguments have been put forward by others to show that soul could not be called body; but this is sufficient.

8[4]. Since soul is of a different nature, we should enquire what that nature is. So is it something other than body but something to do with body, like an attunement? For although the Pythagoreans used the term "attunement" in a different sense, they thought it to be something like the attunement of lyre strings. | For just as in that case when these strings are tightened some sort of affection supervenes on them, which is called "attunement," in just the same way, when our bodies come to exist as a blend of dissimilar elements, a blend of a particular kind produces life and soul, which is the affection supervening on the blend. But many arguments | have already been voiced to show that this view is impossible.

First, that the soul is prior but an attunement is posterior. Secondly, that the soul rules and directs the body and is engaged in many fights against it, which the soul would not do if it were an attunement. Thirdly, that the soul, unlike an attunement, is a substance. Fourthly, that when the blend of bodies | from which we are made up is in proportion, this would rather constitute health;

Fifthly, that there would be a different soul according to the different blend of each part, and consequently be multiple. Sixthly, and most importantly, that there would need to be another soul in existence before the current one producing this attunement, just as in the case of musical instruments | there is the player who imposes the attunement on the strings, having within himself the correct intervals according to which he tunes the strings. For neither in the latter case can the strings, nor in the former case the bodies, bring themselves into attunement by themselves.

In general these people too produce what is ensouled from what is lacking in soul, and they create a haphazard organization from what is disorganized; | they produce the organization not from soul, but say that the soul has received its being from a spontaneous arrangement. But this cannot happen either in parts or in wholes. Therefore the soul is not an attunement.

8[5]. We should next consider what is meant by those who say that the soul is an actualization. They claim that in the compound the soul stands to body as form to matter, that is the body which it ensouls—not the form of all body, nor of body *qua* body, but "a natural body with organs having life potentially." | So if it has been assimilated to what it has been applied to in the way that the shape of a statue is assimilated to the bronze, then first, when the body is divided up, the soul is correspondingly partitioned; and when a part of it is cut off then there is a portion of the soul in the part cut off. Secondly, the withdrawal of the soul in sleep cannot take place since the actualization | has to be part and parcel of that of which it is the actualization—in fact there cannot even be such a thing as sleep.

Thirdly, moreover, if the soul is an actualization, there can be no opposition of reason to desires, but the whole undergoes one and the same experience with no internal conflict.

Fourthly, perhaps perception can occur, but intellection cannot. | That is why they import another soul, intellect, which they suppose to be immortal. So the reasoning soul must necessarily be an actualization—if we must use the term—in some sense other than this.

Fifthly, in fact, since the perceiving soul too retains the impressions of sensible objects | when they are not present, it will accordingly retain them independently of the body. Otherwise these impressions will be in the soul as shapes and images; but if this were the case it would be impossible for them to receive other impressions. Therefore the perceptive soul is not an inseparable actualization.

Sixthly, furthermore, not even the element in the soul that has desires for things beyond the body, not just drink and food, can be an inseparable actualization. |

Seventhly, there remains the vegetative element of the soul, and it might appear possible to dispute the claim that this is a separable entity in this way. But not even this is possible. For if the life principle of every plant is in its roots, and if when the rest of it withers its soul remains in its roots and its lower parts, as is the case with most plants, | then clearly the soul has withdrawn from the other parts and become concentrated in one place. Therefore the soul is not present in the whole as an inseparable actualization.

Again, before the plant begins to grow, the soul exists in the small mass. So if the soul not only retreats from a larger mass into a smaller one but also advances from a small mass into the whole plant, what is there to prevent it from being completely separated? |

Eighthly, how could it be the actualization of a body with parts if it is itself without parts?

Ninthly, the same soul is present in one creature after another. So how could the soul of one creature become that of the next in succession if it were the actualization of a single creature? This phenomenon can be clearly seen in the way that one living creature changes into another.

Therefore the soul does not have its existence | in being the form of anything, but it is a real being and does not owe its existence to becoming established in a body, but exists before it becomes the soul of any particular body. It is not the body of a living creature that engenders its soul.

So what does its real being consist in? If it is neither body nor an affection of body, but action and activity, and if many things are in it and derive from it, then what sort of a thing is it, | given that it is a real being other than body?

Well, it is clearly what we call true being. For everything which is body should be called "becoming," not "being," since "it comes to be, passes away, and could never be truly existent"; it is preserved by its participation in being, to the extent that it participates in it.

9. But the other nature which has its being from within itself is true being in its entirety, which neither comes to be nor passes away. Otherwise all other things will vanish and could not later come into being, if that which guarantees their preservation, especially that of the cosmos, which is conserved and given its order by soul, should cease to exist. | For this is the principle of motion, which imparts motion to other things; it is self-moved and bestows on the ensouled body the life which it has from within itself and never loses, in that it has it intrinsically. For of course not everything enjoys a life that is imparted, otherwise the series will extend infinitely. | But there must be some nature that has life primally, a nature that of necessity is indestructible and immortal in that it is the principle of life for all else. Here all that is divine and all that is blessed must be rooted, living and being of itself, having primary being and primary life, changeless in its essence, | neither coming to be nor passing away. For where could it come from, or into what could it pass away? And if it

is to be properly called "being," then it cannot exist at one moment and not exist at another—just as the color white cannot be white at one moment and not white at another. | But if the white thing were also a real being as well as being white, then it would exist eternally. But as it is it only possesses "white," while whatever has being present to it of itself and primally will be in eternal existence. So this being, which exists of itself and primally, cannot be lifeless like stone or wood, but as much of it as remains isolated | must be alive, enjoying pure life. But anything that is mixed in with what is inferior is barred from achieving what is best, although, of course, it does not lose its own nature but recovers its "previous state" when it rises back up to its proper home.

10. The demonstration that the soul is not body makes it obvious that it is akin to the more divine and eternal nature. Moreover, it does not have even shape or color, and it is intangible. However, all this can also be shown by the following arguments.

Of course, we agree that all that is divine and truly existent | enjoys good and rational life. We should now advance the argument, and our starting point must be the consideration of the nature of our own soul.

Let us not take the embodied soul with all its accretions of irrational appetites and desires and its receptivity to other affections, but the soul which has brushed these off | and, as far as is possible, has no association with the body. A soul of this kind makes it clear that evils are additions which come to a soul from outside, and that when it is purified the noblest things—wisdom and the other virtues—are inherent in it, being intrinsic to it.

So if this is what the soul is like when it returns to itself, how can it fail to be of the nature | which we claim to belong to all that is divine and eternal? For since wisdom and true virtue are divine beings, they could not be engendered in anything inferior or mortal. Rather anything able to host them must of necessity be divine, since it shares in the divine through being akin and of the same essence. That is why any one of us who is of such a nature would differ very little | in his actual soul from those superior beings. His inferiority would amount to no more than the presence of his soul in a body.

So if every man were of this nature, or if there were a large number with this sort of soul, no-one would be so disbelieving as to fail to believe that the soul in them was entirely immortal. As it is, they see that in very many cases | a man's soul bears many scars, and so they do not think of it as they would think of something divine and immortal.

But one should consider each man's nature by concentrating on what is unblemished in him, since any addition always prevents us from understanding the nature of whatever it has been added to. So consider by abstracting—or rather let the man who has abstracted consider himself; | he will then know for sure that he is immortal, when he views himself present in the intelligible and pure realm. For he will see an intellect that sees nothing perceptible, nothing within the mortal sphere, but which apprehends the eternal by means of the eternal, all the contents of the intelligible world, and himself become an intelligible and dazzling cosmos, | flooded with the light of the truth by the Good, which illuminates all the intelligibles with truth.

So often, when he has ascended to the divine, fixing his mind on assimilation to the divine, he will consider the words "Greetings; for you I am an immortal god" to have been well spoken. | If purification gives us knowledge of what is best, then the understanding which is contained within it is revealed, and this is true understanding. For the soul does not, of course, see wisdom and justice by making excursions but by contemplation within itself of itself and of what it was formerly, seeing them firmly fixed within itself | like statues which have become tarnished with the passage of time and which it has now burnished. It is as if gold were ensouled and had purified itself of all dross; beforehand it did not know itself because it could not see any gold, but then, catching sight of itself in its refined state, it marveled at what it saw and realized | that it needed no beauty applied from outside, since it was itself unsurpassed—provided that it was left to itself.

11. What person of intellect would argue that something of this nature is not immortal? It has present to it a life that cannot be extinguished. For how could it be extinguished, since it is in no way acquired from outside, and is not even like the heat that is present to fire? I do not mean that the heat is in the fire | as something acquired from outside, but that even if it is not in the fire as something acquired, it is so in the matter underlying the fire. For it is in this that the fire is extinguished. But the soul does not have life in the sense that it is underlying matter and that life comes to it so as to make it soul. For *either* life is an essence, and soul is a being that has life of itself (which is the object of our enquiry), | and they agree that this is something immortal; *or* they will analyze this too as being something compounded until they reach something immortal and self-moving which simply must not have anything to do with death.

Or if they will say that life is an acquired affection of matter, | they will be forced to agree that the source from which this affection entered the matter is immortal, and cannot admit the opposite of what it brings. But in fact there is a single nature which is alive in actuality.

12. Furthermore, if they are going to say that every soul is liable to destruction, then everything must surely have been destroyed long ago. But if they are going to claim that some souls are liable to destruction and others not

so, and claim, for example, that the soul of the cosmos is immortal but that a man's own soul is not, then they will have to give their reasons.

For each soul is a principle of motion, and each soul lives of itself, | and grasps the same things by the same activity, having intellection of what is in the heavens and of what is beyond the heavens, seeking out everything that has substantial being by ascending to the first principle. Its internal intellection of real being derives from its contemplations within itself and from recollection; this gives it its being prior to body, | and because it enjoys acts of intellection eternally it gives it eternal being.

Everything that can be broken up has acquired its being through composition of parts, and is naturally broken up again into those same parts. But soul is a simple nature, a simplex, that exists in actuality through being alive. So because of this it cannot be destroyed.

But after all, it is a thing of parts | and could be broken into pieces and so destroyed.

No; a soul is not mass or a magnitude, as has been demonstrated.

But it will be destroyed by being qualitatively changed.

No; a destructive qualitative change is the affection of a composite which takes away the form but leaves the matter.

So if the soul cannot be destroyed in any of these ways, it must be indestructible.

13. So if the intelligible world is separate, how does the soul enter body?

The element which is pure intellect cannot suffer affection, and has a life that is purely intellective within the intelligible realm, where it remains eternally, since it has no urge or desire. But any part in that realm next to intellect which receives in addition desire, | by the addition of desire proceeds thereupon, as it were, further afield, and desires to organize according to what it has seen in its intellective phase. As if this had made it pregnant and it were suffering birth pangs it is keen to create, and it becomes a craftsman. In its keenness it stretches out to enfold the perceptible, and together with the entire soul of the cosmos | it transcends what it is organizing outside itself and shares in caring for the cosmos.

But when it wishes to organize a part it becomes isolated in the part where it is. But it does not belong wholly and exclusively to the body, but has something which is outside the body. So not even the intellect of this soul suffers affections, but is sometimes in the body, sometimes outside it. | It sets off from the primary real beings and proceeds as far as the third realities, in this world below intellect, being the activity of the intellect which remains in the same state, filling all things with beauty through the soul, and organizing them—the immortal through the immortal, since it will everlastingly be itself through its ceaseless activity.

14. All the souls of other living creatures which have entered the bodies of animals because they have gone astray are also of necessity immortal. And if there is any other sort of soul, it too must derive from a living nature | and must itself be the cause of life in living creatures. This is particularly true of the souls of plants. For all souls started from the same source, have life as something proper to them, are likewise bodiless, have no parts and are real beings.

If it is claimed that the human soul, being tripartite, will be broken up because it is composite, we will assert that when souls | are released in a pure state they shed what has been added to them at birth like a molding, while other souls retain it for a very long period. But even the inferior part which has been shed does not perish as long as its source endures. For no part of real being will ever perish.

15. We have, then, said what needed to be said in reply to those requiring proof. But what needs to be said to those looking for belief based on the evidence of the senses must be selected from the extensive body of findings on this topic. There are too the oracles of the gods ordering the appeasement of the anger of wronged souls, and the apportionment of honor to the dead | on the grounds that they are aware of them, a practice universal among men. Many souls that were formerly in human beings continued

to benefit mankind after they left the body. By establishing prophetic oracles | they brought many benefits, in particular showing through their own survival that the souls of others have not perished either.

Commentary

Chapter 1

In this chapter Plotinus outlines the area of enquiry—the immortality of the human individual—and promises that the enquiry will be made "according to nature." He begins by stating that the human individual is a composite of soul and body, and proceeds to make some general remarks about body, stressing that at any level body is itself a composite and therefore liable to decomposition. By contrast the soul, which is "the true self," stands to body as form stands to matter.

Lines 1–4

Plotinus begins by stating the scope of his enquiry—the immortality of each one of us—and asks whether the whole person perishes, or whether some part of us perishes while some part endures. He then gives notice of his method: it is to be an enquiry "according to nature" (*kata phusin*). At the outset there is no specific mention of soul, although there is a hint in the phrase "the true self."

1, 1 *Is each one of us immortal*: As the argument proceeds we see that Plotinus is limiting the scope of the enquiry to the soul of the human individual, and does not include soul at other levels such as the soul of the cosmos or Soul the hypostasis, except by way of illustration.

We might have expected the three options to be: (a) is each one of us *entirely* immortal? or (b) is each one of us entirely mortal? or (c) is some part of each of us mortal, another part immortal? Instead the first question is "is each one of us immortal?" with the limiting *entirely* held back until the second option is expressed.

1, 3 *the true self*: Plotinus makes it clear at the end of this chapter, in lines 22–25, that the soul is "the true self." In this he is following Plato *Alcibiades* 130c when, answering the question under discussion "what on earth are our true selves?" (129b) or "what on earth is a man?" (129e), Socrates states that he is neither body nor the composite of soul and body, but that "the man, if anything, turns out to be nothing other than the soul." In a late treatise, II.3 [52] 9, 15ff., Plotinus asks what the true self is, and concludes that it is not the ensouled body, but the soul that is outside the body: "For each of us is twofold, one a compound, the other the person himself." It is the latter that Plotinus has in mind here.

When Plotinus talks about *some parts of us* when referring to the body the plural is appropriate and fits the language of composition and decomposition. When he uses the plural *others* to refer to the soul it is less clear what he has in mind. When he turns to the discussion of the soul at Chapter 8[5] he is at pains to stress the essential integrity of the soul, or at least of its higher parts, for example at Chapter 10, 7 he says, "Let us not take the embodied soul with all its accretions of unnatural appetites and desires and its receptivity to other affections, but the soul which has brushed these off and, as far as is possible, has no association with the body"; and at III.6.5, 20ff., when talking about the purification of the soul, he talks of one part of the soul (the rational) as being "no longer in the body so as to belong to it" and the other part as being the affective part (*to pathêtikon*), observing a broad distinction between the rational and the irrational parts of the soul. The further the soul withdraws from worldly concerns, the more the irrational part ceases to have significance. As Rist (1967, 230) says: "When . . . the higher soul is enjoying its vision of the One, its lower counterparts do not strictly speaking cease to exist, but become irrelevant to the concentrated personality." So perhaps here Plotinus is using the plural loosely to include all three parts of the soul.

This is an early treatise (the second in Porphyry's chronological list at *Life of Plotinus* 4), and it is unlikely that Plotinus is here marking a difference between self and soul. If he is, then it is not a distinction that is taken up in this treatise.[15]

1, 3 *according to nature*: Plotinus is indicating that the enquiry will be analytic—at least until the final chapter where the focus is briefly on an empirical approach. The word "nature" (*phusis*) appears constantly throughout the treatise to remind us of the main focus. There is too perhaps an ironical dig at the Stoics, Plotinus' target in much of this treatise. Their avowed aim was "to live according to nature" (*kata phusin zên*), and Plotinus is perhaps suggesting that they should carry this principle over to their examination of the questions at issue.

Lines 4–7

Plotinus reasserts the distinction between body and soul before proceeding to his analysis of each.

1, 5 *a human*: Plotinus is using the Greek word *anthrôpos* in the broader sense of "each one of us" rather than the more limited sense used by Plato at *Alcibiades* 130c noted above.

15 See further O'Daly (1973) and Gerson (1994, 139–146).

1, 6 *This may be either . . . or*: The two possibilities are not exhaustive. Plotinus prefaces each by the particles *eit'oun*, which Denniston (1954, 418) translates as "whether, in point of fact," and says: "the implication [is] that the fact does not greatly matter for the immediate purposes." This is further confirmed by *all'oun* in line 7, "whatever the case" (Denniston 442–447).

1, 6 *an instrument for our use*: This echoes Plato *Alcibiades* 129c, where Socrates is making the distinction between the craftsman and his instruments (*organa*); see below on 1, 23.

1, 8 *nature and essence*: The nature (*phusis*) and essence (*ousia*) of each is different. Their natures are examined under the general descriptions, that of body following immediately at 1, 7, and that of soul at 8[4], although throughout the treatise there is necessarily an interplay between the two. Their essences are to be defined by their ontological status, following the Platonic distinction between the real world of the intelligible and the less real world of the sensible.

Lines 7–17

Plotinus makes some preliminary points about the nature of composite body, which can maintain its cohesion only when soul is present to it. This is true both on the cosmic and the individual level. On the cosmic level Plotinus takes his cue from Plato *Timaeus*, especially 34b, where we are told that the divine demiurge set soul at the center of the cosmos "and caused it to extend through the whole, and further wrapped its body round with soul on the outside" (tr. Cornford). In Plotinus' special language of emanation the natural world is the outcome of Soul the hypostasis.[16] His clearest statement of the supremacy and ubiquity of soul is to be found at V.1.2. In these lines in IV.7 Plotinus envisages a two-way dynamic. At any level of corporeal being there is a degree of cohesion derived from soul (and therefore ultimately from the One), and a converse tendency to dispersal and decay into constituent elements, ultimately into "the simplest bodies," the four basic elements, viz. earth, water, air, and fire. Even these are further analyzable into form and matter. At this point, which can be reached only by mental analysis, matter is entirely divorced from form and the activity of soul and devolves into incorporeal non-being.[17] The Greek word *sôma* has as many connotations as the English "body." At this point Plotinus narrows the focus from body in general to the human body. What is true of the cosmos at large is true *a fortiori* of our own human bodies, and it is to the human condition that Plotinus devotes the rest of the treatise.

16 For a succinct account see O'Meara (1993, chapters 6 and 7).

17 See O'Brien in Gerson (1996, chapter 7), and Fleet (1995, 164–167).

1, 8 *Body is of course, itself a composite*: Just as the human being is a composite of soul and body, of the immaterial and the material, so too body is composite, and ultimately made up of immaterial (form) and material (matter). But the soul, being non-composite, is indestructible, while body, conversely, being composite is subject to decomposition.

1, 11 *Each of its constituents*: The basic constituents of body are the four elements, and the continuity of any one particular body depends on the harmonization in due proportion of the elements by soul. When this proportion is disrupted beyond a certain point and the organizing power of soul is weakened, the body loses its cohesion and ceases to be that particular body. The destruction of a body can take place at different levels and in different ways; even our senses perceive this happening in certain cases. Plotinus' focus here seems to be on the constituents of bodies seen in terms of the four elements, and he perhaps has in mind Aristotle's discussion of elemental change at *On Coming-to-be and Passing-away* (*De Generatione et Corruptione*) I.8 and II.4 and 5, and perhaps also Plato *Timaeus* 49bff. Again it should be noted that the analysis at this level is notional, since in the natural world no one element can be found unalloyed. He offers three ways in which a constituent element can leave the composite. Either (a) it is "carried to its proper place," as determined by its relative density, with fire, the most rarified element, forming the outermost of four concentric spheres, air next, water next and earth, the densest, the innermost,[18] or (b) one element obliterates another, for example in a conflagration (cf. Aristotle *On Coming-to-be and Passing-away* (*De Generatione et Corruptione*) 327b12ff.), or (c) one element is transformed into another, so losing its identity, as at Plato *Timaeus* 49b and Alexander of Aphrodisias *On Mixture* (*De Mixtione)* 216,14ff. (= SVF 2 473 = LS 48C), where Alexander is discussing Chrysippus' views on mixture. For the composition of body from matter and form see Alexander of Aphrodisias *Supplement* 115, 12: "Just as matter is body lacking form, so it is reasonable to say that form is lacking in matter and body. For the conjoint is made up of these. Further, if body is lacking in soul, why should soul too not be incorporeal?"

Lines 17–20

In a simpler way the physical division of a composite body can result in its loss of identity *qua* that body. Cf. IV.4.27, 9–12: "But what does the soul contribute to the body of the earth itself? We should not think that an earthy body is the same when it is separated from the earth as when it remains part of it, as stones demonstrate; they continue

18 Cf. Simplicius *On Aristotle Physics* 2.263, 26–29 and 287, 30; he quotes Aristotle *On the Heavens* 284b33.

to grow as long as they are connected to it, but when they are removed they remain the same size as they were at the moment of removal."

Lines 20–22

Plotinus draws the conclusion, to give provisional answers to the questions posed at the outset, that the human being, as a conjoint of body and soul, is not immortal, even if the body is seen as a tool, a temporary and thereby mortal possession.

Lines 22–25

Plotinus ends the chapter with a definitive statement of his view, drawing on both Platonic and Aristotelian precedent.

1, 22 *the supreme part*: The phrase echoes Aristotle *On the Soul* 410b13: "Whatever it is that causes the elements to cohere is supreme."

1, 22 *the true self*: See above on 1, 3.

1, 23 *as form to matter*: Although Plotinus, as a Platonist, has fundamentally different views on the nature of the soul from those of Aristotle, he is ready to exploit those parts of Aristotle's doctrines which provide clarification. This is noted in Porphyry *Life of Plotinus* 14: "In Plotinus' works both Stoic and Peripatetic doctrines are interwoven, although they lie under the surface." In this instance Aristotle's form-matter doctrine is exploited to demonstrate the relation of soul to body. Aristotle's clearest statement comes at *On the Soul* 2.1 412a20: "The soul then must be substance (*ousia*) as the form of natural body potentially having life." Plotinus will proceed later in the treatise, at Chapter 8⁵, to attack Aristotle's doctrine that the soul is an actualization; but for the time being this identification of soul as form is entirely acceptable.[19]

1, 23 *as user to instrument*: The language and imagery is that of Plato *Alcibiades* 129bff., where Socrates makes the distinction between the user and his tools. A man *qua* shoemaker uses a variety of tools both external to him, such as leather cutters, and internal to himself, such as his hands and eyes; a man *qua* man uses his whole body and is therefore different from his body; the true user of the body is the soul (130a), and the soul is the true self (130c).[20]

19 For Aristotle's basic soul-matter distinction see *On the Soul* 412a6ff.

20 See also above on 1, 6.

Chapter 2

In this chapter Plotinus considers in broad terms the consequences of saying that the soul is body. As yet he is adopting a broadly anti-materialist position and making some general points. He will turn his attention later in the treatise to specific schools and doctrines. His premise is that "life is of necessity present to soul," so that the correct method of investigation would be to discover what sort of body would have life present to it as something inborn if that body were to qualify as soul. He concludes that it is no single one of the four elements, nor any combination or admixture of them, but that there must be some organizing principle underlying the existence of body. In this latter point he is in fact on common ground with the Stoics.

Lines 1–4

The soul must be body or not body. If the former, then, like all body, it is composite and therefore subject to decomposition. If the latter, then that nature must be investigated.

2, 1 *If it were body . . . if it were not body*: Plotinus uses the optative mood in both alternative protases, suggesting the tentative nature of the discussion at this point.

That soul is body is axiomatic for Stoics, although they are not singled out here; that it is not body is axiomatic for Platonists.

2, 2 *subject to dissolution*: The Greek term is *analuteon*, a verbal adjective based on the verb *analuein*, from which the English word "analysis" is derived. Plotinus uses it in various places both figuratively and literally, often in contrast (as here) to parts of the verb *suntithenai* = to put together, to compose (as at 1, 9 and 1, 17). For both Stoics and Platonists body is a composite of the elements and as such is subject to dissolution or decomposition. For the Stoics the ultimate dissolution came at the periodic conflagration in which all things are returned to fire.[21] Soul, being a material compound of air and fire which pervades matter both at a cosmic and an individual level is thereby ultimately subject to dissolution—even the souls of the righteous, as we are told by Eusebius: *Preparation for the Gospel* (*Praeparatio Evangelica*) 15.20.6 (= SVF 2.809 = LS 53W). For a Platonist, by contrast, soul is not a material composite and is not thereby subject to such dissolution.

2, 4 *that nature too would have to be investigated*: Porphyry (*Life of Plotinus* 13) tells us that on one occasion he discussed the relation between body and soul for three days with Plotinus, and Plotinus himself says at IV.8.1, 27,

21 See M. J. White in Inwood (ed., 2003, 128–130).

talking about Plato's teachings on the soul, "it is clear that he does not always speak with sufficient consistency for us to make out his intentions with any ease"—so much so that in Porphyry's grouping the whole of *Ennead* IV is devoted to questions of the soul, as well as others, for example III.6.1–5. The brief treatise IV.7 is thus only a small part of Plotinus' contribution to the question.

2, 4 *by the same method . . . by another*: "The same method" is the one introduced at 1, 3 "according to nature"; another method would be a non-analytical method, such as is spoken of at I.6.8, 25–27, "you must not look with the eyes, but close them and wake up, and change to a different sort of vision which all possess but few use."

Lines 4–5

Plotinus asks what the material constituents of a corporeal soul might be.

2, 5 *into what constituents this body which they call soul*: Plotinus rarely mentions by name those with whom he is taking issue. In this instance he is referring in general to all those who claim that the soul is bodily, but much of the treatise is devoted to a criticism of the Stoic doctrines. Galen *Doctrines of Plato and Hippocrates* 5.3.8 (= SVF 2.841 part = LS 47H) tells us that Chrysippus describes the breath (*pneuma*) which comprises the soul's commanding faculty (*to hêgemonikon)* as being made up of air and fire, acquiring some moisture from the body it inhabits. Diogenes Laertius *Lives of the Philosophers* 7.156–157 informs us of other Stoic views of the soul, all of which agree that (a) it is material body, and (b) that it is a form of warm breath.

Lines 5–10

Since life is of necessity inborn in soul, then we must discover which of its bodily element or elements has soul present to it.

2, 5 *Life is of necessity present to soul*: Two Greek words, *apsukhos* and *empsukhos* are used in contrast several times by Plato (e.g., at *Sophist* 265c), Aristotle (e.g., at *On the Soul* 413a21) and Plotinus (e.g., at 8^4, 24). Their literal translations are, respectively, "lacking in soul" and "ensouled," but in other contexts are often used to denote "lifeless" and "living." The distinction between life and soul both in philosophical and common parlance became rather blurred, but a distinction is important in Plotinus' argument here. Furthermore both Plato and Plotinus display some ambiguity in making clear the range of items to be considered as ensouled. On the one hand Plato makes it clear in *Timaeus* that the whole cosmos is pervaded by soul (see above on 1, 7–17) and is a single living creature, and Plotinus follows this line of thought in making the cosmos the product of, and pervaded by, Soul the hypostasis. So in this respect there is nothing other than matter (which is pure nothingness[22]) that is lacking in soul. However Plato makes a distinction when he says at *Phaedrus* 246b, "soul as a whole which cares for all that is soulless," a passage quoted three times by Plotinus (at III.4.2,1; IV.3.3, 14; IV.3.9, 13). Plotinus in this treatise observes the common-sense distinction between lifeless things and living creatures. His concern is the human soul, and he is not concerned to prove its immortality, which for a Platonist is axiomatic. His authority for stating that *life is of necessity present to soul* is *Phaedo*, where Socrates develops a general theory of causation, with the distinction between essential and non-essential properties underlying the argument. If one thing, x, is the cause of a property, P, in another thing, y, then x must itself have P of necessity. P is an essential property of x, a non-essential property of y. So, for example, what causes something to become hot is heat—or "more subtly" fire—which must itself be hot. When applied to the case in hand it means that what causes the body to be alive is not just life, but "more subtly"—soul, which must of necessity possess life (*Phaedo* 105cd).

Plotinus uses a number of words and phrases to denote this relationship (in contrast to "something brought

22 See O'Meara (1993, chapter 7, sections 1 and 2).

in from outside"); "present of necessity" (Plato's regular term for the relation of Form to particular is "to be present to"), "inborn" (the Greek word is *sumphuton,* often translated as "innate" or "connate"), "of itself."

2, 7 *So if it were composed . . .* : I.e. the bodily soul. Since body is composite (as established at 1, 8) we need to consider each of its constituents—which are also bodily—to determine which of them has life as an essential property to bring to the compound. If only one of the bodies constituting the compound has life as something essential to it, then this constituent body is indeed soul. Plotinus briefly allows for the possibility that more than one of the constituent elements (or even none of them) might qualify, but he does not pursue the possibility at this stage.

Lines 10–14

Plotinus now shows that no body can have life "of itself," as an essential property. All bodies are either simple bodies, that is, the four elements, or else compounds and ultimately reducible to these four elements. Since all these are lacking in soul "of themselves," any life they have must be imported as a non-essential property ("brought in from outside").

2, 11 *earth*: Jaap Mansfield has suggested that earth is included "for rhetorical effect," since no-one claimed that soul was earth. But Empedocles is said by Aristotle in *On the Soul* 404b12 to have stated that soul was composed of the elements; Aristotle goes on to say that in *Timaeus* Plato too constructs the soul out of the elements (*Timaeus* 42). At Aristotle *On the Soul* 405a2 Hippo is said to "rather tiresomely" claim that soul is water.

2, 13 *there are no bodies other than these*: Graeser (1972, 26) suggests that Plotinus is blocking out any attempt on the part of the Stoics to attribute to the soul a special body different from the regular four elements.

Lines 14–15

Plotinus briefly considers, and dismisses, philosophers who considered that there were elements other than the standardly accepted four.

2, 14 *Even those who thought that there are elements other than these*: Plotinus does not name these materialists. They fall inside the broad category identified by Aristotle at *Metaphysics* 5.3 1014a32: "Those who talk about the elements of bodies mean the parts into which bodies are ultimately divisible, but which are not themselves divisible into parts which differ in form, whether these elements are one or many; this is what they mean by the term element." Previously, at *Metaphysics* 1.3 983b7, he has listed and discussed the views of various of the earlier natural philosophers, and singles out Empedocles as the one who fixed on the four elements, earth, air, fire, and water, which remained fundamental to natural philosophy until the Middle Ages.[23] But Plotinus here hints at some who thought "that there are elements other than these," but does not say whether he is limiting his remarks to those who added an extra element or elements to these four, or whether he is including those who posited elements different from them. In the former group we can include Aristotle himself, who proposed a fifth element, *aithêr*, (e.g., at *Meteorology* 340a1ff.) and perhaps Anaxagoras, for whom the motivating force behind the cosmos is corporeal Mind (*Nous*).[24] In the latter group we can include the atomists, who postulated atoms and void (Aristotle *Metaphysics* 1.4 985b5: "Leucippus and his follower Democritus said that the elements are the full [*to plêres* = atoms] and the void [*to kenon*]"); and even the Pythagoreans, who according to Aristotle *Metaphysics*

23 See Graham (2006, 195–200) and Hankinson in Curd and Graham (eds., 2008, 441): "Here [in Empedocles], for the first time, we have a fully developed element-theory, in which the stuffs of the world are supposed to be reducible to specific compounds of the fundamental elements. Moreover, these really *are* elements—unlike the entities of Anaximander, Heraclitus, Aristotle and the Stoics, they do not intertransmute, but remain intact in the compounds, and serve to explain, reductively, the nature of those compounds."

24 See further Wright in Curd and Graham (eds., 2008, 415–420), and Graham in Long (ed., 1999, 162–165).

1.5 986a2 "assumed that the elements of number are the elements of all things." But of all these the only ones challenged by Plotinus in this treatise are the Epicurean atomists and the Pythagorean "harmonists"[25]—with, of course, the Stoics.

Lines 16–19

Just as no single body *qua* body has life or soul of itself, as Plotinus has stated above (lines 11–15), so he now dismisses the suggestion that a collection of lifeless bodies, *qua* lifeless bodies, can produce life as something emergent.[26] He does not argue his claim at this stage—a claim which is in any case as incontestable for a Platonist as the assertion that "nothing can be created out of nothing"; he returns to it in Chapter 3 of this treatise.

2, 17 *And if each of them could have life*: If each of the bodies could have life of itself there is no need to claim that it is the combination of more than one that produces life; but that any one or more of the bodies can have soul, which comports life, of itself has been denied above at lines 11–12.

25 He argues against the Pythagorean harmony or attunement theory in Chapter 8[4].

26 For emergence see Graham (2006, 215–220) and Clark in Gerson (ed., 1996, 277–281).

Lines 19–25

Plotinus ends the chapter by finding common ground with the Stoics: the cosmos is not the product of random chance, but of an ordering principle.

2, 19 *randomly*: Among ancient philosophers who posited randomness as a principle behind the material cosmos were Empedocles and the Epicureans. Plotinus distances himself and his Stoic opponents from any such belief.

2, 20 *There must, then, be something to order and cause the mixture*: Any explanation of the material cosmos, with the exception of out-and-out Eleatic monism, relied upon positing a mixture of elements. There were as many descriptions of this mixture as there were schools of natural philosophy, and just as many causal explanations. Having ruled out random chance as a causal explanation, Plotinus now alludes to his interpretation of Platonic causal theory, an interpretation which, in Porphyry's words (*Life of Plotinus* 14), has "Stoic doctrines interwoven." Plato *Philebus* 23d has the same expression "cause of the mixture" as the factor combining the definite and the indefinite in the so-called "Anatomy of Entities."

At *Ennead* V.1.3, 6ff. Plotinus tells us that the soul is an image of Intellect (*Nous*), and expands this by saying that "it is the expression (*logos*) of Intellect, the whole activity and life which it (Intellect) pours forth into another being." Atkinson (1985, 49–54) has an excellent discussion of this passage in V.1, in which he shows how *logos* operates as a principle of relationship between priors and posteriors. Plotinus, he says, inherited from the Stoics (and through them from Plato, especially *Timaeus*, and Aristotle) the distinction between *logos* in conception (*endiathetos*) and *logos* in expression (*prophorikos*); the former represents the contents of a hypostasis, the latter its expression in the hypostasis below (where Nature can be seen as a fourth hypostasis). The soul can be said to be a *logos* in that it is the image or expression of Intellect as it (Intellect) pours itself forth as life and activity; it stands to soul as Form to matter, as its very essence.[27] It stands as the ordering factor behind the cosmos in just the same way that, for Plato, the demiurge through the mediation of the soul of the cosmos, ordered the otherwise unruly elements, and for the Stoics, God (albeit a material god) is the ultimate ordering principle of otherwise qualityless matter.

2, 24 *rational principle*: This is a traditional way of expressing in English Plotinus' word *logos* when being used in the above sense. Others render it "formative principle" or "forming principle." See Rist (1966) chapter 7 for a discussion of the term.

27 I have taken this note largely from Fleet (1995, 84–85).

Chapter 3

In this chapter Plotinus answers possible objections to the claims he has made at the end of Chapter 2, that "it is the approach of a rational principle to matter that creates body, and a rational principle could not make its approach from any other source than soul," that is, an immaterial soul. He dismisses the Epicurean position in a cursory manner in lines 1–6 before turning his attention on the Stoics.

Lines 1–6

The first six lines of this chapter have caused commentators much difficulty, but the confusion has been satisfactorily cleared up by Schwyzer in *Gnomon* (1960, 34–35), who allocates both "unification" and "empathy" to the protasis of the conditional sentence, unlike Harder, MacKenna, and Cilento who divide the two between protasis and apodosis, while others attribute both to the apodosis. The point that Plotinus is making is that it is impossible to claim that soulless material particles can produce soul just by coming together, since mere juxtaposition cannot in itself produce unification or empathy.

3, 1 *atoms or things without parts*: The terminology points towards the Epicureans. Although Plotinus mentions

Epicurus by name only once in the *Enneads*, it is likely that Epicurus' doctrines were current as late as the 3rd century CE, as is evidenced by (a) the considerable space allocated to him by Diogenes Laertius (probably early 3rd century CE) in his *Lives of the Philosophers*—the whole of book 10—and (b) the extensive inscription of Epicurus' works erected by Diogenes of Oenoanda in his home town in (modern) Turkey. There was too the Latin of Lucretius' *De Rerum Natura*, but it is uncertain whether Plotinus ever engaged with this work. The Epicureans are not cited by Porphyry alongside the Stoics and Peripatetics at *Life of Plotinus* 14 as being "interwoven in Plotinus' works."

It is possible that "things without parts" is a synonym for "atoms," but the Epicureans themselves made a distinction between atoms that were physically "uncuttable" wholes and their parts. LS (p. 41) state, "Since the atoms varied in shape and size they can hardly have been considered "theoretically" indivisible or partless; they were simply too solid to break into their parts." See further Morel in Warren (ed.) (2009, 73–75), who sees the doctrine of minimal parts as a reply to Aristotle's criticisms at *Physics* 240b8–241a6, and LS section 9 where the doctrine is seen as a riposte to the arguments against motion of Zeno of Elea. In either case the minimal parts of atoms (*elakhista, minima*) are material entities, albeit inseparable from the atom itself of which they are parts. Plotinus' argument is unaffected; a coming together of material parts can have no cohesion without the agency of a non-material organizing principle; without such a principle there would be mere juxtaposition of parts, not a unification.

3, 2 *unification*: The Greek word is *henôsis*, which implies a process (as against *henotês*, the resulting unity). There is a hint of the broader Platonic/Plotinian theme of the yearning of all things to turn toward their priors, ultimately toward the One, and the converse "emanation" or pluralization, towards the non-being of matter.

3, 2 *empathy*: The Greek word is *homopatheia* (lit. = "similarity of experience"), and is picked up by the terms "common affections" and "communality of affections"(*sumpatheia*) in lines 4 and 5. It is unlikely that Plotinus is carelessly using the terms synonymously; the former implies an empathy between soul and entities outside itself, and the latter a sharing of affections within itself, and is found in Plotinus' works often with the sense of "self-reflexivity" (see Gerson 1994, 267n4; Blumenthal 1971, 42; and Emilsson 1988, chapter 3). Gerson (1994, 129) and Armstrong make no distinction; MacKenna offers "the prevailing sympathy" and "self-sensitiveness." Stoics and Epicureans both agree that soul is corporeal, and that only body can affect body. Both use the term *sumpaskhein* and its cognates to describe the interaction; where they differ is that the Stoics had recourse to "total admixture" (a doctrine that Plotinus will examine in Chapter 7) whereas the Epicureans, as Plotinus reminds us here, could call on only juxtaposition (*parathesis*).

3, 5 *no body or even a magnitude*: no body or magnitude *qua* unity can come into being from atoms or *minima*. He is echoing Aristotle *Physics* 231a24: "nothing continuous can be made up of indivisibles." Bréhier (*ad loc.*) says that Plotinus is alluding to the misguided confusion of indivisible mathematicals with atoms which have size.

Lines 6–12

If we consider body *qua* body and adopt the Stoic analysis into qualityless matter and something "holding the rank of form," then that "form" itself, being corporeal, will be liable to the same analysis, and its form likewise, and so on.

3, 6 *Further*: The pair of Greek particles introducing this sentence (*kai mên*—see Denniston 1954, 351–352) indicates a decisive change of topic, away from a criticism of the Epicureans to a much longer discussion of the Stoics lasting as far as Chapter 8[3]. Although, as is his usual practice, Plotinus does not mention his opponents by name, the subject matter makes it clear that he now has the Stoics in his sights. Cf. 1, 17 *Furthermore* . . .

3, 6 *if body is simple*: MacKenna translates, "Perhaps we will be asked to consider body as a simple entity (disregarding the question of any constituent elements)." Cf. II.7.3, 8–15, where Plotinus talks of mentally separating the two components of body, *logos* and *hulê* (matter). So in the rest of this chapter we are asked to consider the implications for the Stoics of viewing body at its simplest level, taking note only of its underlying principles, the material or passive, and the formal or active, and disregarding any supervening qualities. This is to apply an Aristotelian matter-form analysis. Plotinus may well have Alexander of Aphrodisias *On the Soul* 1.4 in mind. Cf. *On Coming-to-be and Passing-away* 329b7ff., where Aristotle says that the four opposites, hot and cold, wet and dry, are at the most basic level of analysis the constituents of all body. Cf. also Alcinous *The Handbook of Platonism* 11, 166, 21, where he talks of "body *qua* body" as opposed to its qualities.

On other occasions (not here) the term "simple" (*haplous*) when applied to body can refer to (any of) the four elements.

3, 8 *matter is something lacking in quality*: the Greek term for "lacking in quality" is *apoios*, which can mean either "qualityless," the negation of the adjective *poios* = of some kind, or else (less commonly) "inactive," the negation of a hypothetical adjective derived from the verb *poiein* = to act. Either or both would suit the context here, although lines 14–15 would suggest the former. See further Graeser (1972, 13). So matter, lacking any quality of itself, can have life only as something imported through the active principle.

3, 8 *the rank of form*: Early Stoics such as Zeno were insistent on reducing Platonic Forms to mere conceptions (*ennoêmata*) perhaps following (as Long 1996, 19nn43–45) Antisthenes' words, "I can see a horse, but I cannot see horseness." See further Burnyeat in Inwood (ed., 2003, 223ff.). Stobaeus *Anthology* 1.136, 21ff. makes it clear that Stoic philosophers had no room for Forms other than as concepts; see further LS section 30 for Stoic Universals. Nor would Stoics be any happier with Aristotelian enmattered forms, which although embedded in matter are not themselves material. So here Plotinus is initially qualified in his terminology, using the periphrasis "that which holds the rank of form," although he later goes on to use the term "this form."

3, 9 *is what comports life*: It was a commonplace of ancient philosophy that life is comported by soul; on occasions little distinction is made between the two. For the Stoics Stobaeus *Anthology* 1.138, 14ff., discussing causation, tells us that Zeno said "soul is the cause of being alive." Plotinus would have no quarrel with this, and would himself need to look no further than the argument from opposites in Plato *Phaedo* 70dff. Here he is probing the Stoic position and showing that it is illogical to posit a material soul as the active principle underlying (living) body.

3, 9–10 *if . . . this form is a substance*: The Greek word is *ousia*. This can either (a) be taken within a Stoic framework as the equivalent of matter (*hulê*) as represented by Diogenes Laertius *Lives of the Philosophers* 7.134: "the passive principle is unqualified substance, viz. matter"; cf. 1,137, Sextus Empiricus *Against the Professors* 9.75 and Calcidius 292 and 293. Or else (b) it can be taken in an Aristotelian sense as in *Categories* 5; this is how MacKenna takes it, translating "But if by this Forming-Idea they mean an essential, a real being," which perhaps gives better sense in this context, since we are about to go on to contrast "substance" and "an affection of substance."

3, 10 *the conjoint*: The Greek term *to sunamphoteron* is used frequently by Plotinus to denote the complex of body and soul, as Plato at *Symposium* 209c. He seems to be applying a Platonic analysis here and arguing that if the Stoics equate soul to "that which holds the rank of form," then it (*per impossibile* for a Platonist) will be a material body and subject to the same analysis, and so on *ad infinitum*.

Lines 12–16

If on the other hand soul (and the life it comports) is no more than an affection of matter, then the Stoics need to explain the cause of the affection—especially important for them in that they taught that there are no uncaused phenomena.

3, 12 *an affection of matter*: The Greek word for "affection" is *pathêma*, and is distinguished by the Stoics from *pathos*, which generally denotes an affection or emotion of the soul, which is not Plotinus' concern here. Both are nouns derived from the verb *paskhein* (to be acted upon), and as we have seen the Stoics distinguished between the two principles of body, the active and the acted upon (or passive). "Affection" here would denote the result of the active principle (*to poioun*) acting on the passive principle (*to paskhon*), in this case life. If the affection is not itself a substance, the Stoics need to give a causal explanation. The un-Stoic possibility that it could be uncaused is not even considered.

3, 13 *the affection and the life*: The soul and the life it comports.

3, 14 *matter . . . does not give itself shape or itself implant soul*: See above on 3, 8. In the first sense of *apoios* (lacking in quality) matter has no quality to pass on to anything else; in the second sense (inactive) it cannot assume a causal role.

Lines 16–28

Plotinus devotes the rest of the chapter to summarizing his own (Platonic) explanation of the soul as a creative and cohesive cosmic cause. Implicit is his own doctrine of "emanation," itself based firmly on Plato's *Timaeus.* At every level in the sensible world soul is what causes the body to exist, to cohere and to survive, in the case of the cosmos at large everlastingly, in the case of individuals for their life-span (see above on 2, 5). But it cannot itself be corporeal. See O'Meara (1993, 15–17) for a succinct summary of Plotinus' position.

3, 16 *any one of the bodies*: This is true for body at any level—simple body as at 3, 6; elemental body (earth, air, fire, water); compound body such as flesh, blood; individual qualified bodies such as animals; the body of the cosmos.

3, 17 *outside but transcending*: Both terms "outside" (*exô*) and "transcending" (*epekeina*) are terms commonly applied by Plotinus to the immaterial, for example, the Forms, which are not only rooted in the intelligible world and so outside the sensible world (cf. *Timaeus* 50c which talks of "copies of real beings entering and leaving the Receptacle") but also transcend the sensible world in a causal role (see Fleet 1995, 235, 268ff. and 276). At *Republic* 509b Plato describes the Form of the Good as "transcending being."

3, 19 *body is in flux*: The picture of flux in the sensible world which Plotinus presents here is another commonplace of ancient philosophy, and goes back to Heraclitus. Both Plato and Aristotle refer to the doctrine of flux, using the verb *rhein* and its cognates, for example, Plato *Theaetetus* 160d and *Cratylus* 439c, and Aristotle at *Metaphysics* 987a32 (see Graham 2006, 113n4 for a fuller list of references). The source for this range of vocabulary is pre-eminently Heraclitus fragment 12 (DK): "Upon men who step into the same rivers different and still different waters flow (*epirrhei*)." (See Kahn 1979, 166ff. for a full discussion of this and fragment 91—labelled by him as 50 and 51.) Plato discusses the materialist claims of Heraclitus at length at *Theaetetus* 179c–183c, and it is probably through the mediation of such passages that Plotinus develops his own arguments against Heraclitus (but see Stamatellos 2007, 125 for Plotinus' possible direct engagement with Heraclitus).

3, 19 *its nature is swept away*: Plotinus may well have in mind Plato *Timaeus* 52e5, where the contents of the Receptacle (equated at a later date with matter—see Fleet (1995, 164–167) are said to be "swept away" in different directions, and are given stability only when "the copies of realities" are imposed on them by soul.

3, 21 *even if someone were to name one of them "soul"*: As both the Stoics and Epicureans did.

3, 21 *the same fate as other bodies*: It would, in the language of line 19, be "in flux" and "swept away."

3, 22 *all things would remain static*: Plotinus goes one stage further and suggests that without some formative immaterial power to give shape to matter, material soul and the cosmos itself would remain static at the level of matter, not even in flux. In Stoic terms it would remain entirely without quality.

3, 24 *perhaps there would not be any matter at all*: On occasions Plotinus identifies matter with non-being. At III.6.7, 7–11 he says "Matter is neither soul nor intelligence nor form nor reason nor limit—for it is lack of limit—nor power—for what can it do? It falls outside all these and could not properly receive the title of Being, but would reasonably be called non-Being." See O'Brien in Gerson (1996, chapter 7 section 1) for a different interpretation of Plotinian non-Being.

3, 26 *a cohesive force of body*: If soul were corporeal.

3, 27 *air and breath*: For the Stoics, at least after Chrysippus, breath (*pneuma*) was a mixture of fire and air (see LS 47H), pervading matter both at the cosmic and the human level as the active force, being the purveyor of *logos*. Blumenthal (1971, 52) suggests that Plotinus is deliberately widening the usual Stoic terminology to include "any doctrine which is based on something like the view which he brings up for discussion."

Lines 28–35

The argument in the rest of this chapter goes one stage further than the conclusion of Chapter 2. Soul gives to body not only its existence, but also the power to create a unified and coherent cosmos; if body lacked that power, then the cosmos would be no cosmos, but a random heap—if its matter existed at all.

3, 28 *all bodies are subject to dissolution*: (MacKenna translates: "all bodies are in a ceaseless process of dissolution"). This is the case if they lack the cohesive force of soul.

3, 28 *anyone who attributes*: Plotinus is casting the net beyond the Stoics here to include any materialist, for example Anaxagoras, whose cohesive force, Mind (*Nous*) is still something corporeal, albeit "fine and pure" (fragment 12 DK); or the Epicureans, whose cosmos is the product of random atomic collision. But he singles out the Stoics in the next sentence.

3, 30 *For what order would there be in breath*: Plotinus reiterates his main criticism of the Stoics, that they are wrong to claim that a corporeal body such as breath can at one and the same time remain corporeal and possess of itself functions which are proper, in Plotinus' view, to non-corporeal soul.

3, 32 *when soul exists*: As best exemplified by the "creation" story in Plato's *Timaeus,* where the demiurge creates the soul of the cosmos as the agent of cosmic order, and the individual soul as the factor of coherence in the individual.

Chapter 4

In this chapter Plotinus goes on to consider the implications for the Stoics of asserting that there must be some part or phase of the soul that is intelligent, while at the same time asserting its bodily nature. He then goes on to examine their claim that life and soul are breath "so disposed," which Plotinus says must be either a meaningless phrase or an indication of something immaterial. He supports his argument by dismissing the Stoic claim that a corporeal soul is able to produce manifold effects in the body.

Lines 1–11

Even the Stoics are forced to admit some intelligent element prior and superior to bodies; to fall back on the formula "body so disposed" needs explanation.

4, 1 *constrained by truth*: The phrase has a range of meaning, from the everyday (MacKenna translates: "by stress of fact") to a more philosophical Platonic meaning; for example in *Republic* 508d the Good is said to illuminate the objects of knowledge (the Forms) with "truth and reality." So Plotinus may well be suggesting that the Stoics unwittingly acknowledge Platonic Forms and admit to the reality of intellective powers "outside and transcending all bodily nature" (3, 17–18).

4, 2 *some phase of soul*: Throughout this passage there is a certain ambiguity as to whether the terms "body" and "soul" are to be applied on a human or a cosmic level. Since Plotinus is concerned in this treatise with the individual human soul, it makes better sense to focus on the latter—although since the individual human soul is "a spark of the cosmic fire" much of what he says can be applied equally to the cosmic. For the Stoics the superior phase of the individual soul is the commanding faculty (*to hêgemonikon*), which Diogenes Laertius tells us (*Lives of the Philosophers* 7.159) is "the most authoritative part of the soul . . . from which rational thought (*logos*) emanates." This is the part of the human soul most akin to the cosmic soul, which is described by the Stoics as "designing fire" (*pur tekhnikon*).

4, 2 *prior to bodies and superior to them*: We have moved on from the simple body of 3, 6–7 and are now thinking of the human body as opposed to soul (a little confusing, since for the Stoics soul was body). "Prior" can have two applications. Either (a) in time, which cannot be the meaning here, since according to Plutarch (*On Stoic Self-contradictions* 1053c = LS 53C) Chrysippus said that the soul comes into being at or after the birth of the infant. Further confirmation is given by the Stoic Hierocles (fl.

c. CE 100) who explains in *Elements of Ethics* 1.5 how the seed changes in the womb into "growth" (*phusis* translated by LS as "physique") from breath (*pneuma*), which is initially dense but becoming finer, only turning into soul when it encounters the world outside the womb. Plotinus discusses this point further in Chapter 8[3]. Alexander of Aphrodisias *Supplement* 104, 13 points out that "it is not that this body first exists without soul and subsequently receives it."

Or else (b) it means ontologically prior, which is Plotinus' point here, as evidenced by what follows.

4, 3 *they make breath intelligent and fire intellectual*: Aetius (4.3.3) tells us that "the Stoics declare god to be intellectual, a designing fire which proceeds to the creation of the cosmos," echoed by Diogenes Laertius (*Lives of the Philosophers* 7.156): "They (the Stoics) think that nature is designing fire, proceeding to creation."

4, 4 *the superior portion*: This phrase echoes "superior to them" in line 2, and refers to the commanding faculty of the soul. Plotinus' point is that if, as the Stoics maintain, this faculty is composed of corporeal breath and fire it is itself corporeal, and in as much as it derives from them it must be posterior to them both chronologically and ontologically. For a Platonist the reverse is the case; the intelligible world is ontologically prior to the sensible world; "body is in soul."

4, 7 *psychic powers*: For Platonists each hypostasis had within itself the power or potentiality to produce the hypostasis below it through the process of "emanation" (see O'Meara 1993, chapters 6 and 7, for a succinct account of emanation; see also Fleet 2012, note to chapter 3, lines 6–16). Blumenthal interprets differently (1971, 25); he suggests that the unitary soul has within it different faculties (the Greek word for "faculty" and "power" is the same—*dunamis*) relating to the appropriate function.

4, 9 *so disposed*: In seeking to give a comprehensive materialist explanation of the cosmos the Stoics developed (probably at the instigation of Chrysippus) their so-called theory of categories. The overarching genus is "something" (*ti*); one of its species is body (*sôma*), and the four sub-species are substrate or substance (*hupokeimenon*), qualified body (*poion*), body so disposed (*pôs ekhon*) and body relatively disposed (*pros ti pôs ekhon*). These are not categories in the Aristotelian sense, but rather (at least in the case of the first three) a progressive description of a body at a particular time. As Rist (1969, 169) puts it: "To introduce the category of disposition is to place the existing object (category one) which is an individual entity (category two) in a particular spatio-temporal situation (category three)." So the analysis of any one item is cumulative, and needs all three factors in its description. Sextus Empiricus (*Outlines of Pyrrhonism* 2.82 = LS 53P) gives a psychic example: "Scientific knowledge is the commanding faculty disposed in a certain way, just as the clenched fist is the hand disposed in a certain way." Other examples are given by Plotinus in his criticism of Stoic categories at VI.1.30 as "3 cubits long," "white," "yesterday," "last year," "in the Lyceum," "in the Academy"; Seneca at *Letter* 113.18 tells us that Dion walking is explained as Dion/his commanding faculty "so disposed." Rist (1969, 171) says "they (the Stoic categories) are meant to guide the enquirers into the status of particular things." Plotinus' complaint is that such an explanation fails to provide "some active principle other than bodies"; how can "breath so disposed" be an adequate description of the (non-corporeal for Plotinus) active principle?

Lines 11–21

Plotinus examines the Stoic concept of "breath so disposed"—the so-called third category—which is either a meaningless concept or one which requires some immaterial factor.

4, 11 *not all breath*: Plotinus perhaps has his eye on Alexander of Aphrodisias *Supplement* 115, 8ff.: "Not all fire and not all breath has this power (of ensouling bodies)."

4, 11 *this state*: The Greek word is *skhesis*, a noun formed from the verb *ekhein*, and is used by Plotinus here as a synonym for *pôs ekhon* (but see below).

4, 14 *is either something real, or is nothing real*: The disjunct is exhaustive—there is nothing outside or between what is something and what is nothing. He deals first with the latter, and his point is that to deny the reality of the third category would be to deny also the second, and we would be left with nothing other than unqualified (*apoion*) matter. If on the other hand disposition is something real, it must be something other than the matter and thereby immaterial. But this is a misrepresentation of the Stoic position, since they would say that it is more accurate to talk of something material being "so disposed" than to talk of an immaterial abstraction such as "disposition" (*skhesis*) as Plotinus does here. "Something so disposed" is more than a mere name.

Lines 21–35

Plotinus produces another in the chain of arguments to show that soul cannot be corporeal.

4, 21 *Furthermore, the following argument*: A central belief of the Stoics was that only body can act on body; the active rational principle breath (*pneuma*, a mixture of fire and air) acts on the passive (a mixture of earth and water). Aetius 1.11.5 (= LS 55G = SVF 2.340) says: "The Stoics say all causes are bodily because they are portions of breath." To this doctrine Plotinus now applies the principle of non-contradiction. Anything "so disposed" must be consistent with that principle, so that no body "so disposed" can produce an opposite disposition in another. But, Plotinus says, the soul manifestly does; therefore it cannot be a body "so disposed." In fact Cleanthes, as reported by Nemesius 78.7 (= LS 45C = SVF 1.158), admits that when the soul feels shame and fear, the body turns red and pale. It would need some ingenious argumentation to show that the soul was itself red or pale.

4, 34 *color as well*: All the other examples Plotinus gives above are of polar opposites (black and white not being true colors).

Chapter 5

In this chapter Plotinus asks how a corporeal soul can perform functions proper, in a Platonist's eyes, to a non-corporeal soul, such as causing movement, growth, memory and reproduction, and in general be present to body in a way other than as a material magnitude. These functions derive from the Aristotelian division of the soul into its different faculties. Blumenthal (1971, 21) comments: "The soul . . . is taken as being divided into certain parts or powers. How Plotinus conceived this division is not immediately clear, since we find both Platonic and Peripatetic doctrines, apparently left in more or less haphazard juxtaposition. Thus we sometimes have Plato's division into a desiring, a spirited and a rational part and at other times a division into faculties of the Aristotelian type. The latter is more appropriate to Plotinus' whole view of the soul, since it fits better with his insistence on its indivisibility and with the idea . . . that certain powers are actualized for specific purposes from a central reserve of what one might call undifferentiated soul"; and at (1971, 26): "Any such divisions of soul may be seen as demarcations or sections of a continuum: in this sense types of soul, or parts of them can be said to differ. The soul is 'like a long expanse of life extended lengthwise, with each of its parts different from the next, but continuous with itself, always other by difference in such a way that the prior part is not lost in the second' (V.2.2, 26–29)." The Aristotelian faculties in question in this chapter are: growth and reproduction in the broad division of "vegetative," movement and memory in that of "perceptive," and getting to know what is appropriate in that of "rational." For a full schematization of the different faculties see Blumenthal (1971, 44). Plotinus goes on to ask the Stoics how their division of the soul into corporeal magnitudes can possibly make sense.

Lines 1–11

Plotinus complains that an active principle which is bodily and within a body is unable to produce movement in the passive principle, other than the simple, single movement intrinsic to all body. The sort of movement that is caused by choice needs a non-corporeal cause. This is especially true of the growth of the living body.

5, 1 *How . . . there are different movements*: These are the words that open the chapter; the noun and adjective are in the accusative case and the verb in the infinitive, requiring us to assume an ellipse of the main verb, either one such as "explain," with its subject the same as that of "make the cause" in line 3, so producing the translation "How will they (i.e. the Stoics) explain . . . " (as MacKenna: "How account for . . . ?" or Armstrong: "Why, I ask . . . ?");

or else (as Bréhier and Lex. Plot.) assuming "soul" to be the subject and "produce" the verb: "How does the soul produce . . . ?"

5, 2 *the motion of every body is single*: The Greek is ambiguous: *pantos sômatos* can mean either "of every body" or "of body as a whole." The former seems preferable, with the sense that every body *qua* body has just one movement intrinsic to it, for example in the case of the elemental bodies fire naturally moves upward, earth downward; Alexander of Aphrodisias *Supplement* 115, 23 says: "Moreover, every body [has] some proper movement of its own, simple of what is simple . . . "; and Simplicius *On Aristotle Physics* 263, 25 makes a further point about composite objects: "A stone and any heavy object can move upwards and sideways only by some agency, but can move downwards of its own accord; fire can move downwards only by some agency but upwards by itself; wood moves downwards of itself, but the bed moves downwards in so much as it is made of wood, not in so much as it is a bed."

5, 3 *choices*: Although the Stoics were strict determinists and might appear to leave little room for choice and "what is up to us" (*to eph'hêmin*) in their explanation of human conduct, they certainly did not preclude it. Plotinus is not concerned here to engage in a debate about determinism and free will (for which see Bobzien 1998); choice, however explained, was an undoubted fact for both Platonists and

Stoics. His question is, given the reality of choice (and "they are right" to make it part of their causal explanation): How can it be something of a bodily nature?

5, 3 *rational principles*: The Greek word is *logous*, a word which (with its cognates) occupies over eight pages in the Lex. Plot. and nine columns in LSJ. Plotinus here suggests that it is a term used by the Stoics to denote something other than choices. So it cannot be something as neutral as "reasons" (as MacKenna and Bréhier); reasoning and calculation (both possible meanings of *logos*) are part of choice, so it is unlikely that Plotinus is offering a mere synonym here. It is better to take it in the more technical Stoic sense of "rational principles," sometimes called "seminal principles" (*spermatikoi logoi*) which, as stated by LS 46 (p. 277), are "the mode of god's activity in matter, a rational pattern of constructive growth which is both the life of god and the ordered development of particular things." These are bound up in the very nature of the world at both unconscious (but not irrational) cosmic and individual levels and are thus different from conscious choices. Cf. lines 42ff. of this chapter where Plotinus illustrates his point with examples of seed (*sperma*) operating unconsciously in the birth of rational and non-rational animals. This doctrine is well-attested in the sources, for example Aetius 1.7, 33 (= LS 46A): "God contains the seminal principles in accordance with which each thing comes about by fate"; and Diogenes Laertius *Lives of the Philosophers* 7.136: "God is the seminal principle of the cosmos."

The Stoics made a distinction between *logos* in conception (*endiathetos*) and *logos* in expression (*prophorikos*), a distinction which Plotinus himself exploited, for example at III.1.7, 4 and IV.4.39, 6ff., and V.9.9, 10; although these are treatises later than IV.7, they may well be in Plotinus' mind here. For a full discussion of this see Atkinson (1985, 49–54), and cf. LS 53T.

5, 6 *this kind of rational principle*: Body *qua* body has no inherent quality but is only, for example, hot or cold in so far as an agent such as soul has bestowed heat or cold on it, as stated at 4, 25ff.

5, 7 *where would body get its power to grow . . . ?*: Growth is a species of movement—the noun used in line 1, *kinêsis*, can mean both movement and change, although *alloiôsis* came to be used for qualitative change; growth implies something of both senses.

5, 8 *It is right that it should* grow: It is right that bodies of living creatures should grow, in order to fulfill their proper function, whether in accord with the teleology of Plato's *Timaeus*, that of Aristotle (as seen e.g. in *Physics* 2.9) or that of Stoic providential determinism. But all that body *qua* body can contribute is "the bulk of its matter" to help soul—"that which causes growth"; the principle of growth is not intrinsic to body. In Platonic terms Plotinus has in mind the Receptacle of *Timaeus* 50c2, which "is the base in which all things are molded, moved and shaped by that which enters it," which Aristotle equates (at *Physics* 2 209b11–210a2) to matter (*hulê*)—which in Stoic terms is qualitiless (*apoios*). See Fleet (1995, 164–167) for a fuller discussion.

5, 10 *what might be received*: In Platonic cosmic terms these are "the copies of real beings, entering or leaving" (*Timaeus* 50c4). Aristotle's ideas on embryology echo this; the mother does no more than provide a place for the embryo to develop; it is the father who provides the form by means of his seed (as outlined at *Generation of Animals* 1.20 729aff.). With the Stoics the picture is more complex; they attribute the growth and nutrition of the living creature to *pneuma* as the active principle. For details see Long (1996, 237–239), rather than to the soul as such. But the three doctrines are essentially the same; matter is impassive and characterless, and can only gain character (quality, form) from outside.

Lines 12–24

Plotinus argues that if soul were a corporeal principle of growth intrinsic to body, it would itself have to grow *pari passu* with the body, and the addition would be either soul or something other than soul. Blumenthal (1971, 10) takes Plotinus to task by saying: "Such an addition could be dispensed with if one accepted the Stoic notion of total interpenetration, but Plotinus does not." In fact he argues against such a notion in Chapter 8[2]. Cf. also II.7 *On Total Interpenetration* (*krasis di'holou*).

5, 14 *either soul or body without soul*: The disjunction is again exhaustive. Before it is added to the soul already in the body, thereby becoming soul, the addition will be either corporeal soul or soulless body. In either case there are questions to be asked—questions to which Plotinus does not here offer notional Stoic replies.

5, 17 *how will it come to be of the same mind?*: This passage focuses on the cognitive aspects of soul—opinion, memory, cognition. Plotinus is questioning the Stoic doctrines he will proceed to examine in subsequent chapters.

5, 20 *the rest of our bodily mass*: I.e. the body as opposed to the soul of the living-creature. If the soul is corporeal it is subject to the same impermanence as all other body—anathema to a Platonist. Bréhier points to Aristotle *On the Soul* 1.2 404a1ff., where Aristotle is discussing the atomists Democritus and Leucippus, and Pythagoras, who say that for the living creature the respiration of particles repairs any psychic loss sustained.

The language of ebb and flow is Heraclitean. For the transitory nature of sensible objects see also Plato *Phaedo* 78dff., *Theaetetus* 155eff. and *Sophist* 245eff.

5, 23 *How will we get to know what is appropriate to us?*: Armstrong and Bréhier both make this an example of the recognition of kith and kin (Armstrong: "how do friends and relations recognize each other when they never have the same souls?"; Bréhier: "How will we recognize our kin if they never have the same soul?"), which assumes that we recognize kith and kin by *their* souls on the principle that like knows like. These both take the Greek word *oikeiôn* as masculine. MacKenna takes it as neuter and translates: "our recognition of *familiar things*." All three take this sentence as an amplification of the previous and relate it to memory. But the Greek word used is *gnôrisis*, and is not the same as *anagnôrisis*, and means cognition rather than recognition. So it is more likely that Plotinus is introducing a new point, about cognition, and relating it to the well-attested Stoic doctrine of *oikeiôsis*, whereby the aspiring Stoic, in his progress toward perfection, seeks to discover what is most appropriate (*oikeios*) for him. Diogenes Laertius (*Lives of the Philosophers* 7.85), after quoting a passage from Chrysippus *On Ends* says: "So it is left for us to say that [nature] in constituting [the living creature] made it like itself (*oikeiôsai*); for in this way it rejects what is harmful and admits what is appropriate (*oikeia*)." So Plotinus' point is that if *our own* soul is never the same, there can be no consistency or stability in our cognitions, especially in those that are important to a Stoic. See further Inwood (1985, 184–194), and Fleet (1995, 104–106).

Lines 24–32

A long and tortuous sentence in which Plotinus lays down some basic principles about the nature of the body. Body, at least according to the Stoics, is infinitely divisible into parts which are not quantitatively the same as the whole, and so not qualitatively the same. Applying these principles to a corporeal soul presents some questions to the Stoics—questions that a Platonic distinction between material body and immaterial quality would answer.

Lines 32–51

These questions are now developed, and Plotinus shows that it is impossible for soul to be quantitatively divided and still remain soul.

5, 32 *each part is soul of the same kind*: If the Stoics admit this principle, then they must admit that the sameness is not quantitative (line 24: "each part is different from the whole"); so the sameness must be qualitative, and they will have to recant and admit that "magnitude contributes nothing to the essence of the soul."

5, 34 *the part of the part*: A reductio argument.

5, 36 *It is present as a whole*: This is a statement of the Platonic non-material soul. The verb "is present" (*pareinai*) is Plato's common term to denote the relationship between intelligible and sensible entities; the former "are present to" the latter without losing their integrity. They transcend the sensible and are indivisible (cf. Plato *Timaeus* 51eff.). If the soul is corporeal, as the Stoics claim, and thereby divisible into distinct parts along with the division of the body, it loses its integrity and cannot perform the functions proper to soul, which is "outside and transcending all bodily nature" (3, 17).

5, 38 *if they deny*: This is the logical outcome of admitting that the part is not the same as the whole. Since all body must be either ensouled (*empsykhos*) or soulless (*apsykhos*) (Plotinus perhaps has his eye on Alexander of Aphrodisias *Supplement* 114, 4ff.) the absurd conclusion is that the corporeal soul will consist of unlike parts lacking in soul.

5, 40 *Furthermore*: On the materialist account as outlined in lines 24–32 a part of a corporeal entity will not be the same as the whole "*qua* body and *qua* magnitude." So Plotinus' point in this sentence is that anything "beyond the lower or upper limit" will not be soul. The arguments in lines 24–40 are about parts of soul, as are the examples given in lines 42–51, that is, soul "at the lower limit." Nothing is said about "at or beyond the upper limit"; hence certain editors follow Eusebius in excluding "or the upper limit" and read *hê* ("the" sc. soul) instead of ê ("either"); Armstrong translates: "And besides, if the size of each soul is limited in both directions, that at any rate which is less [than the minimum size] will not be soul." Others follow the non-Eusebian text, presumably to explain the phrase "in either direction" (*eph'hekatera*). MacKenna translates: "Further, if a definite magnitude, the double limit of larger or smaller, is to be imposed on each separate soul then *anything outside these limits* is not soul"; the italicized words have no equivalent in the Greek text. Bréhier renders: "Further, if each soul has a magnitude contained between two limits, above or below, it will no longer be a soul."

5, 42 *So when from a single act of intercourse*: Plotinus goes on to say that multiple conceptions from the same seed resulting in identical twins, triplets etc.—a Stoic concern as evidenced by Aetius 5.10, 4 (= SVF 750)—tell us that, since the individual soul in each of the multiple offspring is both a whole in itself and identical to its original, then it is not a corporeal fragment of the original, since "when it is divided into a plurality each part is different from the whole" (line 25); what is transferred from the father to offspring is something qualitative, transcending any quantitative magnitude.

5, 51 *rational principles*: This brings us back to the statement in the first sentence of the chapter; what applies to souls applies equally to rational principles.

Chapter 6

In this chapter Plotinus discusses perception, and it is a chapter in which we see Plotinus deploying Platonist and Peripatetic doctrines to combat the errors that he perceives in Stoicism. Platonists, Peripatetics, and Stoics (and even Epicureans) had much to say in common on this topic, so it is unsurprising that Plotinus seeks to establish a clear Platonist position, because Stoic materialism allowed for a consistency of approach that Platonism lacked in its attempt to portray a cosmos in which immaterial and material elements interlocked. The points of agreement are many.

First, all agree that sense data, albeit stemming from the lower part of the cosmic hierarchy, play an important and necessary part in the gaining of knowledge. Deborah Modrak, in Benson (ed. 2009, chapter 10), points to many passages in Plato where this is made clear, notably Meno *82bff.,* Republic *521cff.,* Phaedo *74dff.,* Timaeus *47aff. and* Theaetetus *184bff. Aristotle, at* Physics *1 184a16, insists that we should proceed from the known particular before proceeding to the general; what is most eminently knowable is the individual substance. Similarly the Stoics: according to Aetius 4.11, 1–4 (LS 39E = SVF 2.83), "When a man is born, the Stoics say, he has the commanding part of his soul like a sheet of paper ready for writing upon. On this he inscribes each one of his conceptions. The first method of inscription is through the senses."*

*Secondly, all agree that the sense organs receive the sense data in a raw state. Each organ receives the data appropriate to it, for example sounds are received by the ears, odors by the nose; in some cases data are received by more than one sense organ—Aristotle talks of common sensibles (*koina aisthêta*) such as movement, rest, number (*On the Soul *418a18), which are initially perceived by the sense organs. All give primacy to vision as paradigmatic of sense perception, for example Aristotle at* On the Soul *429a4. What is true of vision, which has the added need of a medium between the object seen and the eye, is true* mutatis mutandis *of all five senses.*

Thirdly, all agree that the sense organs do not themselves form judgments, either simple ones such as "this is white" or ones of a more complex propositional nature.

Fourthly, all include a strong teleological element in their explanations of perception. This is stated most clearly by Plato at Timaeus *47a–c and 68e–69c. Neither Aristotle's biology nor Stoic providential determinism offers a purely mechanistic account of human activity.*

Fifthly, although they offer differing accounts of the mechanics of the reception of sense data by the sense organs, all agree that such reception is a corporeal event, *an affection (*pathos*) of the sense organ. The details need not concern us at this point.*[28]

*Sixthly, they all agree that the affection is transmitted to the rational element of the soul, which, so to speak, processes, evaluates and forms judgments on it. Plato, as we saw above, tended to follow the Aristotelian division into three broad faculties: the rational, the sensitive and the vegetative (of which the first is the recipient of the messages from the sense organs). Aristotle alternatively designated the rational faculty as intellect (*nous*), which he discusses at length in a difficult passage at* On the Soul *3.4–8. For a full discussion of this central faculty of soul in Aristotle see Emilsson (1988, chapter 5). The Stoics called the rational element "the commanding element" (*to hêgemonikon*); five of the other seven "parts" of the soul were the five senses.*

But there is a sharp difference between Platonists and Peripatetics on the one hand, and the Stoics on the other,

28 At *Timaeus* 45bff. Plato gives an account of vision whereby the eye issues a stream of fire that meets a reciprocating stream from the object seen. Cornford (1937, 151ff.) offers an explanation of this process in terms of cones of fire meeting at a midpoint. Aristotle's description is to be found at *On the Soul* 2.7, and that of the Stoics at Diogenes Laertius *Lives of the Philosophers* 7.157 (= LS 53N = SVF 2.867): "Seeing takes place when the light between the visual faculty and the object is stretched into the shape of a cone. . . . The air adjacent to the pupil forms the tip of the cone with its base next to the visual object. What is seen is reported by means of the stretched air, as by a walking stick." Alexander of Aphrodisias *Supplement* 126, 27ff. reviews the various theories.

about the nature of what happens between the reception of the data by the sense organ and the formation in the rational faculty of judgments and ultimately the acquisition of knowledge. For the Stoics it is a purely corporeal process,[29] *whereby the perception is stamped onto the (material) soul as an imprint* (typôsis)*, whether literally like a seal imprint in wax, as Cleanthes said, or figuratively as an alteration in the soul* pneuma*, as Chrysippus is reported as saying (see Fleet 1995, 76–77). By contrast both Plato and Aristotle describe the process as one of the dematerialization of the sense data. Plato makes it clear at* Theaetetus *184cff. that although the individual senses belong to the body, "it seems that the soul views the common features [such as being, not-being and perhaps the Forms in general] of all things* by itself through reasoning (sullogismôi).*" Similarly the whole argument of* Republic 6 *and 7 is based on the assumption of an immaterial soul.*

29 Albeit a complex one, consisting of a "cognizable" presentation (*katalêptikê phantasia*), an assent on the part of the recipient (*synkatathesis*), cognition (*katalêpsis*) and finally knowledge (*epistêmê*); Cicero *Academics* 2.145 (= LS 41A = SVF 1.66) says: "Zeno used to clinch the wise man's sole possession of scientific knowledge with a gesture. He would spread out the fingers of one hand and display its open palm, saying 'An impression is like this.' Next he clenched his fingers a little and said 'Assent is like this.' Then, pressing his fingers quite together, he made a fist, and said that this was cognition. . . . Then he brought his left hand against his right fist and gripped it tightly and forcefully, and said that scientific knowledge was like this and possessed by none but the wise man."

For a Platonist it is an incontrovertible fact that the soul is immaterial, and psychic processes are likewise immaterial, particularly those located in the rational faculty. Aristotle's clearest statement is at On the Soul *2.12, where perception is seen as the reception of form without matter. That is sufficient for Plotinus' purpose, although Aristotle goes on in* On the Soul *3.3–8 to discuss the further point that there is a distinction between e.g. perceiving flesh and perceiving the essence of flesh, leading commentators such as Lloyd (1968, 195–196) to make a distinction between sensible and intelligible forms, mirrored by Aristotle's own distinction at* On the Soul *429b5 between the faculty of sense (*to aisthêtikon*) which is embodied, and intellect (*nous*), which is separate. Alexander of Aphrodisias sums the question up at* On the Soul *60, 3: "We can therefore propose the following definition of "sense" in general as a formula that is valid [for each of the separate senses]: A sense is a power of the soul which, through the instrumentality of certain sense organs, receives and discriminates sensible species separated from their sensible matter." The outcome is that for Plato and Aristotle (and therefore for Plotinus too, despite his reservations about lack of clarity on psychic matters from Plato) perception, although beginning in the material world, is ultimately an immaterial psychic activity. That is the starting point for his criticism of the Stoics.*

Lines 1–15

Plotinus shows that the Stoics cannot posit a single center of perception and at the same time maintain its corporeal nature, which is multiple.

6, 1 *perception, thinking, understanding, virtue*: These are all noble activities in that they occur in the soul, which is closest to the Good (for a Platonist), closest to *nous* (for a Peripatetic) or closest to cosmic reason (for a Stoic). Perception might (for the Stoics) appear to be the odd one out in that unlike thinking, understanding, and virtue it does not seem to involve judgment. But in fact as we have seen (note 29 above) perception cannot take place until the soul, through its commanding element, assents to the impression, which is not the same thing as the perception. According to Calcidius 220 (= LS 53G = SVF 2.879) Chrysippus said: "The soul as a whole despatches the senses (which are its proper functions) like branches from the trunk-like commanding-faculty to be reporters of what they sense, while it itself like a monarch passes judgment on their reports. . . . It is the function of internal reflection and reasoning to understand each sense's affections, and to infer from their reports what it [i.e. the object] is, and to accept it when present, remember it when absent, and foresee it when future." According to Galen *The Doctrines of Plato and Hippocrates* 2.5 (= SVF 2.882) Zeno and Chrysippus both said that the movement must be transmitted (*diadosthai*) to the principal part of the soul for there to be perception. For a Stoic perception is the completed process only starting from the cognizable impression. See further Emilsson (1988, 97).

6, 4 *it must itself be something single*: Platonists, Peripatetics, and Stoics alike agree on the unity of perception. Plotinus' argument is that if, as the Stoics claim, the soul is corporeal, then its parts will be infinitely divisible, with fatal consequences for their doctrine. Alexander of Aphrodisias *On the Soul* 18, 10–23 expands the point. Rather it is the task of the soul to draw together into unity its pluralized perceptions of the sensible world (mirroring the cosmic process of the turning [*epistrophê*] of Soul to its prior, Intellect [*nous*] in increasing unity, and the converse procession or "emanation" resulting in increasing pluralization. [See Atkinson 1985, 64–65 and 110–111.]) So, Plotinus asks, how can a corporeal commanding element, which is itself infinitely divisible and pluralized, be the unifying factor which is at the end of the process of perception? To liken perception to the transmission of sense data along the tentacles of an octopus (LS 53H) is only to suggest a series of disparate sensations in the infinitely many parts of the tentacle. See Alexander of Aphrodisias *On the Soul* 61, 8–19 for a discussion of the apprehension of sense data in the same act, at the same time.

6, 4 *by what is the same*: The same as what? Either (a) the same as its object. At *On the Soul* 429a15 Aristotle, likening the process of thinking to that of perceiving, says: "Thinking must therefore be something which does not suffer affection, but receives the form and is potentially of the same kind without actually being the form," and Alexander of Aphrodisias says at *On the Soul* 38, 21: "Sensation is a power of soul which enables its subject to take on a likeness to apprehended sensible objects by means of some alteration in the [psychic] activity directed towards them, and to pass judgment on these sensibles" and at 39, 12: "The sensible object and the sensory faculty are dissimilar prior to the act of sensation, but they take on a likeness to each other in this act; for the act of sensing comes about through a kind of conformity produced by means of alteration." Or (b) the same as itself throughout, not divisible—perhaps more in keeping with what follows—referring to what Aristotle calls the common sense (*koinê aisthêsis*) at *On the Soul* 425a27, of which Ross (1949, 140) says: "We must think of sense as a single faculty which discharges certain functions in virtue of its general nature, but for certain purposes specifies itself into the five senses and creates for itself organs adapted to their special functions." Cf. Aristotle *On Sleep and Waking* 455a21: "There is one faculty of perception and a single controlling organ of sense (*aisthêtêrion*), but its way of perceiving differs according to each type [of sensible object]." Aristotle denies that there is any sixth sense.

6, 5 *whether a number of impressions*: Plotinus seems to be following Alexander of Aphrodisias 63, 3ff. closely in explaining the unity of the perception of multiple sense data. The analogy of hub/center and radii illustrates in a graphic way this tension between plurality and unity. "Perhaps the ability of the common sense to apprehend in a single act different perceptions produced by different sensible objects could be explained if this sense power were in one respect a unity, but distinguishable into a plurality when considered from another point of view. Now the circle provides an analogy: its radii are indeed many [and separate] when taken at the circumference but come together in unity as they approach the center. All these lines are in fact identical with respect to the point in which they terminate, since they fit their separate termini together to form the center of the circle. This common terminus, the center, is therefore both one and many; it is many inasmuch as it is the focal point for a number of different lines, but a unity in that all these lines blend themselves together within it. Now we may suppose that the common sense is both one and many in a similar way."

6, 10 *otherwise*: Our faculty of perception would be unable to distinguish between different sense data, and we would be unable to pass a judgment.

Lines 15–26

Plotinus shows that it is impossible for the Stoics to maintain both the unity of perception and the corporeality of soul.

6, 15 *But if this center point were extended*: We are asked to imagine our faculty of perception as something corporeal and extended, for example like a line (although this is extended in only one dimension), and thereby divisible into unlike parts (cf. IV.2.1, 60: "Body is one only in continuity; each of its parts is different, each part in a different place"). So (a) if different perceptions reached different points on this line, then the unity of perception could only be maintained if the ends of the line were to be drawn together to meet at some single point, which would compromise its corporeal nature (line 24: "the ruling element will be lacking parts"). Otherwise there will be different perceptions impacting on different points on the line, and the unity of perception will be compromised. Similarly (b) the perception of a complex sensible object with parts such as a face will either be seen as a single thing—which is what happens—or else the perception of the object will be fragmented according to its different features and there will be no unity of perception (cf. Aristotle *On the Soul* 426b19ff.).

6, 23 *they are all the more like thoughts*: Aristotle likens the process of perception to that of thinking at *On the Soul* 429a13.

6, 25 *apprehension*: The Greek word is *antilêpsis*, given as a Stoic alternative to the more usual cognition (*katalêpsis*) by Aetius 4.8.1 (= SVF 2.850).

Lines 26–37

Plotinus exposes the absurdity of claiming that the perceptive faculty is a divisible body, with a string of impossible conclusions.

6, 26 *But in fact the whole is something single:* In the Greek this term (*to pan* = "the whole") is in the neuter gender, and so refers to the commanding faculty (here denoted by the neuter participle *to hêgemonoun* in line 28). Plotinus is careful to keep to Stoic terminology. This statement is common ground for Platonists, Peripatetics, and Stoics alike.

6, 27 *how could it be divided?*: Plotinus again seems to be following the argument of Alexander of Aphrodisias *On the Soul* 63, 12–64, 11, which follows on from the hub/center analogy. Aristotle addresses the same question at *On the Soul* 426b8ff.; at 426b29 he asserts that the judging faculty must be undivided; cf. *On Sensation* chapters 6 and 7.

6, 27 *equal matching equal*: As the subsequent argument shows, Plotinus is thinking of corporeal divisibility, not qualitative likeness; although the ruling element is primarily qualitatively incommensurable with any object perceived, it is *ipso facto* quantitatively incommensurable.

6, 29 *So into how many parts will the division be?*: The division can be only notional and based on the Stoic hypothesis that the ruling element is corporeal.

6, 29 *It will be divided*: HS punctuate this as a question, whereas Bréhier punctuates it as an answer in his Greek text, but as a question in his translation. The sentence is prefaced by the Greek particle ê, which Plotinus often uses as a preface to a reply. To make it a reply perhaps gives a sense of a dialectic between Plotinus and an imaginary Stoic. It is tempting to make the subsequent three sentences question—answer—question (with ê again in line 32). In either case the argument is not affected.

6, 35 *an infinity of perceptions of each object for each observer*: A point dealt with by Aristotle at *On the Soul* 426b8ff. and *On Sensation* 446b20ff.

Lines 37–48

Plotinus concludes the chapter by turning his attention to the Stoic doctrine that perceptions are corporeal imprints on the soul.

6, 39 *like the impressions of signet rings in wax*: The vocabulary of the impressions of a signet ring in wax had long been in common currency in a figurative sense to denote sense impressions. Plato uses *tupos* (as Plotinus here in line 43) on several occasions (*Theaetetus* 171e3, *Republic* 402d3, *Philebus* 51d2) to denote "general character" (not sense impression). But he uses the imagery of wax three times in *Theaetetus* in the context of memory, at 191c9, 194c5, and 196a3. Aristotle *On Memory* 450a31, b6, and b16 uses the same language when talking about memory. Alexander of Aphrodisias says at *On the Soul* 72, 5ff.: "It should be understood that the term "impression" (*tupos*) is being used in a rather loose sense when it is applied to imagination. For "impression" properly describes a shape that is stamped as indentation or relief . . . into some material by the agent which produces this impression—the figures, for instance, produced [in wax] by a signet ring. But the residual images left behind in us by sensible objects are not produced in this fashion; indeed, even the initial apprehension of [external] sensibles does not involve any kind of shape or figure. What, may we ask, is the shape of white, or of color in general? Or how can odor present itself as a figure? Since however there is no precise term to describe that residual trace which remains in us as a result of contact with sensible objects, we employ the word "impression" in a metaphorical sense to designate this residue."

6, 40 *imprinted in blood or in air*: We might have expected, in a Stoic context, to be told that the imprint is made in *pneuma*, a mixture of air and fire. But in describing perception blood and air can be appropriate, since, as Galen says, the Stoics claim that the deliberative part of the soul is situated in the heart (*Foet.* 44.698, 2–9 (LS 53D = SVF2 761) and at *On Hippocrates' Epidemics* 6.270, 26–28 (LS 53E = SVF 2 782) he says: "Everyone who supposes that the soul is breath says that it is preserved by exhalation both of the blood and of the <air> drawn into the body by inhalation through the windpipe." In any case a mixture of blood and air is more malleable than one of fire and air. The same formula is given at 8, 28 and 8, 35. In *Odyssey* 11 Homer tells of the need of souls to drink blood; cf. SVF1.140. Blumenthal (1971, 51–52) says that Plotinus is either (a) being careless, "just unsympathetically lumping together as identical things that are merely connected, or (b) widening the scope of his criticism to "anyone who tries to maintain that the soul is *pneuma* or blood, or anything else of that sort, or (c) himself the victim of a confusion in the doxographical tradition.

6, 42 *as if imprinted on water*: This seems to have been an old proverb. Hackforth (1952, 159n2) says that Plato is using it as "a proverbial phrase for useless labor" at *Phaedrus* 276c (other editors disagree); it is used in this sense by Sophocles (fragment 741) and by various Roman authors, for example Catullus in Poem 70 ("What a woman says to her passionate lover deserves to be written on the wind or flowing water"). Plotinus is certainly using it in this sense here.

6, 43 *there will be no memory*: There is little evidence to indicate what Stoic views on memory were. That they resulted from sense impressions as imprints on the soul was undoubted. Aetius says at 4.11.2 (LS 39E = SVF 2 83): "By perceiving something, e.g. white, they have a memory of it when it has departed. And when many memories of a similar kind have occurred, we then say we have experience. For the plurality of similar impressions is experience." Plutarch *On Common Conceptions* 1084F (LS 39F = SVF 2 847) says: "The Stoics define conceptions as a kind of stored thoughts, and memories as permanent and static printings (*typôseis*)." There was a disagreement between Cleanthes and Chrysippus on the nature of these stored imprints. Sextus Empiricus *Against the Professors* 7 227 and 372 (= SVF 2 56) reports this difference of opinion; the former considered Zeno's term literally as "indentation and relief, like the imprints of a signet ring in wax," while the latter took it to mean "a qualitative alteration (*heteroiôsis*) in the soul," which he describes at *Outlines of Pyrrhonism* 2 70 as "hocus pocus" (*teratalogoumenê*). Cf. Diogenes Laertius *Lives of the Philosophers* 7 50: Chrysippus says that "we should not take "imprint" to mean the stamp of signet ring, since it is inconceivable that there should be many imprints in the same place at the same time." Frede (1987, 167) says: "impressions for the Stoics are mental states that are identified as highly complex physical states, as we can see from the fact that originally they were conceived of quite literally as imprints. When Chrysippus objected to this, it was because he thought that they were much more complex than the term 'imprint' suggested; in calling them 'alterations' or 'modifications' of the mind instead, he deliberately, it seems, left open what their precise nature consists in." In general, Plotinus seems to have taken note of Chrysippus' views over those of earlier Stoics such as Cleanthes. So although in line 43 he attacks the simpler version as put by Cleanthes, in line 48 he seems to be allowing for the more sophisticated view of Chrysippus—although the objection remains in force; even Chrysippus' alteration is a corporeal alteration.

Chapter 7

In this chapter Plotinus continues his criticism of Stoic doctrines of perception, focusing on bodily pain and our awareness of it. His argument is a continuation of that of Chapter 6. Since, according to the Stoics, the soul is corporeal and thereby (infinitely) divisible into unlike corporeal parts, and since only body can affect body, then an affection can be communicated only to the part next to it, and by that part to the part next to it, and so on as far as the commanding faculty. Consequently the commanding element is aware only of the affection in the part of the soul immediately below it in the chain of communication, and not of the pain in its original location.

Plotinus is dismissive of the Stoic position and says little here about the Stoic attempts to rationalize their position, other than to acknowledge their doctrine (if it was as elevated as a doctrine) of transference (diadosis). *He has already commented on and dismissed what they have to say about "communality of affection"* (sympatheia) *in Chapter 3, and about disposition* (hexis) *in Chapter 4, and will return briefly to the latter in Chapter 8[2]. He says nothing in this treatise about Stoic "tension"* (tonos). *But communality of affection, disposition, and tension add up to a more sophisticated and near metaphysical position than he cares to allow.*

Lines 1–7

Plotinus sets out the agreed ground; we all acknowledge that we suffer pain in one part of our body and are aware of it in another. Hence the distinction in the first line between pain and the perception of pain. Cf. Aetius 4 23, 1 (= SVF 2 854): "The Stoics say that the affections occur in the areas affected, but that the perception is in the commanding element."

7, 2 *when a person's toe is said to be hurting*: The Greek word *dactylos* can denote either toe or finger (just as *tarsos* in line 17 can denote either the sole of the foot or the palm of the hand); Armstrong and Bréhier are "toe" men, while MacKenna plumps for "finger." The argument is not affected.

7, 5 *something different*: There is a textual problem here. The main manuscripts add after "something different" the phrase "[from] the breath" (*tou pneumatos*); commentators who accept this reading disagree as to whether it should be translated "the affected area is something different, and the ruling element is aware of the breath" or "the ruling element is aware of the affected area, namely the breath, as something different," both presumably in the sense that the ruling element is aware not of the affected area but of the soul-breath, which is the means of communication between the pain and the ruling element's awareness of it. For soul-breath in this sense cf. Aetius 4 8, 1 (= SVF 2.850): "The Stoics define perception as follows: a perception is an apprehension or cognition through a sense organ (*di'aisthêtêriou*). Perception is spoken of in many senses, as 'disposition,' 'power' and 'activity.' The cognizable presentation occurs, via a sense organ, in the ruling element itself, from which in turn perceptual intellective breaths are said to be stretched from the ruling element." (Although the correct construal of this last clause is not clear.) Vitringa emends "breath" to "affection" (*pathêmatos*); Volkmann suspects it should be "affection" (*pathêmatos*); Müller deletes the phrase altogether, and I follow him in that it may well have been a gloss added by a copyist, and to omit it gives a better contrast between "different" (i.e. from itself) and "same" in the next line. MacKenna captures the spirit well: "The suffering is in one thing, the sense of suffering is another; the entire soul is involved." The point is that the pain and the awareness of it are different phases of a single process. So far the ground is common.

Lines 7–22

Plotinus now outlines the Stoic explanation.

7, 7 *by transference*: The Greek term is *diadosis* (with its cognate verb *diadidosthai*). Although Galen at *The Doctrines of Plato and Hippocrates* 2 5 attributes the verb to Zeno and Chrysippus, it does not seem to have been a technical term used by the early Stoics. Graeser (1972, 46) says that the term is first used in a Stoic context by Epictetus, who possibly inherited it from Posidonius. It is also found in a Stoic context in Alexander of Aphrodisias *On the Soul* 41, 5.

The Stoic explanation of perception is based on their doctrine of "communality of affection" (*sympatheia*) alluded to at 3, 5. At a cosmic level breath (*pneuma*) "so disposed" is the cohesive force holding all things together. The particular disposition which applies in this respect is "tension" (*tonos*) or "tensile movement" (*tonikê kinêsis*); see LS 47G, J & K for supporting texts.[30] On a human level tension is apparent in the "stretching" of the soul as intellective breath throughout the body (see above). The Greek verb for "stretch" is *teinein*; the cognate noun is *tonos*.

However, Plotinus has little time for all this talk of tension, disposition, communality of affection and transference. He criticizes it, calling it "idle talk" at IV.1.2, 12 where he produces much the same argument against the Stoic position as here, but at greater length: "We should have no

30 For the distinction between *hexis* and *diathesis* see Simplicius *On Aristotle Categories* 237, 25ff. (Fleet 2002, 96 = LS 47S).

time for what they say—that perceptions reach the ruling element by transference; they are deluding themselves."

7, 13 *a large or even infinite number*: Infinite, because the soul, being body, is infinitely divisible, like all body.

Lines 22–28

Having shown by this reductio argument that Stoic "transference" cannot account for the unified perception of pain, Plotinus draws the conclusion that the sense faculty must be the same as itself throughout the body—that is, real "communality of affection."

7, 25 *every part of a magnitude is different*: That being the case, every part of a magnitude such as the Stoic soul will have different perceptions, and so there can be no unity of perception.

Chapter 8

In this chapter Plotinus continues his arguments against the Stoic corporeal soul. In the two previous chapters his focus has been on the effects produced in the soul by external factors through sense perception and memories of sense perceptions. He now turns to the inner activities and states of the soul less immediately caused by sense perception—thought and virtue—which are to do with the intelligible rather than the sensible. Although again there was common ground between Platonists and Stoics, in this area the distinctions become sharper and more profound. But again Plotinus does not give a detailed or systematic account of the Stoic position, and we have to wait until Chapter 9 for an exposition of his own views.

Platonists, Peripatetics, and Stoics agree that man is differentiated from other animals by his ability to think rationally, at least after a certain age. Thinking rationally meant making judgments (kriseis) *of a conceptual nature, in particular on moral questions and the choices involved in them (as Plotinus has observed at the start of Chapter 5). For Plato and Aristotle the development of the rational faculty involved a training and education that led a person away from the material world to an understanding of immaterial first principles. Both talk extensively about education and method, for example Plato in* Republic *books 6 and 7, Aristotle in* Nicomachean Ethics *1095a30ff. and 1105a31ff., and* Posterior Analytics *72a16ff. For both the non-corporeality of the soul allowed it to engage not only conceptually with the sensible, but more importantly with the intelligible. Alexander of Aphrodisias* On the Soul *61, 3 talks of the discriminating power of the soul distinguishing between sensible and intelligible objects. Although in the first instance our concepts are based on sense perception (although the recollection [*anamnêsis*] arguments in* Meno *and* Phaedo *perhaps allow for knowledge of the Forms to be given before birth rather than remembered from previous lives). The pinnacle of education, dialectic, is just that—the immaterial soul engaging with immaterial first principles.*

The Stoics put no less emphasis on the progress of the would-be sage, perhaps best exemplified in Seneca's Letters, *in which he gives copious advice to his young Stoic protégé Lucilius. They too admitted incorporeal intelligibles as objects of thought, but unlike Plato and Aristotle they sought to explain the processes of thought in purely corporeal terms (see below note on line 8), and it is on this point that Plotinus takes issue with them. In brief, the soul gives its assent to a cognitive impression by exercising reason, using both memory and preconceptions (*prolêpseis*) to make judgments on the impressions, not only judging immediate sense perceptions but also reviewing existing conceptions (*ennoiai*). Sextus Empiricus* Against the Professors *8 56 (SVF 2 88) says that for the Stoics all thought derives from either sense perception or from experience; Diogenes Laertius* Lives of the Philosophers *7 51 has the Stoics making a distinction between impressions made through the sense organs and those which are not sensual but received through thought (*dianoia*), such as impressions of the incorporeal and other items grasped by reason. Once assent was given, the resulting cognition could lead to impulse (*hormê*). The Stoics nevertheless maintained a strictly corporeal account of the processes of thought, and although reason has an important part to play in passing judgment on impressions, it was no more than breath (*pneuma*) "so disposed"—even if it was at times dealing with the incorporeal (see below on 8, 8). In fact the Stoics had a finely developed theory of dialectic (cf. Diogenes Laertius* Lives of the Philosophers *7 41–44 and LS section 31 for details). Just as Stoic doctrine preserved the unity of the perceptive process, as we have seen in Chapters 6 and 7, so this unity embraced the intellective process. All cognitive activity, whether perceptual or intellectual, was embraced by the concept of* sympatheia. *At each stage, from the initial sense perception through to the formation of a concept and any state or action resulting from it, an affection (*pathos*) of the soul was involved, whereby the corporeal nature of the soul was altered.*

Plotinus, however, makes his opposing position clear at the start of III.6, titled On the impassivity (non-affectability) of the non-corporeal, *where he sets out to show that despite our everyday language, which might suggest that the individual soul, which is closely linked to the body, might somehow share the affections of the body and so be liable to the same destruction as the body, any apparent alteration of the soul is a "different sort of alteration" not leading to destruction. At the start of the treatise he says: "We stated that sense perceptions were not affections . . . affections are to do with something other than the soul—let us say body of such-and-such a kind—while judgment is to do with the soul; it is not an affection"; and at line 21 he continues: "We must beware of giving affections of this kind to the soul, in case we unwittingly make it destructible." So this is an issue of fundamental importance to Plotinus, and in order to maintain the integrity and immortality of the soul he must combat the materialist views of the Stoics.*

Lines 1–7

Plotinus' first argument relies on making a clear distinction between the objects of sense and the objects of thought. He is apparently following Alexander of Aphrodisias *On the Soul* 61, 3–8: "There does in fact exist [within the soul] a single unitary power whose function is to discriminate between sensible and intelligible objects. This is intellect, which comprehends all existents within its cognitive act and determines, moreover, what level of being should be assigned to each existent. For it is the prerogative of sense to differentiate sensible objects on the basis of their purely sensible qualities, but intellect decides how even these sensibles differ among themselves with respect to their reality. And [only] intellect, because it knows objects that are by their nature intelligible, makes judgments about intelligible objects of this sort," developing Aristotle *On the Soul* 426b8ff.

8, 1 *body of any kind*: This phrase qualifies the Stoic premise that Plotinus often prefaces an argument with: "If soul is body." It closes off any possibility of a non-corporeal intellective breath (*noeron pneuma*). O'Meara (1993, 16–17) points the difference between Plotinus and the Stoics on this point: "[The Stoics] had . . . attempted to explain how thinking takes place in a soul that is of a bodily nature. Their conception of soul includes the idea of a unifying tensional force which binds together as a unity different perceptual components in the body . . . The Stoics spoke . . . of a corporeal force, a sort of cosmic life-giving spirit or breath which penetrates and organizes a purely passive matter, creating increasingly complex levels of material reality culminating in rationality. Plotinus, however, takes for granted his own conception of body. He thus assumes that body is incapable of self-movement, of self-organization. It does not have the power to create higher, in particular organic, functions. These functions must be produced by something different, which therefore cannot be body." Not even the most refined Stoic doctrine about body, however disposed, allowed for the soul to be anything other than body.

8, 2 *If sense perception*: Both the Stoics and Plotinus would agree with this premise, but would interpret it in different ways. For the Stoics, as we have seen, the whole process of sense perception was bodily, while for Plotinus, although it started in the bodily organ, it was transformed into a non-corporeal psychic event.

Lines 7–12

Plotinus now includes in his argument the distinction between the objects of sense perception and the objects of thought.

8, 8 *even if they would be reluctant*: The Stoics did admit that there were non-corporeal objects of thought. In their so-called scheme of categories the primary genus "something" (*ti*) was divided into three species: body, the bodiless, and what is neither of these two. Within the second species, the bodiless, were included void, place, time, and "sayables" (*lekta*), as testified by Sextus Empiricus *Against the Professors* 10 218 (SVF 2 331 = LS 27D). In the third species are fictions and limits. It is among the two latter species that intelligibles are to be found. Plotinus is most likely to be thinking here of the second species, especially sayables, although all three species, being "something" are potential objects of thought. At *Against the Professors* 8 409 (SVF 2 331 = LS 27E) Sextus Empiricus talks of "incorporeal sayables" and says that the reasoning faculty is impressed in the face of them (*ep'autois*) rather than by them. Stoic doctrine on this topic is not well documented, but a certain amount is clear about sayables. Diogenes Laertius *Lives of the Philosophers* 7 63 (= LS 33F) tells us that sayables are either complete or incomplete; an example of the former is "Socrates writes" and of the latter "writes." It is the former that are of interest here, and Diogenes goes on to list propositions, syllogisms, questions and enquiries among them. (See further Long 1986, 135–137; Brunschwig 216–219; and Bobzien 85–88 in Inwood, ed. 2003.) We learn little from Stoic sources about how we think about sayables. What is clear is that the thinking mind is corporeal even if its objects are incorporeal. Diogenes Laertius *Lives of the Philosophers* 7 53 (= SVF 2 87 = LS 39D) tells us that "some things are conceived by transition (*metabasis*) such as sayables and place." LS (p. 200) suggest that the transition is between the corporeal entity such as "Cato walking" and the non-corporeal sayable "Cato is walking." Plotinus gives us little indication of his views on this, although at line 18 he talks of separating forms from their matter.

8, 10 *how will a magnitude*: The question—not quite a rhetorical one since a notional reply is given—depends on the principle noted above, that only like can know like. For a Stoic a magnitude, being body, is infinitely divisible. Cf. Aristotle *On the Soul* 407a18: "How will [intellect] think what has parts with what is partless, or what is partless with what has parts?"

Lines 12–23

Plotinus further exploits the illogicality by positing a corporeal soul, which as body has parts, thinking of what is non-corporeal and without parts.

8, 12 *some partless part*: An example of Plotinus' use of apparent paradox; cf. III.6.1, 3 "irrational reasonings" and "unaffected affections," III.6.1, 36 "possesses without possessing and is affected without being affected," and I.1.1, 11 "the animating principle is present without being present." In Stoic terms there can be no corporeal part that cannot itself have parts, since all body is infinitely divisible.

8, 13 *there is no need for the whole to be in contact*: Plotinus is following Aristotle *On the Soul* 406b26ff. (a passage in which Aristotle is challenging Plato's apparently materialistic view of the soul as presented in *Timaeus*): "If it is enough for it [the soul] to be in contact with any one of the parts [of the material magnitude] why does it need to move in a circle or in general possess magnitude?"

8, 14 *primary thoughts*: Primary thoughts are of primary things, the Forms, as detailed in Alcinous *The Handbook of Platonism* 4 6–8 155, 21–156, 23, which the human soul can only engage with fully when it is free of the body, either after death or during the moments of "assimilation to the divine" which Plotinus discusses in IV.8. See Dillon (1993, 66–72), where he explores the suggestion already current in Plotinus' time, that the Forms are the thoughts of God. Plotinus' point here is that primary thoughts must be in the disembodied mind.

8, 16 *entirely pure*: IV.8 is a treatise devoted to describing and explaining the ascent of the soul from body and its subsequent descent. At III.6.6, 15 Plotinus says: "But what would the purification of the soul consist in if it was in no way stained? What is meant by separating it from the body? Purification would be to leave it alone in isolation, or looking at nothing else, having no alien opinions—whatever the nature of these opinions—and for it not to contemplate the images of the affections . . . nor to create affections from them. Is it not true purification if it turns upward in the opposite direction from the world below?" See also I.2.4–5.

8, 17 *And if they claim*: At *The Handbook of Platonism* 4 7 155, 35 Alcinous draws the distinction between primary and secondary objects of intellect, naming them as [transcendent] Forms and enmattered forms respectively: "Intellection (*noêsis*) too will be twofold, the one kind of primary objects, the other of secondary" (tr. Dillon). Aetius 4 11 (SVF 2 83 = LS 39E) explains how concepts are developed: "When a man is born, the Stoics say, he has the commanding-part of his soul like a sheet of paper ready for writing upon. On this he inscribes each one of his conceptions. The first method of inscription is through the senses. For by perceiving something, for example white, they have a memory of it when it has departed. And when many memories of a similar kind have occurred, we then say we have experience, for the plurality of similar impressions is experience. Some conceptions arise naturally in the aforesaid ways and undesignedly, others through our own instruction and attention. The latter are called 'conceptions' as well. Reason, for which we are called rational, is said to be completed from our preconceptions during our first seven years"; this is borne out by Cicero *Academics* 2 21 (LS 39C): "Those characteristics which belong to things we describe as being cognized by the senses are equally characteristic of that further set of things said to be cognized not by the senses directly but by them in a certain respect, for example, 'That is white, this is sweet, that is melodious, this is fragrant, this is bitter.' Our cognition of these is secured by the mind, not the senses. Next, 'That is a horse, that is a dog.' The rest of the series then follows, connecting bigger items which virtually include complete cognition of things, like 'If it is a human being, it is a mortal, rational animal.' From this class [i.e. mental perception in general] conceptions of things are imprinted on us, without which there can be no understanding or investigation or discussion of anything." All this, of course, however developed and sophisticated, is still for the Stoics a corporeal process.

8, 18 *when a body is separated off*: The Greek verb used is *khôrizein*. The process is reciprocal; if body is separated off, then the soul or intellect which does the separating is itself separated. (Bréhier and MacKenna interchange "separate" and "abstract" as translations of the verb.) The separation here is threefold, between body, the soul, and enmattered form. Then separation of body can be either total, in which case only bare matter is left, whose nature is discussed at length by Plotinus in III.6.6–19, or else the separation or abstraction of a particular form will leave the substrate notionally stripped of only one of its predicates. LS (p. 200) summarizes: "Cato's walking is the body Cato 'disposed in a certain way.' There is only one body—the man Cato. In saying 'is walking' of Cato, we abstract a feature of that body, and that abstraction or incorporeal predication is the only way in which the unitary body Cato can be meaningfully described in a sentence. Thus sayables can be regarded as abstractions from bodies—things which are 'body-less.'" The separation of the soul can be seen at two levels, either the complete separation (as mentioned above in line 15) or else, on a (literally) more "down-to-earth" level, the activity of the intellect contemplating not the primary Forms but the mathematical Forms, echoing the distinction made by Plato in *Republic* 6 between the Forms in the uppermost segment of the Divided Line which are apprehended by intellection (*noêsis*) and those in the segment below, the mathematicals, apprehended by discursive reasoning (*dianoia*). It is at the start of the education of the philosopher-king in *Republic* that such activity takes place, and it is this sort of activity that Plotinus points to here with the phrase "in such circumstances." But whether the soul is contemplating primary or mathematical Forms, it must abstract itself from the body. (See also Gerson 1994, 134.)

Lines 23–26

Before turning to consider virtue, Plotinus deals briefly with two of the most important moral and aesthetic Forms.

8, 24 *The beautiful and the just*: These two constitute the pinnacle of the philosophical life in any system or school. (Plotinus tends to equate the beautiful with the good and with the One—cf. I.6.7.) Plotinus isolates them here either because of their pre-eminence among Forms, or else because they are both adjectival epithets (in Stoic terms "incomplete sayables"), unlike the nouns wisdom, justice, and bravery which follow. If this is the case, then MacKenna and Armstrong fail to observe the distinction, translating "beauty and justice" and "nobility and justice" respectively. At I.6.1, 20 Plotinus states that "almost everybody agrees that the beautiful consists in the proper proportion (*symmetria*) of parts to each other and of parts to the whole."

8, 25 *So when they approach our soul*: Plotinus is now talking in Platonic terms. Discursive thinking brings the Forms to our intellect, and in this way the Forms "approach" and the intellect "will receive them." The Greek verb "to receive" (*hypodekhesthai*) recalls the noun used by Plato at *Timaeus* 49a to denote the "receptacle of all becoming" (*hypodokhê*), although we have to distinguish between the reception of Forms by the soul and the reception of their copies (*mimêmata*) in the receptacle. We are asked to consider the reception of Forms in their undivided state. The increasing pluralization of entities as they become further and further away from their source, ultimately the One, is a fundamental tenet of Plotinus' Platonism, and a problem of Platonism that puzzled Plotinus; just how could a Form retain its integrity, as described at *Timaeus* 51e–52a, and yet become divided in bodies? (See O'Meara

1993, chapters 6 and 7 for a succinct discussion of this topic.) Here we are asked to consider the Forms in the intelligible world before the pluralization and dissipation into bodies occurs, when they are still truly partless.

Lines 26–38

Plotinus now considers "the virtues of the soul," which for a Platonist are immaterial Forms, but which for the Stoics were "body so disposed" (cf. Sextus Empiricus *Against the Professors* 11 22: "[For the Stoics] virtue consists in the commanding element so disposed"; also Plutarch *Stoic Self-contradictions* 1034f and Stobaeus *Anthology* 2 68, 18). All would agree that virtue is (or should be) the all-important cause of human choice and action; since for the Stoics only body can act as cause (Diogenes Laertius *Lives of the Philosophers* 7 56), it must be body.

8, 27 *temperance, justice and bravery*: The Stoics followed Socrates in proclaiming the unity of virtue, and that virtue is wisdom. Plutarch *On Moral Virtue* 440e–441d (= LS 61B) reports a wide divergence of opinion among Stoics on its species, but there was a general consensus among philosophers in general that there were four primary, or cardinal, virtues. These were wisdom, temperance, courage, and justice—so that wisdom on occasions seems to have been a species of itself, an illogicality exposed by Socrates in Plato's *Euthyphro*. Plotinus leaves wisdom (*sophia/phronêsis/epistêmê*) out of the list here, accepting the hierarchy whereby wisdom stood above the other three. Plutarch *Stoic Contradictions* 1034c (accepting Pohlenz's insertion) shows how other virtues are no more than wisdom (*phronêsis*) in a certain relationship.

8, 28 *some sort of breath or blood*: See note above on 6.40.

8, 29 *perhaps bravery is the impassivity of the breath*: Plotinus suggests some psychic dispositions to account for the different virtues.

8, 31 *some kind of shapeliness*: Again Plotinus is offering a definition which would satisfy a Stoic. Cf. what he says about visible beauty in I.6.1–3—where his point is that perception of visible beauty is only a means to a greater end, that of perceiving intelligible beauty.

8, 34 *But what need does breath have of wisdom?*: Plotinus ridicules the Stoic notion of soul as a corporeal unity, whose natural inclination *qua* body is not for wisdom but for physical comfort.

8, 36 *to be moderately cooled*: This a phrase from Homer *Odyssey* 10.555. Odysseus is recounting the death of one of his men, Elpenor, who had gotten drunk and gone up onto the roof of Circe's house to get some fresh air, had fallen asleep and in the morning woken suddenly and fallen off the roof to his death. This playful allusion is in keeping with Plotinus' tongue-in-cheek comments. Perhaps the "delight in embraces and touch" and "soft, tender and smooth things" recall Odysseus' own intimacy with Circe.

8, 37 *fair distribution*: This phrase is perhaps picked up by Stobaeus *Anthology* 60, 24 in his mention of fair dealing as a species of justice.

Lines 38–45

The grammar and syntax of these lines is opaque, and translators vary in their interpretation. Plotinus' conclusion in line 44 that "that in which such a thing exists must also be of this nature" must surely refer to the soul. But it is not clear what "such a thing" refers to; the passage offers no obvious answer. MacKenna suggests "the soul's contemplation," Armstrong "the virtues," and Bréhier is non-committal. At the outset of the passage we are offered a choice between viewing virtue as something eternal or as belonging to the world of coming-to-be and passing-away. If the latter, there must still be a cause of its coming-to-be, which would need either itself to be eternal or to have its own cause, and so on (if this is the force of the phrase "in turn" [*palin*] in line 40) in infinite regress, only to be resolved by appeal to an eternal Platonic god or Aristotelian eternal unmoved mover. Such a cause must therefore belong not among bodies. This at least is how *The Theologia* paraphrases: "If they (the Materialists) persist and say that the virtues are all of them physical and concrete, we ask them, saying: Tell us how the soul acquires the virtues and the rest of the abstract things. Is it with their being eternal, not perishing or passing away, or is it with their falling under genesis, and corruption? If they say: It is with their being eternal, imperishable, that the soul acquires them, then they have acknowledged what they had denied of that, and if they say: The soul acquires the virtues with them falling under genesis and corruption, we say: Then who is the generator of them and from which of the elements is their generation? If they say he falls under genesis and corruption, we ask them about that generator too; whether he is eternal or falls under genesis and corruption, and so ad infinitum. If they say he is eternal, imperishable, then they have strayed from their assertion that all things are bodies. We say that if the virtues are eternal and imperishable, like the geometrical figures, there is no doubt that they are not bodies, and if they are not bodies then that which contains them and supports them is necessarily not a body either."

8, 39 *the contemplation:* The Greek word is *theôrêmata* (plural), which can alternatively mean "principles." In which case (as Bréhier) we should translate, "Does the soul grasp the principles of virtue . . . ?" To translate, as MacKenna and Armstrong do, as "contemplation" strains the plural a little.

8, 40 *benefit*: There is little doubt among ancient philosophers that virtue was beneficial. Cf. Sextus Empiricus *Against the Professors* 11. 22 (SVF 3 75 = LS 60G): "The Stoics . . . define the good as follows: "Good is benefit . . . " meaning by "benefit" virtue and virtuous action." (Cf. Plato *Republic* 379b.)

8, 41 *what causes it, and from what source?*: Two Stoic principles underlie these questions: (a) there is nothing in the cosmos that is uncaused, and (b) only body can act on body. So Plotinus is asking how the Stoics would explain both the active and the passive elements.

8, 44 *that in which they are to exist*: The Greek verb "are to exist" (*estai*) is singular, which would suggest that a singular subject should be supplied. But it is a feature of Greek grammar that neuter plural subjects are followed by a singular verb. Since no singular noun can be supplied from the immediate context, various possibilities have been canvassed—either a vague "intelligibles like virtue" construed from the neuter plural "principles of geometry"; or, as Bréhier, "virtue," pluralized by Armstrong and *The Theologia*; or, as MacKenna, "objects of contemplation."

Chapter 8[1]

In this chapter Plotinus brings forward five arguments against the exclusively materialistic Stoic explanation of bodily affection. The arguments are brief, and fall into the pattern of earlier commentators, although they do not match any of the existing arguments, for example those of Alexander of Aphrodisias or Galen.

See note at head of Chapter 9 for the possibility that chapters 8$^{1–5}$ are an interpolation.

Lines 1–17

Plotinus contrasts his own views with those of the Stoics, criticizing their reductionism whereby they attribute all affections in bodies to the activities of corporeal soul, failing to realize (i) that certain bodily affections such as warming and cooling can be produced without any psychic input, and (ii) that psychic activities such as thinking and perceiving are not corporeal but belong to a different order of being.

Platonists took their cue from two passages in Plato's *Theaetetus*. At 156a Socrates, within the context of sense perception, introduces what he claims to be a more sophisticated account than that given by his interlocutors. Opinion is divided on whether this is Plato's own view.

Cornford (1937, 204) says that "*Theaetetus* states Plato's theory of the nature of sensible qualities"; Guthrie (1978, 77) concludes that "This is in fact a refinement on the 'secret doctrine' of Protagoras, and together they present an astonishingly advanced and imaginative theory"; while Brown in Fine (1999, 470n25) says "Whatever the correct interpretation of the *dunamis* proposal, and whether or not Plato endorses it—both highly debated issues—it is manifest that it offers an account of what it is to be, where 'to be' is understood in a complete sense." Whatever the case, for Platonists two important features emerge. Firstly, within the flux of the sensible world there are two types of motion: "one with the power of acting, the other with the power of being acted on," and, secondly, from the interaction between these "twin offspring" are born the perceived object and the perception. Guthrie summarizes: "From intercourse and friction with each other these two motions (i.e. sensible object and sense organ) give birth to twins, an act of perception and a percept (color, sound etc.)." So the idea of active and passive "powers" within the sensible world finds its footing in the Platonist camp.

Then at *Theaetetus* 182a Socrates, discussing the place of perception in the Heraclitean worldview, underlines the distinction between the active and the passive factors on the one hand, and the quality which passes between them on the other (Socrates is apparently coining the Greek word for "quality"—*poiotês*). Then at *Sophist* 247d, where we have left behind the complications of sense perception and the Eleatic Stranger is finding common ground between the materialist "Giants" and the idealist "Gods" in a broadly ontological discussion, he says, "I say that anything whatsoever, whether by its nature it affects something else or is itself affected even in the least degree by the most insignificant agent, albeit on one occasion only—I say that this has true being." This suggestion is accepted provisionally by Theaetetus in the dialogue and is not revisited by Plato. Even so it becomes an important implicit part of his thought. See Cornford (1935, 234–239) for a full discussion, where several passages are adduced from other works of Plato to support the notion of "the power of acting and being acted on" as a mark of what is acceptable to "a reasonable materialist." There is emerging, with regard to the affections of the sensible body—which Plato did not deny—a clear distinction between agent, patient, and quality.

Aristotle advanced the discussion in two significant ways. Firstly, in *Categories* he drew a formal distinction between primary substance (sensible composite bodies) and qualities, which as accidents of material bodies were themselves incorporeal. In this chapter Plotinus is especially interested in "affective qualities"; at *Categories* 9a28 Aristotle says: "The third type of quality comprises affective qualities and affections, such as sweetness and bitterness, and astringency and anything akin to these;

also coolness and warmth, whiteness and blackness." (See Simplicius *On Aristotle Categories* 252, 21ff. for a full discussion.) Secondly, Aristotle developed the notion of different powers (or faculties) of the soul. He does not appear concerned to give a rigid schema of psychic faculties, and gives varying lists in different places. At *On the Soul* 414a31ff. (the work that Plotinus and the commentators such as Alexander of Aphrodisias had mainly in their view) he mentions five faculties—nutritive, appetitive, sensitive, locomotive, and intellective, to which can be added generative (416a19) and imaginative (432b1); elsewhere he talks of the vegetal. Most scholars accept a broad tripartite division into vegetal, sensitive, and rational. Within this context the soul has powers to produce in the individual body such effects as growth, movement, sensation, and thought; further affections of soul as an efficient cause would be, for example, the affections of inanimate substances such as the effect of the carpenter's skill on the wood of the table under construction. And apart from these psychic processes are (teleology apart) the non-psychic effects in the material world such as the rain falling on crops. That qualities are incorporeal is argued by both Platonists and Peripatetics; of the former the most notable is Alcinous in *The Handbook of Platonism* chapter 11 and pseudo-Galen *On the Incorporeality of Qualities* (see Dillon 1993, 111–114 and Sharples 2008, 174–175); of the latter the most strongly argued is Alexander of Aphrodisias *Supplement*

122, 16ff. By far the most extensive discussion of quality is to be found in Simplicius *On Aristotle Categories* 206, 1–294, 15, where he discusses a wide range of issues, for example the question of causation. (See Fleet 2002 for a translation.) Simplicius, of course, was writing some two centuries after Plotinus.

It is assumed or argued as common ground between Platonists and Peripatetics (a) that all qualities are incorporeal, (b) that sensible qualities in inanimate bodies can be produced by non-psychic causes, and (c) that there are psychic causes, some rational such as "thinking" and "taking wise and good care," and some irrational such as nutrition, producing effects that are unlike themselves in the patient.

By contrast the Stoics, insisting on a purely corporeal explanation, accepted the active and the passive principles; but for them the former was breath (*pneuma*), a combination of air and fire, which was co-extensive with the passive principle, which was composed of earth and water. The complexity of objects in the sensible world depends on the tenor or mixture of breath in them. The cosmic breath is all-pervasive; it mixes with the otherwise unqualified passive principle to produce the so-called second category, "the qualified." The Stoics were somewhat ambiguous on the status of qualities; in principle a quality was no more than a corporeal disposition, as testified by Aetius 1.11.5 (= SVF 2 340 = LS 55G): "The Stoics call all causes corporeal because they are portions of breath," summarized by LS (p. 271): "to predicate a property of a subject is to describe a quality or disposition of god in matter"; this is the tenet that Plotinus is arguing against here. But Sextus Empiricus *Against the Professors* 9.211 (= LS 55B) tells us that the Stoics made a distinction between the corporeal cause and the incorporeal effect: "The Stoics say that every cause is a body which becomes the cause to a body of something incorporeal." For instance the scalpel, a body, becomes the cause to the flesh, a body, of the incorporeal predicate "being cut." So there does seem to be a distinction between the bodily cause and the bodily end result, for example the cut body which is qualified body (*poion*) or even body "so disposed," and the quality itself, which is a "sayable." Simplicius gives a different version at *On Aristotle Categories* 217, 32: "The Stoics say that the qualities of bodies are corporeal. Their error is due to the fact that (a) they think that causes are of the same substance as their effects, and (b) they assume a common account of cause in the case of both bodies and the bodiless."

8[1], 3 *they locate the soul in this world*: Plotinus would not deny the cosmic role of soul in the workings of the cosmos. His meaning here is that it is wrong to claim, as the Stoics do, that the soul is itself something corporeal.

The Greek word for "in this world" is *entautha*, which is commonly used by Plotinus in contrast to "in the intelligible world" (*ekei*)—here denoted by the phrase in lines 8–9: "some other kind of existence."

8¹, 3 *as if stationing it in a field of action*: There are two strands to this phrase. Firstly the verb "station" (*tattein*) has a military ring to it; secondly the word denoting "of action" (*drastêrios*) echoes the Stoic active principle—Galen (SVF 2 405 and 406) tells us that the Stoics considered heat and cold to be "active" (*drastikos*), especially heat, which is "the most active of the qualities." Plotinus' point is that the Stoics are foisting an inappropriate bodily causal role onto soul (cf. Simplicius *On Aristotle Categories* 217, 32).

8¹, 6 *powers*: The Greek word is *dunameis*, which has a wide range of connotations. In this context the appropriate one (as shown above in the discussion of *Theaetetus*) is "power" or "faculty" rather than "potential."

8¹, 7 *thinking, perceiving etc.*: Platonists, Peripatetics, and Stoics would all consider these to be activities of the highest, rational, faculty of the soul (cf. Sextus Empiricus *Against the Professors* 8 275 = LS 53T = SVF 2 223).

8¹, 8 *wise and good care*: Henry originally wished to emend the reading of Eusebius and Stephanus from "good" (*kalôs)* to "bad" (*kakôs*), comparing a similar phrase in a list of psychic activities in Plato *Laws* 10 897a2. But he has since accepted the Eusebius/Stephanus reading.

8[1], 11 *It is evident from what follows*: This refers to the immediate point made in lines 11–17 rather than to the arguments of the rest of the chapter.

8[1], 11 *powers . . . empowered . . . power*: Plotinus rather labors the repetition to make his point.

8[1], 13 *all body is quantitative but not all body is qualitative*: Quantity is given priority over quality by Aristotle in the order of categories in that it is found at the first level of substantial being after pure matter, and awaits the arrival of quality in order for substance to come into being. Cf. Simplicius *On Aristotle Categories* 120, 25–121, 13—see Fleet (2001, 99) for translation. *The Theologia* on this passage says: "Nor is it possible for a body to be without quantity; this the Materialists acknowledge."

8[1], 14 *for example matter*: For Platonists and Stoics alike (and for Aristotle in the sense of bare or prime matter) matter is lacking in quality. But its quantitative status is ambiguous. On the one hand Plotinus on some occasions is following the description of the Receptacle at Plato *Timaeus* 48eff. and underlining the utter non-being of matter; at III.6.7, 1–7 he says: "But we must return to the underlying matter and to the things said to be based on it—from which it will be recognized that matter has no real being and is not subject to affections. It is on the one hand bodiless, since body is posterior to it and is a compound formed by matter and something else. For it is because both being and matter are different from bodies that matter shares this description with being—because of its bodilessness." In fact the bulk of III.6 is devoted to demonstrating that matter is not able to receive affections in that it is not body. On the other hand, in that it is space (*khôra*—one description given by Plato of the receptacle) it has at least a semblance of quantity although it is entirely without qualities, and any descriptions of it are negative. But it appears that at some time after Plato's death the idea of matter as portrayed by Plotinus in III.6 became fused with the idea of matter as a material substrate to corporeal bodies. In fact Plato does not use the term "matter" (*hulê*) (see further Fleet 1995, 164–167). See also below on line 28.

Lines 17–35

Plotinus adds a further series of brief arguments against the Stoic position. It is tempting to see them as a set of observations made at the end of one of the seminars and incorporated by Plotinus in his write-up. They are similar in this respect to the series of arguments found in other commentators such as Alexander of Aphrodisias, although their content is rather different.

8^1, 18 *as was stated earlier*: Plotinus is referring back to the argument at 5, 24–52, and applying it here to show that qualities cannot be corporeal. The conclusion at the end of Chapter 5 was that neither soul nor rational principles (*logoi*) are corporeal. It is on the latter of these two items that the argument now focuses. For a Platonist there was a distinction between Form in the intelligible world and the quality or enmattered form in the sensible world, which shades into, but remains distinct from, the *logos*, a distinction made by Simplicius at *On Aristotle Categories* 218, 31, where he establishes a hierarchy of Platonic Form, *logos*, quality and qualified thing.

8^1, 21 *sweetness . . . honey*: Sweetness in honey is an example of an affective quality used by Aristotle at *Categories* 9a28.

A further post-Plotinian refinement mentioned by Simplicius at *On Aristotle Categories* 219, 17 to account for any apparent quantitative feature of quality is that of "latitude" (*platos*), a term used by the commentators to explain an apparent paradox: How can anything acquire different degrees of a quality which itself does not admit of degrees? Their answer was that the mixture of elements in a thing, through remission and intension (*anesis* and *epitasis*) in the mixture, allows a range or "latitude" in the participation in the quality.

8[1], 23 *if powers were bodies*: Plotinus now turns his attention to the power (*dunamis*) rather than the quality itself, although the dividing line between powers and qualities is not always sharply drawn, for example at III.6.8, 1: "As a general rule anything that is to be affected must be such that it is in possession of the powers and qualities opposite to the ones that come in on top and cause the affection" (see Cornford 1935, 236–237). The point is the same: powers are not divisible in the way that bodies are.

8[1], 28 *matter, being body*: For the Stoics at the most fundamental level of analysis of the cosmos there were two principles (*arkhai*), the active and the passive; it is the latter that Plotinus now considers. This principle is variously termed "matter" (*hulê*)," the substrate" (*to hupokeimenon*) or "unqualified substance" (*apoios ousia*). It can be termed "body" in that it exists and is extended, although in itself it is entirely lacking quality; this is its persisting sameness. That it remains the same *qua* body is attested by Stobaeus *Anthology* 1 132, 27ff. (SVF 1 87 and 2 317) who tells us that both Zeno and Chrysippus made primary matter everlasting and not subject to any alteration in quantity; cf. also Alcinous *The Handbook of Platonism* 166, 21; "One body does not differ *qua* body from any other, but differs in quality (certainly not in body); so therefore qualities are not bodies" and 163, 3: "It is likewise proper to all receptive matter, if it is to receive the forms thoroughly, not to have subsistent in itself any of their nature, but to be without quality or form in order to be the receptacle of the forms." That its only attribute is extension is attested by Apollodorus quoted by Diogenes Laertius *Lives of the Philosophers* 7 135 (SVF 3 Apollodorus = LS 45E): "According to Apollodorus in his *Physics*, body is what has threefold extension—length, breadth and depth; this is also called solid body"; to this can be added "resistance" as attested by Galen *On Incorporeal Qualities* 19 483, 13 (SVF 2 381 = LS 45F)—which conforms with Plato *Theaetetus* 155e. Supervenient qualities that combine with it to produce what is at the second level of Stoic analysis, "qualified body," do not contribute anything bodily to what is already bodily in its own nature.

8¹, 32 *breath or blood*: The argument is either the same as at 6, 40, or else Plotinus is making a more general point that no corporeal entity is able to comport life.

Chapter 8[2]

*In this chapter Plotinus discusses the Stoic doctrine of total blending (*krasis di'holôn*), not only criticizing the consequences of its materialist assumptions but also extracting from it support for his own Platonic account of the soul. We move from the Stoic position outlined in the first sentence (*if soul . . . bodies are blended*) through a series of arguments directed against it, finally reaching a conclusion in the last two sentences (*So it is not possible . . . therefore it is bodiless*). His task in this chapter is to show that although soul does blend totally with the body, it cannot do so in the way that the Stoics claim. In doing so he at least gives negative parameters for his own ideas on how soul is present to the body, a deeply problematic issue for him as a Platonist, as we have already seen (note on 2, 4). But it must be said in fairness to the Stoics that he presents their doctrines in a grossly materialist manner which does not do them justice, and he gives no scope for a more sophisticated interpretation—for which see LS (pp. 293–294). Plotinus returns to the question in a brief later treatise II.7 titled* On Total Blending.

Stoic ideas on the total blending of two or more bodies had been adumbrated by Presocratics such as Anaxagoras and Empedocles, who had been criticized by Aristotle, for example at On the Soul *418b17, where, defending his statement that light is not a body, he says "For it is impossible for two bodies to be together in the same place at the same time," going on to point to Empedocles as one of the culprits; at* On Coming-to-be and Passing-away *327a30ff. Aristotle conducts a lengthy discussion on material mixture, making a basic distinction between combination (*sunthesis*) where the ingredients retain their identity in actuality (*energeiai*)—his example is a heap of grains of wheat and barley—and blending (*krasis*) where the ingredients are subsumed in the blend into a new homogeneous substance, still retaining their identity but only in potentiality (*dunamei*). Of these only the latter, he says, is a true mixture. The resulting homogeneous mixture is capable of (infinite) division into like parts; at 328b18 he adds a further refinement—a mixture in which the ingredients are destroyed—although it may be that Aristotle is using the verb* diaphtheirein *here in the sense of* sumphtheirein *= "blend totally" (as Diogenes Laertius* Lives of the Philosophers *VII.151). Certainly Plotinus' focus here is on the blend in which the ingredients are recoverable (how else would the soul survive the death of the body?) such as that noted by Stobaeus* Anthology *1.155, 5–11 (= SVF 2 471 = LS 48D): "If one dips an oiled sponge into the water that has been blended with wine, it will separate the water from the wine" (an experiment I tried with some success). Cf. also* Physics *4 209a5, where Aristotle denies* *that place, although having the three dimensions of length, breadth, and depth, is itself a body, for if it were two bodies it would* per impossibile *occupy the same space.*

It is on the basis of this analysis of different types of mixture that the Stoics built their doctrine of total blending, although they disagreed with Aristotle in his claim that two bodies cannot occupy the same space at the same time. Stoic doctrine goes back possibly to the founder, Zeno of Citium, if we are to believe the testimony of Hippolytus and Themistius (SVF 2 468 and 469). Most of our sources, mainly from the 1st and 2nd centuries CE, point to Chrysippus as the originator of the doctrine, for example Diogenes Laertius Lives of the Philosophers *7 151 (= SVF 2 480 = LS 48B), Stobaeus* Anthology *1.17.4, 153, 24, and Alexander* On Mixture *216, 14. This last is printed in Todd (1976, 52ff.), whose introduction to his commentary on this work gives a full and scholarly account of the antecedents to Alexander's book, a text which is fundamental to Plotinus' discussion here in IV.7.8*[2]*. Cf. also Alexander* Supplement *117, 9ff. and 138, 3ff. Alexander shows how Chrysippus refined Aristotle's classification to: juxtaposition (*parathesis*), where the ingredients retain their substance and quality (i.e. they continue to exist in actuality), fusion (*sugkhusis*) where the ingredients lose their substance and quality as in the case of certain drugs, and mutual co-extension (*antiparektasis*) as in the case of wine and water, where the ingredients exist only in potentiality* *as long as they are in the mixture, but are separable into their original states. Of these mutual co-extension and fusion differ in that in the former the ingredients retain their identity, at least potentially, and are recoverable, while in the latter they are irrecoverably destroyed—the distinction hinted at by Aristotle at* On Coming-to-be and Passing-away *327b2ff. Soul and body are mutually co-extended, and it is on this type of mixture that Plotinus directs his attention (juxtaposition in the case of soul and body is the preserve of the Epicureans, and is not considered here by Plotinus). Alexander at* On Mixture *217, 33 says that among the examples given by the Stoics of mutual co-extension is "the way in which the soul, which has its own substantial existence (*hupostasis*), just like the body that receives it, pervades the whole of the body but retains its own being (*ousia*) when it mixes with it; for no part of an ensouled body lacks soul." ("Pervade" is one of the terms used to denote total blending.) See LS section 48 for a full analysis of this and other relevant texts.*

This then is the starting point for Plotinus' discussion in this chapter, as outlined in the first sentence. The terminology and the arguments he deploys suggest that Alexander's works, especially On Mixture, On the Soul, *and* Supplement *were to hand at Plotinus' seminar(s) where this topic was discussed.*

Lines 1–7

A material soul cannot blend with material body without losing its existence in actuality.

8², 3 *in actuality*: Plotinus is taking his lead from Aristotle *On Coming-to-be and Passing-away* 327b23: "Since some things exist in potentiality and others in actuality, it is possible that the ingredients in a mixture exist in one way, but not in another. The resulting mixture is something different, which exists in actuality while each of the ingredients is still potentially what it was before the mixture, and is not destroyed." Alexander discusses the point at *On Mixture* 231, 12–233, 14, where he expands Aristotle's point, saying at 231, 15: "they quickly become a single body in both substrate and quality, which is none of the ingredients in actuality, but all of them in potentiality." The distinction between potentiality and actuality (perhaps first made by Plato at *Sophist* 246e) was fully formulated by Aristotle and quickly became part and parcel of philosophical thinking. This passage is an example *par excellence* of Plotinus calling in Aristotle to amplify and support Plato's thoughts. For Aristotle the soul, as defined at *On the Soul* 412b5, is "the first actuality of a natural body with organs." Plotinus would have no quibble with this, that the embodied soul exists in actuality; but he would disagree, however, with Aristotle on the nature of the soul, which for Aristotle is enmattered form and is thereby inseparable from the body other than conceptually, whereas for Plato and Plotinus soul is a separable entity which belongs primarily to the intelligible world. So to suggest that the soul, by its presence in the body, loses (albeit temporarily) its being so as to exist only potentially ("so that we have no soul") is anathema to Plotinus. (Cf. Alexander of Aphrodisias *Supplement* 116, 5.)

8², 6 *when sweet and sour are blended*: The Greek is ambiguous; the terms "sweet" and "sour" could denote either qualities or qualified bodies, although for the Stoics there is no difference, since both refer to "matter so disposed." The implication here is that this is an example of blending rather than fusion, and seems to go against Aristotle's point at *On Coming-to-be and Passing-away* 327b3, that if one of the ingredients is destroyed while the other persists (here the sweet and sour respectively) then it is not a mixture. Perhaps the argument is compressed and in full would be: "just as the sweet does not exist in actuality when sweet and sour are blended, so neither does the sour, although both exist potentially in the blend."

Lines 7–22

To posit total blending of corporeal soul and body engenders impossible conclusions; therefore soul is not body.

Plotinus starts by giving a description of Stoic total blending (*krasis di'holôn*), which has the following characteristics (using as an example the blending of two bodies, although it applies equally to a blending of more than two bodies—in fact Stoic soul as breath [*pneuma*] was itself a blend of two bodies, fire and air, just as the body too was a blend of many bodies):

1. The bodies are co-extensive and equal. The terminology echoes Alexander of Aphrodisias *Supplement* 140, 1, where we are told that at least in some cases in a mixture one of the bodies receives the other and becomes "co-extensive and equalized with it." The first term, co-extension (*parektasis*), is expanded by some writers such as Stobaeus and Alexander, to "mutual co-extension" (*antiparektasis*). Here Plotinus ridicules the idea, saying that it is impossible *for the lesser to become equal to the larger.*

2. There is no increase in either of the ingredients. However, Alexander of Aphrodisias at *Supplement* 140,31ff. expresses some puzzlement at the apparent Stoic inconsistency in saying that in some cases the total volume of the mixture is greater than the volume of either of the ingredients (as in the case of two liquids), while in others the volume of one of the ingredients is not added to that of the other, as in the case of fire "going through" iron. He resolves the question (in a way unacceptable to the Stoics) at *On Mixture* 220, 3ff., where he says that in cases of mixture where the resulting volume is no greater than that of one of the ingredients, it is not a case of mixture: "There is no body

for which the mixture of bodies preserves a volume equal to one of the ingredients; for where it seems to remain equal it is not a mixture of bodies, but a case of either form and matter (as soul and body) or body and quality (as iron and heat) or a given change occurs into some other thing, as happens with ash. But neither qualities nor forms are bodies and certainly would not receive another body in themselves" (tr. Todd, slightly adapted). This is a position that Plotinus would be entirely happy with.

Interestingly, at *On Coming-to-be and Passing-away* 328a26, Aristotle says that a single drop of wine, when mixed with a large amount of water (he gives a notional figure of 30,000 liters), loses its form (*eidos*). Later Peripatetics preferred to use the term "mutually co-extensive" and to claim that even in such a case the wine retains its form at least potentially.

3. The Stoics, like Aristotle, believed in the infinite divisibility of material body, although Chrysippus, according to Diogenes Laertius *Lives of the Philosophers* 7 151, made a distinction between "division to infinity" and "infinite division," since there is no terminal point. A body which is homogeneous, "full of itself," has no internal divisions which would allow it to be divided up into atomic parts. In a total blend this principle holds good, so that division is infinite, as Alexander says at *On Mixture* 222, 4: "The consequence for those who describe division as continuing

to infinity is that it is impossible to speak of a body being in actuality divided through and through and of bodies being in this way also totally mixed by being in actuality divided into infinities" (tr. Todd). Since division is infinite, with the division never terminating but always leaving a homogeneous residue, total blending in Stoic terms is never possible, since, as Todd (note *ad loc.*) puts it: "bodies are totally blended insofar as they are divided, and since the previous argument has shown that such division can neither be limited nor exhaustive, then the only alternative is that constituents must be divided to infinity. This must involve division into an actual infinite set of parts, since infinite division as an incompleted process would not explain total blending. However, once one admits that total blending can only be explained by division into actual infinite sets, and says that these are composed of bodies, various paradoxes ensue, which, given that these bodies are not atoms, cannot be evaded by saying that the infinite sets are composed of incorporeal entities which cannot be the parts of a body."

8[2], 15 *Even so*: Plotinus accepts that if for the sake of argument total blending and infinite division are compatible, the outcome must be the one alluded to in the previous note, that the terminal point must be non-corporeal, since any corporeal part must admit of further division and so preclude total blending, *which is impossible*. The logical outcome of infinite division (which is a necessary condition for total blending) where there is (theoretically) no body remaining to divide is that we are left with geometrical points that lack magnitude—but that is absurd since a magnitude cannot be made up of parts lacking magnitude. (Cf. 3, 5 "no body or even a magnitude could come from what is lacking in parts"). Cf. Aristotle *On Coming-to-be and Passing-away* 316a26: "If no body or magnitude is to be left and yet division is to take place, the body will consist of points and its constituents will be things with no magnitude, or else it will be absolutely nothing."

8², 18 *If it were possible*: Again Plotinus accepts for the sake of argument that if such infinite division is possible, it must for the Stoics be actual, not potential, as it is for Aristotle. Cf. *On Coming-to-be and Passing-away* 316b20: "It is in no way absurd that every perceptible body should be divisible at *any point whatsoever* and also indivisible. For it will be potentially divisible and actually indivisible."

Chapter 8[3]

In this chapter Plotinus attacks the Stoic doctrines on the generation of the (corporeal) soul through his criticism of their doctrines on the hierarchy of priority-posteriority.

Lines 1–6

Plotinus dismisses the Stoic doctrine that the soul comes into being at birth when the breath (*pneuma*) which has been conveyed into the womb at conception by the male seed becomes cooled and hardened at birth.

8³, 1 *They say . . .* : The fullest description of the Stoic account of the generation of the human soul is given by Hierocles (a 1st–2nd century CE Stoic) *Elements of Ethics* 1.5ff. (= LS 53B): "If the seed falls into the womb at the right time and is gripped by the receptacle in good health, it no longer stays still as before but is energized and begins its own activities. It draws matter from the pregnant body, and fashions the embryo in accordance with inescapable patterns, up to the point when it reaches its goal and makes its product ready to be born. Yet throughout all this time—I mean the time from conception to birth—it remains in [in the form of] physique (*phusis*—otherwise translatable as "nature"), i.e. breath, having changed from seed and moving methodically from beginning to end. In the early stages the physique is breath of a rather dense kind and considerably distant from soul; but later, when it is close to birth, it becomes finer. . . . So when it passes outside, it is adequate for the environment, with the result that, having been hardened thereby, it is capable of changing into soul." This is confirmed by other writers who add that at the moment of birth the "physique," which has been nurtured in the heat of the womb like a plant, is chilled by the outside air, is tempered like hot iron plunged into cold water, and becomes soul, as Plutarch says at *On Stoic Self-contradictions* 1052: "He [Chrysippus] thinks that the fetus is nurtured in the womb by nature like a plant. When it is brought to birth the breath is cooled (*psukhomenon*) and tempered by the air, changes and becomes a living thing. So it is not absurd to call it soul (*psukhê*) from the cooling (*psuxis*)." The would-be soul, while still in the womb, is variously termed "seed" (*sperma*), "breath" (*pneuma*), "embryo," "fetus" (*brephos*) and "nature" or "physique" (*phusis*).

Two features of this account are important for Plotinus. First, while still in the womb the embryo is no more than a plant whose controlling principle is nature, and whose functions are purely vegetal (cf. Galen *On the Doctrines of Plato and Hippocrates* 6.3.7 (= SVF 2 710): "The Stoics did not call the principle that controls plants 'soul,' but 'nature.'") The soul is generated at the end of the process. Secondly, the generation of the soul is the effect of antecedent material causes.

8³, 4 *For many living creatures*: Plotinus' first point is that the Stoics are inconsistent in claiming that all souls are the result of cooling and hardening, since "*many living creatures are born in heat and have souls that are not cooled.*" He does not give any examples. The most obvious possibility is that some creatures are born in a hot climate (at least as hot as the interior of the womb). Otherwise he could be referring to the heavenly bodies; Plutarch *On Common Conceptions* 1084e (= SVF 2 806) observes that the Stoics "engender the hottest thing by means of cooling, and say that the sun became ensouled when the moist changed into intellective fire"—but Plotinus is not concerned with the souls of the heavenly bodies here. Or possibly we could note Galen's observation at *On the Doctrines of Plato and Hippocrates* 5.5.8ff. (= LS 65M) that Posidonius criticizes Chrysippus for failing to see that impulse is often caused by a movement in the passionate part of the soul: "animals and men that are broad-chested and hotter are all the more competitive by nature." At *On the Soul* 403b1 Aristotle says that most philosophers ascribe anger to the boiling of the blood round the heart, and at *On Respiration* 479a29 he says that birth is the first participation of the nutritive soul in the hot. Finally at *On the Generation of Animals* 732b29 he says: "The more perfect living creatures are those which are by nature hotter and more fluid." This remark is followed by a classification of creatures by temperature, from the hot and fluid (human) to the cold (insect).

8³, 5 *even so, they say that nature is prior to soul*: Whether or not the soul is the result of cooling, the Stoic doctrine that the soul is generated only at birth leads to absurd conclusions, which Plotinus points to in the remainder of the chapter. His argument hinges on the interpretation of the term "prior," and his point is that the Stoics have, literally, got their priorities wrong.

At *On the Generation of Animals* 742a20ff. Aristotle draws the distinction between (a) temporal and (b) ontological priority. He differentiates between "that for the sake of which" (*to hou heneka*) and "that which is for its sake" (*to toutou heneka*); of these the former, *to hou heneka*, is the term used in *Physics* 2 to denote the final cause, reminding us of the overriding teleology of Aristotle's metaphysics; in *Physics* 2, after identifying the four generic causes (*aitia*) as material, formal, efficient, and final, he goes on to say that in the case of natural entities the last three can often be subsumed under a single heading of form, and concludes at 199a30: "Since nature is twofold, both as matter and form, and since the latter is the end, and since everything else exists for the sake of the end, then form will be the final cause." In *Generation of Animals* he says that *to toutou heneka* is prior in generation (*genesei*) while *to hou heneka* is prior in real being (*ousiai*). This is confirmed at *Parts of Animals* 646a25: "The case of generation is the opposite to that of real being. For what is later in generation is prior in nature" (where "nature" is the equivalent of "real being").

Simplicius *On Aristotle Physics* 380, 13 summarizes Alexander's conclusions on this point: "Alexander says 'it seems to me that from this he [Aristotle] proves that the cause is more properly the form than the matter . . . for if the matter exists for the sake of the form then the form would be more properly the cause than the matter.'"

If we apply this principle to the human then we can draw two conclusions. First, that the soul as the form of the body is prior to it ontologically and is the final cause of the body (*On the Soul* 415b8: "The soul is the cause and principle of the living body"). Second, that the body stands to soul as matter to form, and is accordingly posterior to it ontologically.

In his account of the development of the living creature Aristotle insists that the soul and the body develop *pari passu* and that neither can exist in separation from the other (cf. *On the Soul* 414a19 and 413a4). This is in keeping with his general point that form is inseparable from matter. In his description of the development of the soul Aristotle employs the basic division into nutritive, sensitive, and rational "parts." Of these, at the outset of pregnancy, the mother alone provides the nutritive, which develops first (*Generation of Animals* 735a17) so that the physical growth of the embryo starts at conception. The sensitive part develops second and the rational part last of all, and both these parts are provided by the male through the seed. The entire soul is present from the moment of conception, though in each case there is a development from potential to actual. *Generation of Animals* 735a9 tells us: "It is clear that the seed possesses soul and that it is soul in potentiality." The nutritive part develops as it draws nourishment, "and it is clear that we should say the same about the sensitive and rational soul, since it is necessary to possess all the parts in potentiality before possessing them in actuality." The acquisition of intellect is problematic, and Aristotle never quite makes up his mind, but suggests at *Generation of Animals* 736b27 that "intellect alone comes in [into the seed] from outside and alone is divine; for corporeal activity (*energeia*) has nothing in common with its activity" (cf. *On the Soul* 413a6, 413b25, 430a6, and *Metaphysics* 1070a25). Alexander *Supplement* 106, 18–113, 25 has a long discussion on the nature of intellect. In each case the vehicle by which the parts of the soul receive their functions is "innate breath" (*sumphuton pneuma*) "actualizing the latent potentiality of the material, bringing about in it the alteration of which it is capable" (A. L. Peck in Loeb *Aristotle; Generation of Animals* 580; see his Appendix B for a full discussion of *sumphuton pneuma*). Alexander at *On the Soul* 19, 15ff. draws a clear distinction between soul and *pneuma*—a distinction which he complains the Stoics fail to observe.

In short, for Aristotle soul grows *pari passu* with the embryo/infant. Each stage is (temporally) prior in generation to the next, but (ontologically) posterior in reality, in that each stage is going forward to the perfection (*telos*) of the living creature for whose sake each preceding stage exists.

Plotinus clearly welcomed the Peripatetic arguments as put forward by Alexander in both *On the Soul* and *Supplement,* and would accept many aspects of those arguments. But he would disagree with Aristotle on certain fundamental points. First, Forms, as intelligibles, are entirely separable from the sensible particulars in which they are imaged. Secondly, soul is no exception to this principle; it (if not in its entirety at least in its rational part) is separable from the body both before, during (see IV.8) and after its engagement with the body. Thirdly, although Plato does not indulge in Aristotle's systematic embryology but often has recourse to myth, it is clear that before birth the human soul is a fully formed being with rational knowledge of the Forms, as exemplified in the doctrine of Recollection in *Phaedo* and *Meno.* In *Timaeus* the lower parts of the soul are added later by the lesser gods after the demiurge has created and implanted the immortal part. Plato's division between rational and irrational parts is broadly the same as Aristotle's, but their order of acquisition, at least in *Timaeus*, is reversed. In *Phaedrus* the chariot of the soul has its three parts all the time. But in his criticism of the Stoics Plotinus could find his greatest support in the writings of Alexander, which were specifically directed against the Stoics in a way that Plato's, of course, could not be. And there is nothing in Alexander's criticisms of the Stoics on this issue about which Plotinus would have serious concerns.

8^3, 6 *comes into being because of external circumstances*: The Greek word for "circumstances" here is *suntukhiai*, which might suggest a random and unpredictable cause, since *tukhê* often represents the element of chance; but that would not fairly represent Stoic views on causation. For them all causes were material, and any set of given causal factors could produce only one outcome. So Plotinus is not exploring or exploiting any apparent difficulty here, but merely saying that for the Stoics the soul comes into being as the necessary outcome of the coincidence of a number of material factors. He is using the term *suntukhiai* in a more colloquial sense; cf. 8^4, 24.

Lines 6–25

Plotinus attacks the Stoic doctrine of the corporeal soul by showing the absurd implications of positing a single order of priority and posteriority based solely on materialist causation.

8³, 6 *So the result is*: The Stoic order of psychic generation is, as we have seen, a temporal one, so that what to a Platonist or Peripatetic is superior, i.e. intellect, is created later and thereby, in Stoic terms, inferior. The hierarchy that Plotinus attributes here to the Stoics is: at the lowest level (in Plotinus' estimation) there is "state" (*hexis*), "something still worse," in the middle is "something inferior," and last of all (in the Stoic temporal priority) intellect.

"State" (*hexis* can be rendered variously as "disposition," "tenor," "*habitus*," "condition") is the noun derived from the verb *ekhein* (= to have, to be in a certain state); Aristotle at *Metaphysics* 1022b4 offers one sense of *hexis* as "a disposition (*diathesis*) according to which the item disposed is either disposed well or badly *per se,* or else in relation to something else." It can be applied widely; for example Alexander uses it of a state of the intellect at *On the Soul* 81, 2ff. Here Plotinus is restricting its application to the Stoic hierarchy whereby *hexis* refers to the state of inanimate entities, as opposed to nature (*phusis*), which is the state of plants (*phuta*) and soul, which is the state of living creatures. Philo, the Stoicising Jewish Platonist philosopher of the 1st century CE, (SVF2 458 = LS 47P) gives at *Allegories of the Law* 2.22 an extended hierarchy in which the higher faculty depends cumulatively on what is below it: "State is common to lifeless things such as stones and timber (and our bones, which resemble stones, share in it); nature extends also to plants (and our nails and hair are like plants); nature is state already in motion; soul is nature which has the addition of mental impression (*phantasia*) and impulse (*hormê*); this is common to irrational creatures. Our intellect too has something that conforms to the soul of an irrational creature, but furthermore its discursive power is particular to intellect." Elsewhere we have a simpler version, for example at Plutarch *On Moral Virtue* 12 451b (SVF 2 460): "The Stoics say that some things are controlled by state, others by nature, others by the irrational soul and others by soul that has reason and discursive thought." (Cf. also Alexander *Supplement* 140, 27.) Plotinus has telescoped the items into three, so that "something inferior" seems to refer to nature plus irrational soul.

8³, 9 *Now if intellect is prior to all things*: Which it is in the Aristotelian scheme of things; in Platonic terms, as seen by Plotinus, Intellect is prior to all things with the exception of the One—which, in that it is beyond and transcending all things, is not one of those things. The Stoic hierarchy is the consequence of wrong-headed materialist thinking. Had they seen the truth (as Plato and Aristotle did) they would have reversed the order.

8[3], 11 *So if god as the equivalent of intellect*: Diogenes Laertius *Lives of the Philosophers* 7 135–136 (= SVF 1 102) says that according to Zeno: "God, Intellect, Fate and Zeus are one—and are given many other names too."

8[3], 12 *posterior, created and having intellection added to it*: According to Diogenes Laertius *Lives of the Philosophers* 7 136 Zeno said that God is the seminal reason (*logos*) of the cosmos and (as the cosmos) is indestructible and ungenerated. So Plotinus is saying here, ironically, that the Stoics, in employing their inverted scale of priority, do away with the very creative principle of the cosmos and so contradict their founder. The existence and pre-eminence of God in the Stoic system is well attested. For a full discussion see Algra in Inwood (ed., 2003, chapter 6).

8[3], 15 *For what will there be*: Plotinus' position is firmly grounded in Aristotle's doctrine of the unmoved mover, expounded in *Physics* 8 and *Metaphysics* 12, of which the points relevant to Plotinus' argument here are: First, there must be a primary principle of motion which is itself unmoved; second, since movement and change imply potentiality, the prime mover, being unmoved, must exist in actuality, since what exists in potentiality does not need to actualize that potentiality; third, the prime mover acts as final cause to whatever it moves as the object of its desire and intellection; what is moved is moved by looking at something else which will exist in actuality; fourth, the actual is prior to the potential, and the prime mover is pure actuality.

8³, 18 *Yet if what is in potentiality*: This is an impossible condition, but Plotinus adds it to show that *any* change from potential to actual is better than nothing. Bréhier excludes *Yet if what . . . bring about an actuality* as a gloss.

8³, 20 *So the superior is prior*: The superior is the prime mover, which Aristotle equates to god in a purple passage at *Metaphysics* 1072b26: "Life belongs [to God]; for the actuality of intellect is life, and he is that actuality. And his essential actuality is the best life, and is eternal. We say that God is the best living creature, so that life and continuous and everlasting eternity belong to God; for God is just that."

8³, 22 *prior to nature*: I.e. *nature* in the Stoic sense as outlined above, note on line 6. In the line above he has used the word in a more general sense.

8³, 22 *Other arguments:* Especially those of Alexander.

Chapter 8[4]

Plotinus now turns his attention away from the materialists such as the Stoics and Epicureans, who claimed tout court *that the soul is a corporeal entity, and examines, albeit briefly, the doctrines of those who make soul to be something supervening on body, not an independently existing substance. In Chapter 8[4] his focus is on those Pythagoreans who said that soul is an attunement (*harmonia*) supervening on the compound body. The corpus of Pythagorean writings was certainly available to Plotinus. They are now generally agreed to be largely a spurious compilation of the 3rd to 1st centuries BCE (see H. Thesleff, 1965), but Plotinus almost certainly accepted them as genuinely pre-Platonic. However, his treatment of the topic in this treatise is brief and consists of a number of arguments against the thesis, all (bar one) of which can be found in either Plato* Phaedo *or Aristotle* On the Soul*; two arguments are attributed to the lost work of Aristotle,* Eudemus, *by Philoponus, who says that Aristotle offered more in that dialogue. This is supported by other post-Plotinian Neoplatonic commentators such as Simplicius, Themistius, and Olympiodorus, whose testimonies are collected under fragment 45 (Rose). Alexander has a short passage in* On the Soul *24, 18–26, 30 in which he follows and expounds Aristotle's remarks* *in his* On the Soul, *but Plotinus does not make use of this passage. This would suggest that Plotinus is consulting either a limited range or a compendium of works from the 4th century BCE, so that we should not expect any elements of later Pythagoreanism to appear, which would be in keeping with his general veneration of "the ancients." See note on line 17 for a further possibility.*

I have indicated the sequence of arguments by adding in the translation First, secondly, *etc.; these words do not appear in the original text.*

8[4], 2 *something other than body but something to do with body*: The Greek phrase I have translated as "*but something to do with body*" is *sômatos de ti*, suggesting that in some people's view soul is not itself body, but still not independent of body.

8[4], 2 *like an attunement*: The Greek word is *harmonia*, which together with its cognate verb *harmozein* denotes the balanced relation between two or more parts in a compound, for example at *Republic* 430e and 431e Plato talks of *harmonia* as the balance between different elements in the soul, and by analogy between the different elements in society. It is a term widely used in music (see LSJ *s.v.* IV), especially to refer to the attunement of the strings of the lyre (although presumably a single string can be attuned by producing a balance between the different forces at play in the instrument—as in "the attunement turning back on itself, like that of the lyre" in Heraclitus fr. DK51, and the tension (*tonos*) of the Stoics discussed in Chapter 8[3]). Here we are dealing with the balance between different strings and between the different parts of the lyre.

8[4], 3 *For although the Pythagoreans*: The Greek phrase for "the Pythagoreans" is *hoi amphi Puthagoran*, which literally means "those around Pythagoras"; but it could be a periphrasis (as commonly, e.g. in Plutarch) for "Pythagoras." But in view of the subsequent argument it seems more likely that Plotinus is singling out a group of Pythagoreans who have departed from Pythagorean orthodoxy and are using "attunement" in a different sense. The orthodox sense is exemplified by a fragment of the 5th century BCE Pythagorean Philolaus, quoted by Stobaeus *Anthology* 1 21d7 (and KRS 429) which talks of cosmic harmony which holds together in balance "all things that are unlike, not akin and of a different order from each other." The unorthodox sense is the one used in *Phaedo* in which the soul was thought to be something like the attunement of lyre strings and taken up here by Plotinus. We are not told of whom this group consisted, but it seems to be the Pythagoreans specified in *Phaedo*; at 61a the two interlocutors who later propound the theory, Cebes and Simmias, are said to have spent time with Philolaus in Thebes, and the narrator of the dialogue, the Pythagorean Echecrates, says at 88d that he had heard and been attracted by the theory. Diogenes Laertius *Lives of the Philosophers* 8 46 says that Echecrates of Phlius was a pupil of Philolaus. So although there is no direct link made by Plato in *Phaedo* (or by anyone else) between Philolaus and the *harmonia* theory of the soul, it is tempting to include him among "those who thought . . . " Whatever the case there is a discrepancy between this doctrine and what we can be certain *is* an original Pythagorean doctrine, that the soul exists both before, during, and after its association with the body. How can that discrepancy have come about? Another feature of Pythagoreanism we can be certain about is the importance of number, especially the so-called *tetraktys*, the numbers 1, 2, 3, and 4. Not only do these numbers add up to 10, an all-important number for the Pythagoreans, but they also represent the three basic musical intervals—1:2 the octave, 3:2 the fifth, and 4:3 the fourth. See Sextus Empiricus *Against the Professors* 7 54, (= KRS 277) and C. Huffman in Long (ed., 1999, 74). It may have been that some over-enthusiastic Pythagoreans, perhaps Philolaus himself, extended this numerical scheme to the description of the soul, failing to see its implications *vis-à-vis* the immortality of the soul. Cicero at *Tusculan Disputations* 1 41 suggests that Aristoxenus was so fond of music that he even tried to transfer its notions to the field of psychology. Certainly in *Phaedo* both Simmias and Cebes accept the Recollection argument (that souls know the Forms before birth, forget them at birth and recollect them during life) as proving the soul's pre-natal existence. For an extended discussion of these points see H. B. Gottschalk in *Phronesis* 16 (1971). Gottschalk gives references for another group of Pythagoreans headed by Dicaearchus and Aristoxenus, both mentioned by Cicero in *Tusculan Disputations* 1 21, and summarizes: "Instead of an immanent relationship between the elementary bodily constituents, the soul was for Aristoxenus the end-product of the activity of living creatures." Gottschalk suggests that this group may be Aristotle's source of information about the attunement theory. Simplicius at *On Aristotle on the Soul* 53, 23 denies that the Pythagoreans made attunement a substance. See also Bostock (1986, 11–12).

8⁴, 5 *For just as in that case*: The details of the analogy come from *Phaedo* 85e–86d, where Simmias suggests that just as the attunement of the lyre, which is incorporeal, comes into being when the parts of the lyre are in proper balance, and is destroyed when the lyre is broken or its strings cut, so the soul comes into being when the mixture of dissimilar elements—hot, cold, wet, dry, etc.—is in proper proportion, and is destroyed when that proportion is destroyed.

8⁴, 6 *some sort of affection supervenes*: The attunement is merely a property which depends entirely on the condition of the composite body of which it is a property. It does not, as we shall soon be told, have an independent existence of its own.

Lines 9–23

Six arguments are put forward, drawn from Plato *Phaedo*, Aristotle *On the Soul*, and possibly from Aristotle *Eudemus* to show the weakness of the attunement doctrine.

8[4], 11 *First*: The terms prior and posterior can be used either in the Aristotelian sense as in Chapter 8[3], that the soul is ontologically prior to body and to any of its properties; or else Plato is looking to *Phaedo* 86eff., where it is agreed by all the interlocutors that soul does exist before birth (cf. *Laws* 896c: "So in saying that soul has come into being before body, and that body has come into being second and later, we would have spoken correctly, authoritatively, most truthfully and perfectly"). Perhaps closer to the Aristotelian sense is *Phaedo* 92aff., where the argument is that an attunement, being composite (*sunthetos*) cannot exist before/be prior to the elements of which it is a compound. Socrates says: "Do you not realize that you are in fact admitting this [that the composite attunement exists before its components] when you say that the soul exists before entering the form and body of a man and that it is a compound of things not yet in existence? No, attunement is not what you liken it to; the lyre, the strings and the notes exist before they are brought into attunement, while the attunement is the last thing to come into being and the first to perish." Then Socrates asks Simmias to choose between saying that knowledge is recollection and saying that the soul is an attunement. Cf. Themistius (Rose fr. 45): "In the body there is the primary element, viz. the soul, and attunement comes later."

8^{4}, 12 *Secondly*: That the soul rules the body and on occasions conflicts with it is a theme to be found in more than one of Plato's dialogues, for example *Phaedrus* where the conflict is rather portrayed as one between reason and passion within the soul—the passions being ascribed to bodily desires. More immediately we should look at *Phaedo* 80a: "Consider it in this way, that when soul and body are together in the same place, nature ordains that the one should serve and be ruled, and that the other should rule and have mastery," and 94b: "When heat and thirst are present, the soul pulls the body in the opposite direction . . . and we see the soul conflicting with the body in many other ways." Plato's argument is that an attunement can perform neither of these roles but can "only follow and never lead" (94c), and: "It is not possible for an attunement to lead the elements of which it is composed, but only to follow." Cf. *Laws* 896c: "It is natural that the soul should rule and body be ruled."

8^{4}, 14 *Thirdly . . . the soul is a substance*: Plotinus is either relying on the distinction made by Aristotle in *Categories* between a substance (*ousia*) and its properties (*pathêmata*) such as quality and quantity, with an eye to *On the Soul* 412a20: "So soul must be substance as the form of a natural body having life potentially." Cf. also *On the Soul* 408b18: "Intellect (*nous*) seems to be engendered as a substance and is not destroyed." Hicks (1907, *ad loc.*) says: "The exact relation of the thinking part of the soul to the rest of the soul is nowhere made perfectly clear," but Simplicius *On Aristotle On the Soul* dismisses the problem, saying: "The human soul, which he [Aristotle] calls Intellect . . . in fact other souls are substances, for all life is substance" (this is supported by Themistius and Philoponus). Or else Plotinus is claiming, as a Platonist, that the soul belongs to the realm of true being, the intelligible world. Throughout the treatise there is an ambiguity in the use of the Greek word *ousia,* which is a noun cognate with the verb "to be," and is used sometimes in a more technical Aristotelian sense of "substance" as in *Categories,* sometimes in a quasi-technical Platonic sense of "real being" as opposed to "[transitory] becoming," sometimes in a more neutral sense as "existence"; it is not always easy to see which sense is being used in any particular context, as here; Fotinis (1979, 175) marks the distinction well, saying: "Plotinus holds that the soul possesses being because it is an absolute reality rather than a form of something, since it pre-exists its body. The soul has existence of itself before it ever belongs to a body and not from the fact that it is in a body . . . Alexander as an Aristotelian views the soul as a form, as an actuality; being therefore a substance in the sense of form the soul pre-supposes actuality." Further, one of the arguments attributed to Aristotle in *Eudemus* by Philoponus is: Harmony has an opposite, but soul has no opposite (substances do not have opposites, as Aristotle tells us in *Categories* 3b25); therefore the soul is not a harmony. Simplicius (Rose fr. 45) raises an objection to this, saying that the opposite of soul is "negation (*sterêsis*) of soul." See further Blumenthal (1971, nn9 and 10) and on *nous* see Gottschalk (1971, 189).

8⁴, 14 *Fourthly . . . this would rather constitute health*: The point is made by Aristotle at *On the Soul* 408a2: "It is more harmonious to denote attunement as health, and generally as bodily excellence, rather than as soul." This is expanded by Alexander at *On the Soul* 25, 5, and in *Eudemus* (Rose fr. 45) where disharmony in the body is said to be disease, weakness and ugliness, and harmony to be *health*, strength, and beauty. We could also add that health, unlike soul (*pace* Simplicius) has an opposite.

8⁴, 14 *Fifthly, there would be a different soul*: The argument is drawn from Aristotle *On the Soul* 408a10ff., where Aristotle has established that one sense of attunement is the due proportion of the elements in a compound mixture—and there are many such compounds in the body; he goes on to say: "It will follow that there will be many souls throughout the body." Philoponus (Rose fr. 45) says: "They thought that the soul was an attunement of the body and that the different aspects (*eidê*) of the soul corresponded to the different attunements in the body." Bréhier omits Plotinus' argument here from his translation, but not from his text.

8⁴, 17 *Sixthly, and most importantly*: It does not seem possible to identify this argument in any of the sources mentioned above. Either, then, Plotinus is adding an argument of his own, which is out of keeping with the rest of the chapter, or else he is looking to some other source not available to us, perhaps *Eudemus*. Alexander offers a similar argument at *Supplement* 114, 24–35, which is directed at the Stoics: "Moreover, if the soul is a body, it is held together either by something [else] or by itself. But it is not possible [for it to be held together] by itself because it is single and similar throughout. For it is impossible for the same thing in the same respect both to hold together and to be held together. So it remains for part of it to hold together, and part to be held together. But if so, the part that holds together, and not that which is held together, would be the soul, and this [the soul], if it is also itself a body will either be held together by [something] else, or by itself, and so ad infinitum. . . . And in general none of the things that [other] things possess also itself possesses [itself]: not heat or sweetness or shape or color or health or attunement, and not virtue or knowledge either. But the soul is a thing of this sort" (tr. Sharples).

The argument is: In the case of an instrument the attunement is produced by a musician who has internalized/knows (from Recollection) the correct proportions; but in the case of the soul what is it that produces the soul *qua* attunement? What plays the part of the knowledge and the musician together? Answer: the soul, which *is*, not *has*, the proportion; cf. Aristotle *Politics* 1340b19: "Some philosophers maintain that the soul *is* an attunement, others that it *possesses* it."

Lines 23–28

Plotinus summarizes his objections against "these people too," these Pythagoreans. The inclusion of "too" broadens the criticism to the materialists in general who have been under discussion since the start of the treatise, although the last sentence returns the focus to these Pythagoreans. Twice in these lines he uses his favorite paradox "ensouled . . . lacking in soul" and "organization . . . disorganized."

8⁴, 24 *what is ensouled*: Bréhier translates *ta empsukha* simply as "soul." But Plotinus' point is slightly different: Just as the musician, starting from the materials, produces a well-tuned lyre, not just an attunement, so the Pythagoreans try to produce from the bodily ingredients not just a soul, but an ensouled being.

8[4], 24 *haphazard*: The Greek phrase is *kata suntukhian*, a term used at 8[3], 26 ("because of external accidents"). Plotinus is accusing his opponents of a non-teleological attitude, which can be applied at either cosmic or individual level. See Sedley (2004) for a full account of this issue. Plotinus' words here echo Aristotle *On the Heavens* 280a8: "[Those that say the world is indestructible but generated] say that order arose from disorder; but a thing cannot be at the same time in order and disorder. The two must be separated by a process involving time" (tr. W. K. C. Guthrie).

8[4], 26 *its being*: Plotinus uses the Greek word *hupostasis*, which later became an important term for his Neoplatonic successors, denoting any of the three levels of true being, the "Hypostases": the One, Intellect and Soul, of which Plotinus gives his fullest treatment in V.1 *On the Three Principal Hypostases*; see Atkinson (2004) for a translation and commentary. Here, assuming that at this relatively early stage Plotinus has not yet formalized his metaphysical terminology, he may be using it in its broader sense as a synonym for *ousia* = "being," to distinguish it from his use of *ousia* in line 14 as "substance." Otherwise (as BP) Plotinus is using it here in its more technical sense, and his point is that soul *has* real being.

8[4], 26 *spontaneous*: The Greek word is *automatou*, discussed at length by Aristotle in *Physics* 2.4–6, a concept that both Plato and Aristotle, firm in their teleological attitude, oppose.

8[4], 27 *in parts or in wholes*: As Armstrong, “in parts of bodies or whole bodies”; Bréhier renders “in particulars or universals,” and MacKenna “the sphere of the partial . . . that of wholes,” and BP “in particular beings or in others.”

Afterthoughts

It may seem strange that Plotinus does not in this chapter invoke Plato *Timaeus*, which was an important text for him and one that he frequently alludes to, containing much on the creation and composition of the soul, both cosmic and individual. Why that is the case is not immediately obvious. From the extremely complex description of the creation of the cosmic and individual souls at 34aff. and 41dff. respectively three points germane to this treatise emerge.

First, soul, at both levels, is prior to body. In the terms of the *Timaeus* myth this is initially a temporal priority; if we demythologize the priority is ontological, as at 34c: “The god made soul prior to body, and more venerable in birth and excellence, to be the body’s mistress and governor.”

Secondly, the cosmos revealed in *Timaeus* is teleologically designed by the divine craftsman (demiurge) after the divine model; although some scope is given in the account for the random “works of necessity,” the order imposed on the whole by the divine craftsman is rational, in conformity with *logos*.

Thirdly, the parts of the soul are mixed together in due proportion (*logos*) from the Same, the Different, and Being, and an increasingly complex structure of psychic movements in the heavens is built up from different musical intervals arranged in harmonious proportion. But this harmony is within the soul, not the body, and there are no grounds for suggesting that the soul itself is the attunement of the parts of the body. Cornford (1937, 72) says: "But in the *Timaeus* the harmony resides in the structure of the soul." So we can be as scrupulous as Plotinus in observing the distinction between the attunement within the soul itself, which it *has* but not *is*, and the attunement of the bodily parts which the soul engenders as something other than itself.

Chapter 8[5]

In the preceding chapters Plotinus has employed mainly Peripatetic doctrines to criticize what he sees as the out-and-out materialism of the Stoics and the attunement theory of some Pythagoreans, whereby the soul is posterior to and dependent on the body. He now turns in a near volte face *to attack the very core of Peripatetic doctrines on the nature of the soul, which portray the soul as supervening on the body in the way that form supervenes on matter. Unable now to employ those doctrines in order to attack them, he has recourse to his own Platonic views.*

That is not to deny that that Plotinus owes much to Aristotle in his attempts to grapple with the many problems bequeathed to him by Plato, and it would be impossible for him to ignore or challenge much of the groundwork done by Aristotle in various areas of psychology. One notable feature common to both philosophers and to the fore in this chapter is the division of the soul into "parts" or "faculties." Neither philosopher is concerned to give a dogmatic schema of the different faculties, but both accept a broad division into three—the rational, the sensitive, and the vegetative,[31] within which there are variable sub-divisions.

31 Plato's division is into rational (*logistikon*), spirited (*thumoeides*), and appetitive (*epithumêtikon*), or sometimes into two, rational and irrational.

Aristotle mentions five faculties at On the Soul *414a31: nutritive (*threptikon*), appetitive (*orektikon *corresponding to Plato's* epithumêtikon*), sensitive (*aisthêtikon*), locomotive (*kinêtikon*), and intellective (*dianoêtikon *corresponding to Plato's* logistikon*); he adds two further faculties, the reproductive (*gennêtikon*) at 416a19, and the imaginative (*phantastikon*) at 432b1; and at* Nicomachean Ethics *1102b28 he mentions a further one, the vegetative (*phutikon*). Of these Plotinus singles out in this chapter the sensitive, the appetitive, and the intellective. Blumenthal (1971, 44) gives a table showing these broad and subsidiary divisions applicable to both Aristotle and Plotinus.*

I have indicated the sequence of arguments by adding in the translation First, secondly, *etc.; these words do not appear in the original text.*

Lines 1–5

Plotinus summarizes the Peripatetic view of the soul as the actualization of the body of a living creature, drawing on Aristotle's designation at *On the Soul* 412aff.

8^5, 1 *the soul is an actualization*: The Greek word is *entelekheia*, sometimes rendered in English as "entelechy," which Plotinus uses ten times in this chapter. The term is rooted in the word *telos* ("end," "goal") and implies completion. On occasions it is used by Aristotle in contrast to *energeia* ("activity"). Ross (1924) on *Metaphysics*

1046b30 says: "Strictly speaking *energeia* means activity or actualization, while *entelekheia* means the resulting activity or perfection. Yet *energeia* is not a movement towards something other than itself; this is the difference between it and *kinêsis*. For the most part Aristotle uses the words as exact synonyms." Waterlow (1982, 186) says: "Aristotle's *energeiai* are *teleiai* ('complete,' 'perfected') in the sense of being ends in themselves, so that even as they continue, the ends (i.e., themselves) for the sake of which they are engaged in have already been realized for some length of time." But Aristotle does, in *On the Soul*, make a distinction not between the two different terms but between two senses of *entelekheia*, designating them as first and second actualizations, and it is to Plotinus' detriment that he apparently in this chapter fails to note the distinction, although he has observed it at 8[3], 14: "If the potential were to come into being without the prior existence of what is in activity (*energeia*), then it could not come into actualization (*entelekheia*)." At the start of *On the Soul* 2, where he is outlining his own view of the soul (after having reviewed previous doctrines in book 1), Aristotle begins by naming three senses of the term "substance" (*ousia*), as matter (which he equates to potentiality), as form (which he equates to actualization) and as the compound (*sunthetos*) of these two. Within the context of *On the Soul* the matter of the individual creature is body *qua* body, the form is the soul and the compound is the individual creature. This reflects Aristotle's general account of form, matter and the compound in *Metaphysics* 7, 8, and 12. It is on the second of these, soul as form, that Aristotle focuses his attention. But before attempting his account (*logos*) he makes a further distinction within soul as form; his words at 412a10 are: "Matter is potentiality, and form is actualization, and that term has two senses, one being, for example, knowledge (*epistêmê)* and the other contemplation (*to theôrein*)," i.e., the possession of knowledge as opposed to the exercise of it. Aristotle's language can be a little confusing. For example this first actualization (knowledge) is in one sense also a potentiality too; it is in itself an actualization, but it is at the same time the potentiality for the exercise of knowledge as contemplation. So on occasions this first actualization is referred to as a second potentiality (the first being the living child before it has developed into a rational adult). This duality of psychic function is further illustrated at being asleep and being awake, a point that Plotinus takes up in line 9. See further Waterlow (1982, 183f.).

A further point that Aristotle makes, at 413a3ff., is that at least in some cases soul and body cannot be separated—although he suggests that where a part of the soul is not an actualization of any part of the body then it might be separable, a point that he takes up at 413bff. (see further Barnes in Barnes, Schofield, and Sorabji (eds., 1979, vol. 4 34–36). Again this separation has two senses—either the separation of soul from body, and the separation of different parts of the soul from each other, more properly termed "division."

8^{5}, 2 *They claim*: I.e. the Peripatetics.

8^{5}, 3 *viz. the body which it ensouls*: This phrase, *to sôma empsukhon* (lit. "the body ensouled") has caused commentators some difficulty. Some render as "holds the rank of form in relation to the ensouled body" (Armstrong), "holds the rank of form to the matter, which here is the ensouled body" (MacKenna). But this is to ignore (a) the fact that in Greek the adjective is regularly placed between article (*to*) and noun (*sôma*) unless it has some special force (e.g., in English the difference between "I painted the red house" and "I painted the house red"), and (b) that the matter is not the ensouled body, but the body *qua* body, which only becomes ensouled by the presence of the form. BP translate "holds the rank of form in relation to matter when the body is ensouled, following Dodds and Blumenthal, who add a participle *on* ("being") after the adjective." (Armstrong accepts this emendation, but does not use it to good effect in his translation.) Bréhier adds a second definite article before the adjective and renders "holds the rank of form in relation to the matter, which is the ensouled body." See Blumenthal (1971, 58–62) for a different explanation: "The body to which soul and nature are attached is not itself devoid of soul, but has a trace of it."

8^5, 4 *of a natural body with organs having life potentially*: Aristotle gives three slightly different descriptions of soul: (a) 412a20 "Soul must be substance as the form of a natural body which has life in potentiality," (b) 412a27 "the soul is the first actualization of a natural body which has life in potentiality, viz. any body which has organs, and (c) 412b5 "[soul] would be the first actualization of a natural body possessing organs." In (b) "first actualization" has explained "in potentiality," and in (c) has replaced it. Otherwise the three descriptions are equivalent. But it is important to note that Plotinus does not employ the term "first."

8^5, 5 *If it has been assimilated*: One of Aristotle's favorite examples of the form-matter compound is the bronze statue, where the form is the shape and the matter is the bronze. In what sense is it possible to say that the form has been "assimilated" to the bronze? Aristotle uses the term at *On Coming-to-be and Passing-away* 324a10 in a discussion of agent and patient, and says that in a change to an opposite state the agent assimilates the patient to itself, for example in the process of heating the hot "will assimilate to itself" what is cold. But form and matter are not opposites, so the analysis does not apply in the strict sense; the bronze is no less bronze when it is an unshaped mass than when it has been shaped, and it has some shape before the sculptor gets to work on it. Plotinus uses the verb and its cognates generally, but not exclusively, of an inferior being made like its superior, notably the assimilation of the soul to the divine (see Fleet 2012, 38ff.), where the one party is made like the other in quality. Certainly Plotinus would deny that the soul could become assimilated to anything corporeal—that would entail an affection of the soul, a possibility denied throughout the early part of III.6 (as indeed it is of matter in the latter part). So perhaps "assimilated" is being used here in the loose sense, "matched up."

A further possibility is that the assimilation takes place in the sense organ, as Aristotle suggests at *On the Soul* 2.7 (see Fleet 1995, 260–261; Emilsson 1988, chapters 3 and 4; and Burnyeat in *Phronesis* 47.1 (2002) 28–90). But the nature of sense-perception is not the issue here, and it does not seem likely that Plotinus is introducing any point about assimilation in the strict sense.

8[5], 7 *then first, when the body . . .* : Plotinus applies a blunt and somewhat materialistic argument: according to Aristotle the soul is located in the whole body, so that any division in the body necessarily involves a material division and separation within the soul—anathema to a Platonist, and somewhat unfair to Aristotle. Blumenthal (1971, 12) comments: "His discussion is to a large extent based on the Platonic view of the soul as a separate entity, and he does not seem to make a serious attempt to see how far Aristotle's view of the soul as the principle of life is valid," and p. 13: "His criticism that if a part of the body is cut off a part of the soul too would be cut off seems to miss the point: one could answer that this was true in so far as the soul would be incapable of performing certain functions that depend on the part missing. So the entelechy of a man who had lost his legs in an accident would be different from that of a normal man." Aristotle broaches the subject at *On the Soul* 413b14ff. Plotinus offers no amplification of his statement, or reasons for it, and he does appear to confuse the material parts of the body with the immaterial "parts" of the soul. The soul is the operative principle of, say, the appendix; but an appendectomy in no way diminishes the soul as an operative principle.

8⁵, 9 *Secondly, the withdrawal of the soul in sleep*: Plotinus again appears to be giving Aristotle little credit, suggesting that, *per absurdum*, there cannot be such a thing as sleep, since sleep involves a cessation of consciousness—but our active intellect never ceases thinking (*On the Soul* 430a22). Plotinus ignores the point that sleep is the first actualization in relation to the waking state, the second actualization—a distinction which Plotinus himself employs when talking of the undescended soul, for example in IV.8.8: "there is always some part of the soul in the intelligible world." Blumenthal (1971, 13) comments: "To make it a reproach that the withdrawal of the soul in sleep cannot happen since an entelechy must be attached to that of which it is the entelechy assumes the truth of a Platonic view, while to amend this objection to the statement that there can be no such thing as sleep at all ignores the word "first" (which Plotinus does not mention) in Aristotle's definition of the soul."

8⁵, 10 *part and parcel*: In Aristotelian terms form and matter are separable only in concept. But again Plotinus ignores the possibility raised by Aristotle at *On the Soul* 3.5 430a22 that intellect may be separable: "when it is separated it is purely and simply what it is—this alone is immortal and everlasting."

8⁵, 11 *Thirdly, moreover*: Plotinus' point is that an actualization does not admit of degrees—as at *Categories* 3b33ff. The Platonic soul, with its tripartite structure, does allow conflict between its parts, especially between the rational and the irrational, whether that is seen as a single part or divided into the spirited and appetitive, as is seen in the struggle between the charioteer and his two horses (standing for the rational, spirited, and appetitive). When these are brought into line under the control of reason, then the soul is said to be virtuous (cf. III.6.2, 5–18). For Aristotle too the human condition involved a conflict between reason and appetite. To resolve that conflict so as to achieve the greatest good was "up to us" (*eph'hêmin*). This is the basis of his major ethical work, *Nicomachean Ethics,* and in *On the Soul* too he marks the distinction between reason and appetite (his Greek terms are *nous* and *orexis*) which are inseparable elements in our personalities. At *On the Soul* 433a21 he suggests that both appetite and reason are subsumed under the single faculty of appetition: "intellect does not prompt us to action, since will is an appetite, and when actions are done in accord with calculation it accords with will, but appetite produces action contrary to calculation. For desire is a kind of appetite. Intellect is always right, but appetite and imagination can be right or wrong." So although they may comprise a single faculty, there is still internal conflict being waged. So Plotinus' question is: How can that process of conflict be consistent with actualization, which is a perfected state. Again he seems to ignore the distinction between first and second actualization, the progression from the incomplete to the complete actualization, where desire and reason are one and the same.

8⁵, 14 *Fourthly, perhaps perception can occur*: Plotinus is adopting the Platonic position in these lines (14–25), which is based on the distinction between the sensible (*aisthêton*) and the intelligible (*noêton*) worlds and the corresponding distinction between the soul's apprehension of them, perception (*aisthêsis*), and intellection (*noêsis*) respectively. The soul can only move from perception of the sensible world to knowledge of the intelligible by withdrawal from the former to the latter (see Fleet 2012, *Introduction* for a discussion of this "ascent"). Plotinus' point is that an Aristotelian embodied (unascended) soul can have only perception. Aristotle's position is that the embodied soul can have both perception of enmattered forms (as described at *On the Soul* 2.12 424a17ff.) and can have intellection of those forms; perception stands to intellection as knowledge to the exercise of it, i.e., as first to second actualization—not the privileged Platonic intellection. Aristotle's doctrine allows for a seamless intellective process entirely within the parameters of the embodied soul. But see next note.

8[5], 15 *That is why*: Plotinus is alluding to *On the Soul* 3.2 430a22–25, a passage which has caused much debate, to the extent that some have suggested that this chapter is a late interpolation designed to bring *On the Soul* into line with Aristotle's discussion of divine intellect in *Metaphysics*12; see Ross (1961, 41–48) and Hicks (1907, 488–510); both refer to the ongoing debate among Peripatetics and non-Peripatetics. But in *On the Soul* Aristotle is talking about human intellect as distinct from the divine intellect of *Metaphysics* 12, and is certainly suggesting that human intellect may be separable and immortal. At 408b19 he says, tentatively, that "intellect seems to be a substance engendered in us and to be imperishable," and at 408b29 "perhaps intellect is something more divine and imperishable"; further at *Generation of Animals* 736b27 he says: "so it remains that intellect alone enters [the soul] from outside, and that it alone is divine, since bodily activity (*energeia*) has nothing to do with its activity." So Plotinus grudgingly allows Aristotle something approaching the noetic activity of the Platonic soul—which he is reluctant to call an actualization.

The Theologia attributes this argument to "the materialists," but this seems unlikely in a chapter whose linking theme is Aristotelian actualization.

8⁵, 19 *Fifthly, in fact*: Here Plotinus turns from his discussion of the rational faculty to the activity of the sensitive faculty taking in and retaining impressions. He suggests that according to Aristotle's account of such a process it is not possible for the sensitive faculty to be an actualization. He seems to be relying for his account on *On Memory* 450a22ff., where Aristotle uses the imagery picked up here by Plotinus of "impressions" (*tupoi*); The word *tupos* and its cognates were common currency among philosophers in a figurative sense, with a wide range of connotations from "shape," "form" to "impression." Plato uses *tupos* of "general character" on several occasions, although he does not use it anywhere as a metaphor for perception. But he uses the imagery of the wax tablet (in which the impression is made) three times in *Theaetetus* in the context of memory. Similarly Plotinus uses similar vocabulary, for example at III.6.1, 8, where he says: “one could say of the so-called impressions (*tupôseis*) that they are made in a way quite different from what has been supposed.” This would be in keeping with what Aristotle says about the reception of forms without matter in *On the Soul* 2.5, and he is not imputing to Aristotle a materialist account of memory, as is implied by the words “the impressions of sensible objects when they are not present.” But, Plotinus objects, if the sensitive soul is the actualization of an ensouled body, it must have something of the body about it, and as such cannot accept what is purely immaterial, which it could do if it were separable from the body. Therefore it must be separable if it is to perceive what is separable—like perceives like. See further Sorabji in Barnes, Schofield, and Sorabji (eds., 1979, 53–56).

8^{5}, 21 *as shapes and images*: As impressions are in such materialist accounts, such as the Stoic and Epicurean.

8^{5}, 23 *Sixthly, furthermore*: The argument concerning the appetitive faculty—part of the sensitive faculty—is the same *mutatis mutandis*.

8^{5}, 23 *Seventhly, there remains the vegetative element*: The lowest faculty of the soul, common to all living creatures, includes the faculties of nutrition, growth, and reproduction; in the psychic hierarchy each higher faculty depends on the one below it (*On the Soul* 415a14ff.).

8^{5}, 26 *it might seem possible*: The two key phrases in this part of the argument are *in this sense* and *in the whole.* The Greek of the first sentence is ambiguous, since the phrase "to dispute the claim" (*amphisbêtêsin . . . ekhein*) is followed by a negative (*mê*), and could mean "dispute the claim that this is *not* an inseparable entity"; but such verbs and verbal phrases are often followed by what is called "the redundant negative," in which case the meaning would be "dispute the claim that it is an inseparable entity." The conclusion of the argument in lines 31–32 states that the soul is not present *in the whole,* i.e., it is present in the surviving part of the plant, the root, and so it is separable in that way, in contrast to the way that the desiring element is present—this seems to be the meaning of *in this sense* in line 26. A further ambiguity lies in the second sentence *But clearly not even this is possible.* What is not possible? The claim, or the denial of it? The various translations replicate the ambiguity: "There might seem to be some possibility of questioning whether this might not be an inseparable entelechy in this sense" (Armstrong); "which might seem to suggest the possibility that, in this phase, the Soul may be the inseparable Entelechy of the doctrine" (MacKenna); "one could doubt whether it is in this sense an inseparable entelechy" (Bréhier); "it seems that a disagreement could occur: might it not be an inseparable entelechy in this sense?" (BP). Blumenthal says (1971, 13): "Such an answer [that the entelechy of a man who has lost his legs in an accident would be different from that of a normal man] could also be made to Plotinus' contention that the withdrawal of soul into the root of the plant that has withered shows that it is not in the whole as an inseparable entelechy, and that therefore the definition is not even applicable to the vegetative soul."

8^5, 32 *Again*: Plotinus takes the argument one stage further, and suggests that the vegetative soul might be *completely* separable, on the rather dubious grounds that if it is partly separable, as seems to be the case both when a plant withers and when it grows, it might be *completely* separable.

So Plotinus' point in lines 26–35 is that if the vegetative soul can be seen as something separable, Aristotle's whole contention that the soul is the [inseparable] actualization "of a natural body with organs having life potentially" is undermined.

8^5, 35 *Eighthly, how could it be*: We should distinguish between "separable" (*khôristos*)—this has been the topic of a previous part of the chapter—and "divisible" (*meristos*), which can have either a material sense, "divisible into corporeal parts"(*merê*) or a non-material sense as is the case with the division between the non-material faculties of the soul (*moria*). Plotinus' point is again somewhat crudely materialist, and picks up, without amplification, his words at lines 7–9.

8^5, 36 *Ninthly*: The argument can be applied at two levels. Plotinus inherited from Plato, who in turn probably inherited it from the Pythagoreans, a belief in re-incarnation (see Fleet 2012, 18 for Platonic references), and so Plotinus could here be alluding to that belief. The individual soul retains its identity throughout successive rebirths, and the words *exists before it becomes the soul of any particular body* would suit this interpretation. But Aristotle did not share these views, and so it is more likely that Plotinus' argument is based on the biological fact, one that Aristotle would have accepted, of the metamorphosis of the insect from egg, through larva and pupa, to full-grown adult (*Generation of Animals* 3.9 gives details of Aristotle's observations). The words *one living creature changes into another* suits this interpretation, and the words *before it becomes . . . any particular body* do not preclude it.

8^5, 40 *Therefore*: Plotinus' answer starts here, and the rest of the chapter outlines the broad distinction between the Aristotelian and the Platonic concept of soul.

8^5, 40 *the soul does not have its existence . . . it is a real being*: The soul belongs first and foremost to the intelligible world and is thereby prior to anything in the sensible world; it does not stand to body as form to matter in the Aristotelian sense, where the soul supervenes on the body and depends on it for its existence—or rather the relationship is one of mutual dependence. In Plotinus' Platonic view soul engenders the body.

8^5, 42 *before it becomes*: The Greek verb *ginesthai* is commonly used in contrast to the verb "to be" (*einai*, as used in line as 47–48; cognate parts of it are used sixteen times in lines 40–50, while parts of *ginesthai* appear four times) to refer to the sensible world of becoming as opposed to the intelligible world of real being. The soul, although seated in the intelligible world, does engage with the sensible world, so it can be said "to become the soul of a particular body."

8^5, 44 *it is neither body nor an affection of body*: Chapters $1–8^3$ have dealt with soul as body, and Chapters $8^{4–5}$ with it as an affection of body.

8^5, 44 *action and activity*: The distinction is broadly between affection (*pathos, pathêma*) and action, a distinction that we have seen employed by the Stoics to differentiate between the active and the passive cosmic principles; it is a distinction made by Aristotle in *Metaphysics* between the unmoved mover and what is moved. In this treatise Plotinus has dismissed the Stoic claims, and ignored

Aristotle's metaphysics, focusing on individual souls in the sublunary world. Similarly he seems to pay little attention to what Aristotle says in *On the Soul* 3.4–5. In Chapter 5 he divides intellect into active and passive intellect, and he characterizes the former as an intellect that makes all things, is separable, impassive, unmixed, is in activity by its essence, is immortal and eternal. Aristotle had himself questioned Plato's theories, especially those put forward in *Timaeus*, on the grounds that they did not satisfactorily explain how an immaterial entity could affect body, and this was a difficulty that Plotinus too was aware of; at IV.8.1, 23ff. he expresses his reservations, which are perhaps reflected here by the introductory *If.* Plotinus' answer to the question he poses takes up the remainder of the treatise. He has now nailed his colors to the mast. *Action and activity* denote the force of emanation, ultimately from the One, through Intellect and Soul to the natural cosmos.

Lines 46–50

Plotinus uses words from *Timaeus* 28a3–4 to draw the distinction that is fundamental to a Platonist's worldview. The *truly existent* is all the things that the transitory sensible world is not; the sensible world's only claim to any sort of being is through its *participation* (Plato's regular term for the relation of sensible particulars to eternal Forms) in the intelligible world. The relation is not reciprocal. The soul belongs to this intelligible world, from which it descends to the sensible world before re-ascending to its true home.

Chapter 9

At the end of the previous chapter Plotinus has turned our attention away from rival philosophical claimants for whom soul is either body or an affection of body, to the Platonic soul as incorporeal "true being." Chapter 9 prefaces the remainder of the treatise by offering an outline of Plato's teachings on the character of the intelligible world, drawing upon a number of seminal passages in the dialogues.

Alternatively, John Dillon suggests that Chapters 8^1*–*8^5 *may have been included in a later version of the treatise, written by Plotinus as part of a separate attack on materialist and supervenient theories of the soul, included in the version of Eustochius and taken up by Eusebius; this would mean that these five chapters had somehow eluded the attention of Porphyry. Certainly there does appear to be a smooth transition from the end of Chapter 8 (*For the entire nature of body does not endure, but is in flux*) to the start of Chapter 9 (*But the other nature which has its being from within itself is true being in its entirety, which neither comes to be nor passes away*).*

Plotinus is concerned to outline the place held by Soul in the intelligible world, and in this chapter he gives a broad picture of that world before turning more precisely to the soul in Chapter 10. Consequently there is very little mention of the One, the first Hypostasis, which is beyond being; it is the equivalent for Plotinus of Plato's Good, which is referred to at line 36 of Chapter 10. More at issue is a question that remained unresolved for Platonists both before and after Plato: the relationship between Intellect and Soul.

As early as Aristotle a distinction had been made between the prime mover as divine intellect and the individual soul. He describes the former at Metaphysics *1072b18ff., emphasizing two characteristics; its thought—"thinking in itself is concerned with that which is best in itself," and its life—"its life is like the best which we have for a short time . . . for the actuality of reason is life, and god is that actuality, and his essential activity is the best and eternal life. We hold then that god is a living being, eternal and most good, and so life and continuous and eternal duration belongs to god; for this* is *god" (tr. G. E. R. Lloyd). At 1074b15ff. he examines the nature of god's thinking. This is clearly the model, with some modification, for Plotinus' second Hypostasis, Intellect. See O'Meara (1993, 33–37) for a succinct history of the concept; O'Meara points out that there was a group of Middle Platonists who identified the demiurge of Plato's* Timaeus *with Aristotle's divine intellect. This is the goal of "assimilation to god" (*homoiôsis tôi theôi*) mentioned by Plato at* Theaetetus *176b, which became a mantra for subsequent Platonists. See Fleet (2012, 19, 34, 38ff., 70–71).*

*But Plato himself did not hypostasize intellect; for him intellection (*noêsis *rather than* nous*) was an activity of the human soul (as in* Republic*) and the soul of the cosmos (as in* Timaeus*). The consequence for Plotinus is that he has no obvious Platonic text on which to draw for his discussion of intellect. On the other hand he does have a wealth of Platonic material—albeit inconsistent, as Plotinus admits—on which to draw for his discussion of the soul.*

In this chapter, then, he does not differentiate between Intellect and Soul, but applies Plato's texts to the intelligible world as a whole. An easy (facile) solution to the question might be to suggest that in this early treatise Plotinus had not yet fully developed his doctrine of emanation, and that there is as yet no clearly formulated distinction between the hypostases. But this seems a solution ruled out by the apparent distinction made in Chapter 13. See also A. H. Armstrong in Oxford Studies in Ancient Philosophy, *Supplementary Volume (1991) 117–127. (Armstrong notes Plotinus' care in indicating the distinction and the continuity between hypostases.) As far as Intellect is concerned there is no real problem for Plotinus. Intellect is firmly and totally rooted in the intelligible world, as he points out at the start of this chapter. But the nature of soul is less clear cut in that (a) at least in some of its phases it shares with Intellect in "true being . . . changeless in its essence, neither coming to be nor passing away" (lines 14–15), but*

(b) it is associated with the body both at a cosmic and an individual level, and thereby, at least at the level of individual soul, shares some of the impurity of body and some of the non-being of matter.

In Plato's account of the relation between soul and intellect we can pick out three features. First, in the Divided Line passage of Republic *6 he emphasizes the cognitive role of the individual soul, which stands apart from the objects of its cognition and straddles the intellectual and the sensible worlds, itself remaining incorporeal but engaging with both worlds. There is no hierarchy of hypostases. Secondly, both at cosmic and individual levels soul has a causative role, using the contents of the intelligible world as models for the sensible world. It is this aspect that Plotinus seizes on both generally in the* Enneads *and in particular in this treatise, where he emphasizes its power of bringing life to ("ensouling") material bodies. Thirdly, individual soul is described variously by Plato as being a composite of three "parts" as in* Republic *and* Phaedrus*, or as a unity as in* Phaedo *(see Fleet 2012, 8, 17, 25, 102). This distinction is not at issue in this treatise, but is hinted at in Chapter 10.*

The tone of this part of the treatise is doctrinal rather than discursive. Plotinus is stating, not defending, what he sees as the truth about the nature of the intelligible world, in particular the individual human soul. Chapter 9 must be seen as a preamble to Chapter 10, where we are shown the immortality of the soul as displayed in its noetic activity, when it is at its closest to the Divine. Plotinus is showing us the reverse side of the increasing pluralization of emanation; in the reverse direction we see increasing unification, so that by the end of Chapter 10 we have a picture of the noetic activity of soul, in which, like Intellect, it contains within itself the objects of its intellection—true assimilation, if not quite identity.

See Bréhier (1927, 185–188) for an analysis of this part (chapters 9–14) of the treatise.

Lines 1–5

The intelligible world, of which soul is a part, comprises true being, as opposed to the inferior sensible world, which owes its order and preservation to the intelligible world.

9, 1 *the other nature*: This phrase has been used at Chapter 8[4], 1 to differentiate soul from body; here it differentiates the whole of the intelligible world—"true being in its entirety"—from body. This first sentence (and the final sentence of Chapter 8[5]) are derived from *Timaeus* 27d, where Plato opposes "that which is eternal and has no becoming" to "that which is (always) becoming but never (really) is," a distinction which was common among ancient philosophers, perhaps originating with Parmenides. But see the note at the head of this chapter for the possible link to the end of Chapter 8.

9, 1 *which has being from itself*: O'Brien (1997, 61) takes HS to task for their idiosyncratic use of smooth and rough breathings (non-aspirate and aspirate) in instances like this and at line 14, particularly in the case of the pronoun *auton/hauton*, the former being (in classical Greek) non-reflexive and the latter reflexive. Sleeman and Pollet in Lex. Plot. 280 comment: "It is important to note that Plotinus often uses *autou* etc., instead of the usual reflexive forms with the rough breathing (*hautou*), and it impossible to be always sure what he wrote." But they may be led astray by HS' practices. HS_1 print *autês*, which if taken non-reflexively would mean "has its being from it"—presumably from the participation mentioned at the end of the previous chapter. HS_2 print *hautês*, with the meaning "from itself." This feature is not explicit in the passage of *Timaeus* referred to. But the interpretation "has its being from within itself" fits in well with Plotinus' doctrine of "emanation": the One, in its sheer oneness, overflows (the Greek verb is *ekrhein* = the Latin *emanare*, hence the English term); the as yet undefined overflow turns back (*epistrephetai*) to contemplate its source and in so doing gains definition as intellect (*nous*); the overflow of this contemplation of its prior likewise gains definition as soul (*psukhê*); the overflow of soul's contemplation of its prior is the raw material of the cosmos, but unlike the One and Intellect, which take no notice of their emanations, soul is concerned with the ordering of what comes after it, and the result is organized matter, the cosmos. Part and parcel of this description of the intelligible world is its being, which is not derived from the One—how could it be, since the One is "beyond being"? So the intelligible world has its being as something underived, "of itself." What Plotinus does not make clear is the extent to which Soul can be said to have its being derived from Intellect. In one sense, since it is an emanation of Intellect, any being that it has is thereby derived; but Plotinus here, as we have seen, is not concerned to make a distinction within "true being in its entirety." Rather he goes on to talk about the causal role, which more properly belongs to Soul, as the references to the Platonic texts make clear. O'Meara (1996, 76) summarizes: "If the world depends on soul, soul cannot be regarded as the absolute prior by nature, Plotinus argues, because soul presupposes and depends on intellect, which must consequently be independent of, and different from soul."

9, 2 *Otherwise*: Plotinus now turns from his brief consideration of the ontological status of "the other nature" to that of its causal functions. Important to our understanding is the contrast between prior (*proteros*) and posterior (*husteros*). O'Meara (1996, 66–81) offers an excellent discussion of these terms as used by Plotinus to designate his "hierarchy of being": "I suggest taking the terms 'prior' and 'posterior' as expressing a way of ordering things. Plotinus himself uses these terms in connection with the structure of reality and uses them reflectively, that is in connection with discussion of the kinds of order which these terms serve to express. In this he is following the example of Plato's Academy and of Aristotle." In Plotinus' view that which is later/posterior depends on what is earlier/prior, but not *vice versa*; the relationship is not reciprocal. Within the intelligible world the hierarchy is that of the three principal hypostases, where the priority is not one of time but rather, as O'Meara puts it, quoting *Republic* 509d, one of "power and dignity." By contrast, it is at the level below soul, sometimes called "nature" (*phusis*) by Plotinus, that priority/posteriority of space and time come into play. In each case, however, the posterior depends for its being on its prior, so that to remove the prior inevitably entails the removal of the posterior.

9, 5 *the cosmos*: The account of the ordering of the cosmos at large by the soul of the cosmos is the subject matter of Plato *Timaeus,* especially 34a–40d. See Gerson (1994, 137–138) for a discussion of this passage.

Lines 6–16

The intelligible world is the self-moved primary source of motion for all that comes after it; the particular motive function of soul is to bestow life on bodies, which thereby become "ensouled."

9, 6 *For this is the principle of motion*: Plotinus keeps to Plato's term "motion" (*kinêsis*) to denote change, which is rooted in motion. Other words are *alloiôsis* (qualitative alteration) and *metabolê* (change). This creative activity on the part of the soul of the cosmos is echoed by that of individual souls, which conserve and give order to "other things," and in particular to the ensouled body, which is the subject of *Timaeus* 40d–47e. Plotinus turns for his authority to *Phaedrus* 245c–e, where Plato is discussing the activity of "divine and human soul": "All soul[32] is immortal. For that which is in motion but is being moved by something else ceases to live when it ceases to move. Only that which moves itself, since it never abandons itself, never ceases its motion; this is also the principle of motion in other things which are moved. But a principle is ungenerated, since it is necessary that anything that is generated should be generated from a principle, while the principle is not generated from anything; for if the principle were generated from something, it would no longer be a principle.[33] And since it is ungenerated, it must also be imperishable. For if the principle is to be destroyed, then it cannot come to be from anything nor could anything come to be out of it, since all things must come to be from a principle." Cf. Aristotle *On the Soul* 432a17, and

32 See below for a discussion of this phrase.

33 Reading *ouk an eti arkhê* after Burnet for *ouk an ex arkhês* of the manuscripts.

Gerson (1994, 137–138) for a discussion of this passage of *Phaedrus* and Plotinus' response to it—though I feel that Gerson is wrong to limit this activity to soul—or at any rate, if Plotinus is referring to soul alone here, he reverts to a more general subject at line 10. For Plato, at a cosmic level, the soul of the cosmos ensouls the entire cosmos, which is a copy of the Ideal Living Creature of *Timaeus* 30c–31a, and which thereby has its own imparted natural motion, for example in the movement of the four elements to their proper place (cf. Simplicius *On Aristotle Physics* 287, 30: "It is clear that none of these things moves itself. But they do have a principle of movement, not in the sense of acting or causing movement, but of being moved . . . for example fire, which is only moved upward, and earth, which is moved towards the center.") And at the level of the ensouled body it is the individual soul that bestows life. Plotinus' reference to the life of the ensouled body in line 7 suggests his main interest in this treatise; see below on line 10.

9, 8 *the life which it has from within itself*: What distinguishes the ensouled from the unensouled body is life. Bodies can be ensouled to different degrees, from the simplest plants to the most complex rational creatures, according to the level of complexity of the soul present in them. But they are all living creatures, and it is soul which is the cause of life at every level. Soul, as cause, is prior to body, as effect, and as cause it must possess what it produces in another. Plotinus' authority for this is Plato *Phaedo* 105c–d (Socrates is questioning Cebes):

> "What must come to be present in a body for it to be alive|?
>
> Soul.
>
> Is this always so?
>
> Yes, of course.
>
> So the soul brings life to anything that it takes possession of?
>
> Yes.
>
> Is there, or is there not, something which is the opposite of life?
>
> There is.
>
> What?
>
> Death.
>
> So soul—according to our previous agreement—will never admit the opposite of that which it brings?
>
> Of course not."

Bostock (1986, 189–193) objects to this argument (for the immortality of the soul), but Plotinus is either unaware of any such objection, or chooses to ignore it. In any case, he is not indulging in polemic in this part of the treatise.

9, 10 *otherwise the series will extend infinitely*: Although neither Plato (in the passage quoted) nor Plotinus (here) states unambiguously that each individual soul is a self-moving principle of movement, he certainly does not preclude the possibility—as we have seen the whole of the chapter avoids making a distinction between Soul and Intellect. *Timaeus* 42e–43a talks of the demiurge instructing the lesser gods to fashion the soul, "the immortal principle," to be implanted in each living creature. This principle is thus in one way derived from the activity of the demiurge and the lesser gods, but in another it is, as an immortal principle, self-moved and able to follow the desire of the demiurge expressed at 41c, that some part of the individual living creature should "share the name of the immortals, being designated divine." This accords with the general teleological tone of *Timaeus* and *Phaedrus* and the metaphysics of *Phaedo*. The principle of an unmoved mover was clearly spelt out in the passage of *Phaedrus* quoted above, and is confirmed by Aristotle *Metaphysics* 11. It is less certain that we can apply this principle of self-movement to the individual soul and there has been much debate on this topic, largely stemming from the translation of the first phrase of the quoted *Phaedrus* passage, *pasa psukhê*; is it collective, "soul as a whole," or distributive, "every soul"? The Greek can bear either sense. There is a succinct discussion at Ferrari (1987, 123–125). Ferrari's conclusion is that the ambiguity is deliberate, and that the claims that follow are applicable to either collective or individual soul; the one does not preclude the other. Plotinus is committed to the immortality of the individual soul, which lies at the core of this treatise. The undoubted immortality of the soul of the cosmos is not central to the discussion—but neither is it excluded. There is no contradiction involved. Rather Plotinus is gradually narrowing the focus from the intelligible world, through soul in general to the individual soul of living creatures. He is echoing and exploiting the ambiguity in *Phaedrus*. It is not until Chapter 10 that we finally focus on the individual soul.

9, 10 *some nature that has life primarily*: The broad description that follows is of the intelligible world. So much of what is said in lines 10–19 can be applied to Intellect; the possession of life is not the preserve of Soul, but abounds throughout the intelligible world. Atkinson (1983, 77) on V.1.4, 7 says: "The belief that the intelligible world was alive can be traced back to Plato's *Sophist* and *Timaeus* and to Aristotle *Metaphysics* 1072b26–27. Plotinus characteristically develops what he found in Plato and Aristotle. "His world is boiling with life . . . every Form has a life of its own . . . there is nothing in Intellect which is not alive." Cf. Gerson (1994, 53): "Intellect is the *arkhê* of essence. That is, its activity, intellection of all Forms, is the paradigm of life. It is *per se* essence and life, whereas everything else that has essence and life is so *per aliud*. So the perplexity remains: why does Plotinus draw upon Platonic texts which are to do with the soul to illustrate the nature of Intellect?"

9, 11 *primally*: Non-derivatively; Intellect has a life that is prior to the life of all posterior to it. But the perplexity lurks in the background.

9, 11 *indestructible and immortal*: O'Brien (1997, 59) prefers to see *Phaedo* 88b5 and 106e9 as Plotinus' Platonic source for these words, rather than HS' 95c. There are also possible allusions to Parmenides DK 8.3 and 8.19.

9, 13 *all that is divine and all that is blessed*: This religious-sounding language is more suitably applied to the realm of Intellect which subsumes that of the soul of the cosmos. Cf. III.8.11, 32, where Intellect is said to "live a blessed life"; there are also echoes of Aristotle's god.

9, 14 *of itself*: The same difficulty arises here as that noted at line 1 concerning the rough and smooth breathings. But better sense is given by adopting the reflexive form here.

9, 15 *changeless in its essence:* Atkinson (1983, 77) says: "There is nothing in Intellect which is not alive. Unlike the life of the physical universe, however, the life of the intelligible world is stationary." Cf. Gerson (1994, 60) who, grappling with the perplexity, says: "Another way of describing the kind of *arkhê* that Soul is is to say that it is the *arkhê* of transitive motion. I use the term 'transitive' to distinguish the motion of which the Soul is the *arkhê* from the kind of 'intransitive' motion that can be attributed to Intellect and is synonymous with its activity."

Lines 16–26

Plotinus contrasts true being with color, which holds an intermediary position between true being and the material world. Like the former it has (or is) a changeless quality; like the latter it lacks life and true being.

9, 19 *the color white*: Plotinus' language is ambiguous, and reflects an ambiguity in Greek expression which stems from the use of a neuter definite article + adjective, which can denote either a sensible particular, "the white thing," or a non-sensible universal, "the white, whiteness."[34] Often Plato will prefix the expression with *auto* to denote a Form, as *auto to kalon,* the Form of the Good in *Republic.* Here Plotinus' phrase is *to leukon, auto to khrôma* (lit: the white, the color itself). But Plotinus cannot here be

34 Cf. the confusion shown by Euthyphro in the dialogue named after him. Initially he is unable to distinguish between the two senses of *to hosion,* (a) the pious act, and (b) piety.

talking about a Form of color or of whiteness, but rather using the phraseology to mean "the white—I mean the color, not the white sensible object." Alternatively we could re-punctuate and place the comma after *auto*, so rendering "the white itself, I mean the color." He is using the term to demonstrate two points. First, *like* the color white, the principle of life cannot be anything other than itself, just as the color white (as opposed to the changeable sensible object) cannot be anything other than the color white; secondly, *unlike* the color white, which is a quality[35] not possessing real being (and so not possessing life), the intelligible world is/has real being and life "of itself and primally." See Fleet (2012, 123) for a further Neoplatonic refinement on the way that qualities are present in sensible particulars. There is no clear suggestion in Plato's works that color is to be viewed as a Form, although color and white are more than once linked, for example *Meno* 74c–76d, *Theaetetus* 153d; cf. also *Phaedo* 101cff., *Philebus* 12e and 53a–c, *Timaeus* 67c. *Phaedrus* 247c talks of "the colorless, formless and intangible real being."

9, 20 *But if the white thing*: The Greek phrase is *to leukon*, which as we have noted above is ambiguous. Here, in contrast to *to leukon, auto to khrôma* in line 19, it refers

35 Cf. Plato *Lysis* 217d for a further distinction within whiteness as a quality—the accidental property of dyed hair as opposed to the intrinsic whiteness of an old person's hair. See Guthrie (1975, vol. IV, 148).

to a white sensible particular, and Plotinus' point is that a white object is not a real being, so any property that it has—the color white—is not "of itself" or "primary" and it too is not a real being. By contrast in the intelligible world the life that soul possesses shares its real being.

9, 23 *So this being*: Soul, in that it (or at least that part of it that remains isolated) exists in the intelligible world has its life as something intrinsic, primary and eternal, unlike a sensible particular such as a stone or wood, which has no life. The choice of stone and wood reflects *Sophist* 246a–b, where the materialist "Giants" are said to "pull everything down from heaven and the unseen world, literally grabbing hold of rocks and trees." The part of the soul that does not remain isolated is mentioned in the next sentence.

Lines 26–29

Plotinus focuses on that part of the intelligible world germane to the treatise—the individual soul, which in its higher phase belongs entirely to the intelligible world, but makes forays into the contaminated and impure sensible world.

9, 26 *But anything which is mixed with what is inferior*: As at the end of Chapter 8[5] Plotinus introduces the subject matter of the next chapter, the human soul, which by its descent into the sensible world (the subject of IV.8 in this series) becomes mixed with what is inferior and thereby less pure.

9, 28 *its previous state*: The phrase is from *Republic* 547b, where Plato is discussing the decay of the ideal republic, when its four elements, designated as gold, silver, bronze and iron become mixed, and the better mixture, gold and silver, pulls toward "virtue and the previous state."

9, 29 *rises back up to its proper home*: The Greek verb is *anatrekhein* (lit. "runs up/back"), which Plato and Plotinus commonly use as part of the imagery of the ascent of the soul from the sensible to the intelligible world. *Ana-* as a prefix can have both senses of "up" and "back again," both appropriate here. See Fleet (2012, 19ff.).

Chapter 10

Having in Chapter 9 described the nature of the intelligible world, Plotinus now turns to consider the rational part of the human soul, which is part of the intelligible world. He employs a range of Platonic texts.

Lines 1–6

Soul is akin to intellect, enjoying a good and rational life.

10, 1 *it is akin to the more divine and eternal nature*: In the process of "emanation" there is a gradual dilution of unity and being, as Hypostasis flows into Hypostasis and beyond. Nearest to the One at the center (Plotinus often uses the image of concentric circles or spheres) we have Intellect (*Nous*), whose contemplation of its contents, undivided Forms, is carried outside itself to produce soul, which is "the image of Intellect" (V.1.3, 7; see Atkinson 1985, 50–54 for a good discussion including Platonic and Aristotelian precedents). The conveying principle is *logos*, and Plotinus describes the higher soul as the *logos* of Intellect at V.1.3, 8. As the higher soul, next closest to the center, turns back to contemplate Intellect, it begins the process of division; it is at this stage that the Form gains "some trace of what it is to become." See also Fleet (2012,

93–95 and 164–165) for a discussion of this increasing pluralization. The One, unity itself, is entirely undifferentiated. At the next level Intellect is differentiated from its objects, the Forms, which are themselves differentiated from each other by the mediation of Soul (cf. *Sophist* 254bff. for the "five greatest forms," being, motion, rest, sameness and difference, which give the Forms their most basic differentiation). So each Form can be described as both akin to and different from its fellows (IV.4.32, 37). This analysis is repeated in the sensible world where the pluralization is much greater—although Plotinus would deny that there is a kinship between intelligible Form and sensible particular; III.6.15, 9 talks of "the utter lack of kinship."

Soul presents a paradox, straddling as it does the intelligible and the sensible worlds and apparently displaying some kinship to both. In this chapter Plotinus shows that the soul in its most rational phase ("the rational part") is akin to intellect; consideration of the lower phases, or parts, of the individual soul is excluded. This is entirely consistent with Plato's doctrines, as we shall see as the argument unfolds.

10, 1 *the more divine and eternal nature*: This is the intelligible world, as presented in Chapter 9. This is an echo of *Republic* 611e, where the soul is said to be "akin to the divine and the immortal everlasting being."

10, 3 *it does not have even shape or color, and it is intangible*: *Phaedrus* 247c tells us that the supracelestial region (i.e., the intelligible world when demythologized) is occupied by "intangible true being, which is colorless and without shape"; Plato is denying these three qualities of material objects to the intelligible in order to spell out its non-material nature (cf. Hackforth 1952, 80ff.). Color and shape are the most evident qualities of material objects, and at *Sophist* 246a the materialists are said to "maintain that true being belongs only to that which can be touched or handled." Shape (and size) are the minimal requirements for the extension of material bodies (cf. III.6.6, 13 and II.4.8, 21). Color and shape are included in the third and fourth types of quality of sensible substances in Aristotle *Categories*. Of the senses color is perceived by sight, shape by sight and touch, tangibility by touch.

10, 4 *we agree that all that is divine and truly existent enjoys good and rational life*: This echoes *Republic* 521a where Plato says that the rulers of the ideal republic will be rich "not in gold, but in what the happy person must enjoy—a good and wise life." See Fleet (2012, 34–37) for the same principle couched in a broader context by both Plato and Aristotle. Through contemplation we most nearly actualize the immortal part of us.

Lines 6–26

We should consider the individual human soul in its best state, removed as far as possible from the concerns of the sensible world. Every human soul is akin to the divine, even if its involvement with the body makes this hard to discern.

Plotinus brings forward an issue fundamental to Platonism, the paradoxical nature of the human soul, which at its best is removed, as far as possible, from the concerns of the body and achieves "assimilation to the divine." The most important texts are *Republic*, *Phaedrus*, *Symposium*, *Letter 7*, *Phaedo*, *Timaeus*, and *Theaetetus*. See Fleet (2012, 19–34) for a detailed discussion of the relevant passages, and 37–38 for the development of the principle in the Middle Platonists.

But at its less than best the human soul becomes embroiled in the material world. Plato's most vivid account of its dual nature comes at *Republic* 611c: "Well then, that the soul is immortal is established beyond doubt by our recent argument and the other proofs; but to understand her real nature, we must look at her, not as we see her now, marred by association with the body and other evils, but when she has regained that pure condition which the eye of reason can discern; you will then find her to be a far lovelier thing and will more clearly distinguish justice and injustice and all the qualities we have discussed. Our description of the soul is true of her present appearance; but we have seen her afflicted by countless evils, like the sea-god Glaucus, whose original form can hardly be discerned, because parts of his body have been broken off or crushed and altogether marred by the waves, and the clinging undergrowth of weed and rock and shell has made him more like some monster than his natural self. But we must rather fix our eyes, Glaucon, on her love of wisdom and note how she seeks to apprehend and hold converse with the divine, immortal and everlasting world to which she is akin" (tr. Cornford).

10, 8 *irrational appetites and desires*: For Plato the human soul is divided into the rational and the irrational, and the latter further divided into the appetitive and the desiring faculties—the model for his analogy in *Phaedrus* between the rational, appetitive, and desiring elements in the soul, and the charioteer and the two horses drawing the chariot of the soul. Plotinus is here inviting us to consider the soul in its purest state, when it is purified "as far as possible." He gives a description of such a state at III.6.5, 13ff.: "But what would the purification of the soul consist in if it was in no way stained? Purification would be to leave it alone in isolation, or looking at nothing else, having no alien opinions—whatever the nature of these opinions—and for it not to contemplate the images of the affections, as has been said, nor to create affections from them. Is it not true purification if it turns upward in the opposite direction from the world below?"

Plotinus' contribution to the debate was to claim—apparently without Platonic authority—that one part of our soul remains always in the intelligible world, a claim explored in IV.8.8, 1–3: "Furthermore—if I may venture to state my convictions more clearly against the opinion of others, as I must—not even our own soul sinks in its entirety, but there is always some part of it in the intelligible world."

10, 11 *evils are additions which come to a soul from outside*: Plotinus takes an optimistic view of the human soul—in keeping with the passage from *Republic* quoted above, which distinguishes between (a) the soul's "real nature" when she displays "love of wisdom" and "seeks to hold converse with the divine, immortal and everlasting world to which she is akin"; and (b) her "affected state." Plotinus examines the distinction further in III.6.1–5 where he poses and answers the question: What do the so-called affections of the soul consist in? Cf. also *Timaeus* 42aff. where the young souls are battered into confusion *from outside*.

10, 13 *wisdom and the other virtues*: At *Symposium* 209a Plato talks of those whose souls conceive and give birth to what is appropriate to them, "wisdom and virtue in general" (Waterfield renders: "virtue and especially wisdom").

Wisdom is singled out as being the virtue most akin to rational thought. Bréhier (1927, 206n2) comments: "The whole of this second argument assumes a theory of virtue particular to Plotinus, a theory laid out in *Ennead* I.2[19], according to which virtue is not an acquired quality as it is in Aristotle, but on the contrary is the product of purification, the activity whereby the soul casts off its own nature and detaches itself from all that it has acquired."

10, 14 *when it returns to itself*: The verb used is *anerkhesthai*, which, like *anabainein* in line 39 and 12, 8, can also bear the sense "ascend"; cf. note on 9, 29. The ascent or return of the soul to its true self is described at IV.8.1: "I often wake up from my body into my true self, so that being within myself and outside all other things I enjoy a vision of wonderful beauty. It is then that I believe most firmly that I am part of the nobler realm, living a life of perfect activity; I have become at one with the divine."

10, 16 *wisdom and true virtue*: See above on line 13.

10, 19 *through being akin and of the same essence*: For Platonists it was problematic to posit a strict dualism of two entirely separate worlds, the intelligible and the sensible, which are not akin and not of the same substance. The two worlds are related, and Plato attempts to capture the relationship by using terms such as "the participation of sensible particulars in intelligible Forms" and "the presence of Forms to particulars." Plotinus' answer was his doctrine of emanation whereby the difference between sensible and intelligible is maintained but within an overall unity. As we have seen, the human soul presents a special case, both ontologically, in that it has its being both within and outside the body, and epistemologically, in that it has cognition of the intelligible world through rational thought, and of the sensible world through the senses. Here Plotinus is stressing: (a) that the human soul is at its best when it has "returned to itself" (and is "an intelligible and dazzling cosmos") and is able to host wisdom and virtue; (b) that intelligible and divine beings such as wisdom and true virtue belong entirely to the intelligible world and can be hosted only by what is "akin and of the same substance"—Intellect itself and the other Forms by communion, and here particularly the rational soul; and (c) that the human soul achieves the divinity of wisdom and virtue when it is no longer present in the body and its irrational phase is in suspense.

10, 19 *of the same essence*: The Greek word is *homoousios*, perhaps coined by Plotinus and used only on one other occasion by him, at IV.4.28, 55, where the different parts of the soul are said to be "akin and of the same essence." The word had an unfortunate history in early Christianity, when one camp used it to describe the nature of Christ as being of the same essence as God and the Holy Spirit, as opposed to those who claimed that his nature was only of similar essence, *homoiousios*, perhaps giving rise to the expression "an iota of difference." See MacCulloch (2009, 146–147 and 214–223).

10, 25 *a man's soul bears many scars*: An echo of *Republic* 611b quoted above: "marred by association with the body"; the verb used there by Plato and here by Plotinus is *lôb-asthai* (MacKenna: "soiled").

Plotinus ends this section on an uncharacteristically pessimistic note; not only do most of us bear the multiple scars on our soul of its embroilment in the material world, but most of us fail to realize its true nature.

Lines 26–37

We should strive to put aside all that distorts our self-vision, and to see ourselves as we truly are.

Much to the forefront here is a passage from *Phaedo* 65a–c:

"Socrates: So what about the acquisition of knowledge itself? Is the body a hindrance, or not, if a person enlists its support in the search? I mean something like this: Do men's sight and hearing offer any truth, or—as the poets are forever telling us—do we neither hear nor see anything accurately? Yet if these bodily senses are not accurate or clear, the others are hardly likely to be, since they are inferior. Do you agree?

Simmias: I certainly do agree.

Socrates: So when does the soul attain to truth? For when it tries to consider anything along with the body, it is clearly deceived by it.

Simmias: True.

Socrates: So is it not in thought, if anywhere, that something of true being becomes clear to it?

Simmias: Yes.

Socrates: So its thinking is at its best when none of these things trouble it—hearing, sight, pain, pleasure—but when it is, as far as possible, alone by itself, taking leave of the body, avoiding, as far as possible, all bodily contact and association, and reaching out to real being."

10, 27 *what is unblemished in him*: Bréhier (1927, 207n1) suggests that Plotinus might have in mind a passage from *Philebus* 52d, where Plato is making a distinction between pure and impure pleasures, and says: "In all matters let us consider the pure sorts." Perhaps more pertinent is Socrates' remark at *Republic* 534b that the man who cannot abstract the Form of the Good from everything else cannot truly know the Good itself or any particular good; cf. Gerson (1994, 216), and *Phaedrus* 247de, *Phaedo* 79a, and *Republic* 611a–612a.

10, 30 *abstracting*: The Greek word is *aphelôn*, the word used by Plato at *Republic* 534b, where the true philosopher is said to abstract the Form of the Good (Adam 1963 *ad loc.* suggests that this may be a reference to the Platonic process of division, for which see Guthrie 1975, vol. 4, 47). I have followed this interpretation. Others (Bréhier, Armstrong, BP, MacKenna) suggest "stripping" away all accretions; either way the philosopher is left with the truth.

10, 34 *by the eternal*: I.e., by the element in the soul which is akin to the eternality of the intelligible.

10, 35 *an intelligible and dazzling cosmos*: Cf. V.1.3, 12: "Coming from Intellect, then, the soul is intellectual, and its own intellect."

10, 36 *flooded by the light of the truth by the Good*: At *Republic* 508d Plato draws an analogy between (a) the sun, which brings growth and light to the sensible world, giving its contents visibility and the soul the power of sight, and (b) the Good, which gives being to the contents of the intelligible world and the power of knowing to the soul. Plotinus is here transferring the vocabulary of (a) to (b).

Lines 37–52

The soul in its purest state, assimilated to the divine, will have true understanding of the Forms, which are inside his soul.

10, 37 *when he has ascended to the divine*: For a full account of the ascent of the soul and its assimilation to the divine see Fleet (2012, 19–42). For "ascent" see note on 10, 14.

10, 38 *"Greetings; for you I am an immortal god"*: This is a quotation from the opening of Empedocles' poem *Purifications* (DK 2 112.4). Empedocles is greeting the inhabitants who live on the heights above Acragas. See KRS 313–314 for a discussion of the possible context, possibly Pythagorean. Plotinus is using it here to highlight the arrival of the soul in the intelligible world, when it has been purified and assimilated to the divine. Empedocles continues: "I am no longer a mortal." MacKenna seems to miss the point, and translates: "Farewell; I am to you an immortal god."

10, 40 *knowledge of what is best*: It is only in its purest state of assimilation to the divine that the soul can have knowledge (*gnôsis*) of "what is best." Cf. 9, 26–27: "But anything that is mixed with what is inferior is barred from achieving what is best."

10, 41 *the understanding which is contained within*: "Understanding" (*epistêmê*) is a key word in the metaphysics of Platonic epistemology. Plato does not employ a developed technical vocabulary, and other words such as *gnôsis, noêsis*, and *dianoia* can all be rendered similarly, although they tend to denote the processes of thought that culminate in the acquisition of a state of understanding. Most importantly, in the context of IV.7, *epistêmê* is used by Plato in *Republic* to indicate the grasp by the soul of intelligibles, in contrast to the perception (*aisthêsis*) of sensibles. As the philosopher-kings proceed through their higher education they acquire the understanding appropriate to each stage before moving on to the next. The curriculum is divided into two parts, the first comprising mathematics, plane geometry, solid geometry, astronomy and harmonics, all of which are grounded in sensible objects and are self-contained, so that an understanding of one does not entail that of another and does not lead the student to an overall view. This is acquired only as the culmination of the second part of the curriculum, where dialectic leads through a study of the higher Forms to an eventual overall understanding of the Good. Since at each level an understanding is achieved, both Plato and Plotinus can talk of "understandings," which is clumsy English. Others keep the plural and translate as "sciences," but that does not give the correct sense, so I have kept to the singular "understanding." At I.3.4 Plotinus sums up dialectic and concludes that "it converses (*dialegetai*) about good and its opposite and whatever is ranged under the good and its opposite, about what is eternal and what is not eternal, with understanding, not opinion. It ceases from its wanderings in the sensible world and establishes itself in the intelligible, where it busies itself, putting aside falsehood, feeding the soul on what Plato calls "the plain of truth" (*Phaedrus* 248b), using division to distinguish the Forms, their essences, and the primary genera, weaving together intellectively what derives from them, until it has traversed the whole of the intelligible world."

10, 41 *the understanding that is contained within . . . by contemplation with itself of itself*: Plotinus gives his own twist to the argument by saying that the soul contemplates the Forms not as external objects of thought, but as intrinsic to itself; each man becomes "an intelligible and dazzling cosmos." In this he is likening the noetic activity of the soul to that of Intellect as portrayed by Aristotle; see note at head of Chapter 9.

10, 43 *wisdom and justice*: Cf. *Phaedrus* 247d, where the charioteer of the soul "sees justice itself, sees wisdom, sees understanding—not the understanding that comes into being and varies as it is contained in different things, which we in our present state call real beings, but the understanding which resides in true and real being."

10, 44 *by contemplation*: The Greek word is *katanoêsis*, used again at 12, 9. See Rist (1967, 43) for some comments on Plotinus' use of this word.

10, 45 *what it was formerly*: This is either a reference to the doctrine of Recollection (cf. 12, 9) or to the soul's periodic assimilation to the divine.

10, 46 *seeing them firmly fixed within itself*: Cf. *Symposium* 216d, where Alcibiades suggests that if one opened Socrates up one would see the divine and golden images (*agalmata*) inside. Plotinus goes on to combine this picture with *Republic* 611c (see above, note on lines 6–27), adding his own contribution, of which Armstrong says: "The image of living gold hammering away its own dross is one of Plotinus' most original dynamic images."

10, 48 *dross*: The Greek word is *geêron* (lit. "earthy"), which BP notes as occurring at *Republic* 612a as describing the accretions clinging to Glaucus' body.

So by the end of the chapter we have a picture of the immortality of the soul as displayed in its noetic activity, when it is at its closest to the divine. That noetic activity is of a special kind, beyond what Plato himself had envisaged. O'Meara (1993, 21) sums up admirably: "Intelligible reality is discovered within ourselves, as soul, and further investigation of the roots of our nature discloses the primary form of intelligible being, intellect. In a sense

Plotinus internalizes intelligible reality, as opposed to an external conception that sees it as another world outside and beyond this world. For Plotinus intelligible reality is to be found in the depths of our own nature."

Chapter 11

In Chapters 11 and 12 Plotinus turns to consider possible objections to the immortality of the soul. His starting point is the argument put forward by Socrates at Phaedo *102d–107b, which itself looks back to the discussion at 69e–72e, the so-called Argument from Opposites. The former has occasioned much debate among commentators, the majority of whom see the argument as flawed, especially in the conclusion at 106eff., where Socrates (with Cebes' agreement) claims that because the soul is immortal (*athanatos*) it is also imperishable (*adiaphthoros*). For various analyses see Keyt (1963), Guthrie (1975, vol. IV), Frede (1978 = 2001), Bostock (1986 and 1999) and Weller (1995 = 2001). In the main their unease lies in the way that Socrates uses the term* athanatos *and his poor understanding of opposites and contradictories. Plotinus clearly sees no difficulty; rather his argument is that precisely because the rational soul belongs to the intelligible world, which is immortal and thereby imperishable, so too is the soul, which is incorporeal and not subject to the same analysis as the corporeal.*[36] *Much of his terminology is Aristotelian, and*

36 It is possible that Plato is introducing a deliberate ambiguity in order to exercise his students in the Academy as in *Euthyphro* and *Theaetetus*. If that is so, Plotinus passes it by without comment.

part of his argument relies on Aristotle's analysis of change at Metaphysics *1069b3ff. With material objects there is an underlying material substrate, in which the arrival or departure of a particular quality marks a qualitative change (*alloiôsis*). So, to take Plato's example in* Phaedo, *water as the underlying matter will be changed to steam by the arrival of heat, or to snow by the arrival of cold. Heat and cold can be described as immanent forms, which for Aristotle cannot have a separate substantial existence. Further, at* On Coming-to-be and Passing-away *329a24ff. Aristotle, in his analysis of the four primary bodies, earth, air, fire, and water, reduces their constituents to combinations of pairs of the four basic tangible (*haptos*) qualities; for example the two tangible qualities of fire are the hot and the dry. It is not entirely clear what he means by "tangible"; it cannot be synonymous with "material," but rather denotes a non-material quality which when present in a substrate is detectable by touch. Thus Plotinus can agree that in the sensible world the underlying matter, for example combustible wood (the Greek word he uses is* hulê, *which can denote either "matter" or "wood") can acquire from outside fire, one of whose two essential qualities is heat. The fire burning in the wood can be extinguished by the introduction of something cold (although nowadays we would hardly say that it is the coldness of water that douses a fire), and when this happens the heat is necessarily lost—"for it is in this that the fire is extinguished"* *(line 9). So the analogy that Plato uses in* Phaedo *is valid only to a certain extent. Soul has as its essential quality life just as fire has heat. The difference is that fire is not presented as a Form by Plotinus (whether Plato envisaged a Form of fire is debatable—he himself asks the question at* Timaeus *51b), and can be extinguished along with its heat. But the soul that we are considering in this part of the treatise is the rational, or noetic, soul. So while the irrational parts of the soul perish when the body perishes just as fire perishes along with its heat "in the matter underlying the fire," the noetic soul, which is "akin to the more divine" and thereby immortal, is by the same token imperishable. So the apparent inconsistency in* Phaedo *106e disappears and no further argument is needed, and we can accept the conclusion reached at* Phaedo *106de:*

*"Socrates: It would be agreed by everyone that god, the very Form of life, and anything else that is immortal (*athanatos*) is never destroyed.*

Cebes: All men would certainly agree, and even more so all the gods would, in my opinion.

Socrates: Since the immortal is also indestructible, then would not the soul, if it actually is immortal, also be indestructible?

Cebes: Of course.

Socrates: So when death comes to a person, the mortal part of him, it seems, dies, but the immortal part withdraws in the face of death, and departs safe and indestructible.

Cebes: So it would seem.

Socrates: So it is absolutely certain that soul is something immortal and indestructible, and that in truth our souls will exist in the Underworld."

Lines 1–11

Plotinus reiterates his own view of the nature of the soul. It is a noetic being, and life is essential to it; it is not to be compared with the essential qualities of material entities.

11, 1 *What person of intellect*: The Greek phrase is *tis noun ekhôn* (lit. "Who, having intelligence . . . ?")—ironical in that we all have a noetic soul, if only we would exercise it.

11, 3 *in no way acquired from outside*: Life is essential to soul, as Plotinus has told us at 9, 8ff.

11, 5 *I do not mean*: In the next few lines Plotinus points to the difference between fire manifested in the sensible world, and the noetic soul which belongs entirely to the intelligible world (see note at the head of the chapter). MacKenna translates: "This is no case of a Matter underlying and a life brought to that matter and making it into soul (as heat comes into matter and makes it fire)."

11, 9 *either . . . or*: Plotinus' Greek is ambiguous, and commentators are divided in their interpretation.

MacKenna: "Either life is Essential Reality, and therefore self-living—the very thing we have been seeking—and undeniably immortal; or it, too, is a compound . . ." This reading relies on deleting "the soul" in line 11.

Armstrong: "For life is rather a substance, and soul is a substance of this kind, living of itself, which is the thing we are looking for—and they will admit that it is immortal, or they will treat it also as a compound . . ." This reading relies on taking "the soul" in line 11 not as part of the parenthesis ("the thing we are looking for, namely the soul") but on making it the subject of the second "is" in contrast to "life," the subject of the first "is." Armstrong further apparently takes the first word in the Greek, ê, not in the sense "either," but as an emphatic particle strengthening "For."

Bréhier: "For either life is a substance, but such a substance is alive of itself; now this is precisely what we are seeking, and they will admit that it is immortal; or else it is a composite . . . " Bréhier, as MacKenna, deletes "the soul" in line 11.

BP: "In fact life is either a reality, and a reality of the kind that possesses life of itself—which is precisely the object of our enquiry—and they will agree that this is an immortal thing; or else they will see it as a compound . . . " This reading relies on keeping "the soul" as part of the parenthesis, and "life" as the subject of both occurrences of "is."

A further difficulty is presented by the Greek word *ousia*, used twice in line 10. It can bear all of the meanings offered by the above quartet—essential reality, substance, reality; it can also mean, *inter alia*, "being" and "essence." To Plotinus, of course, it is just *ousia*, and so I have taken the liberty of translating the two instances differently here.

Lines 11–18

Plotinus dismisses the claims of the Peripatetics and Pythagoreans.

11, 11 *and they agree . . . or they will analyze*: Aristotle does not give a dogmatic view of the parts, or faculties, of the human soul. At *On the Soul* 414a31 he mentions five faculties—nutritive, appetitive, sensitive, locomotive, and intellective. To these can be added generative (416a9) and imaginative (432b1). Yet another account is given at *Nicomachean Ethics* 1102b28, where the vegetal is added as a faculty of the irrational part of the soul and said to include nutrition and growth, and set against the appetitive and impulsive. Most scholars accept a broad tripartition into vegetal, sensitive, and rational. Plotinus' point is that the human soul for a Peripatetic is immortal and self-moving, whether viewed as the rational faculty (which survives the death of the body) or a compound where the other faculties are mortal and subsumed under the rational. He may well have in mind a much-debated passage at *On the Soul* 430a23: "When it [intellect] is separated it is just what it is, and this alone is immortal (*athanatos*)."

11, 14 *or if they will say*: Plotinus' target here is in particular the Pythagoreans and their doctrine of the soul as an affection of matter; he has answered them already in Chapter 8[4]. The affection is "acquired" when the parts are in a certain arrangement, like the attunement of the strings of a lyre. The argument could equally be directed against the Stoics and the Peripatetics and any who saw the soul as an affection of body.

BP notes that Plotinus' source for the self-movement of the soul is *Phaedrus* 245cd, and his source for "must not have anything to do with death" is *Timaeus* 41b. Plotinus' phrase for "must not" is *mê themis*, a religious term which echoes the passage in *Timaeus*, where the divine craftsman is issuing orders to the lesser gods.

11, 17 *But in fact*: The "single nature" is the soul, which has life essentially. It is alive in actuality—its life is not a potentiality to be realized, unlike the living creature defined by Aristotle at *On the Soul* 412a27 as "that which has life potentially."

Chapter 12

Plotinus now deals with the Stoics, whose doctrines he finds inconsistent. They follow the distinction between the soul of the cosmos and the individual human soul which Plato affirms in Timaeus, *but claim that it is only the soul of the cosmos which is indestructible, while individual human souls sooner or later perish. The soul of the cosmos is equated to god (see LS 54B and I) who transcends the cosmos. During the periods between conflagrations* (ekpurôseis) *god pervades the cosmos as a providential force, but at each conflagration, when the entire cosmos is consumed, god is then pure fire. But although all else is destroyed god, as "matter so disposed" remains as the creative force behind the new order, which is an exact repetition of all former worlds. So according to Stoic doctrine the soul of the cosmos is not liable to destruction, and Plotinus' claim (if it in fact refers to the Stoics) is not quite fair. With individual souls the situation is different. In a way each soul is destroyed, if not at death then at least at the conflagration, when it is reabsorbed into the cosmic soul-fire. Eusebius* Preparation for the Gospel *15.20.6 (= SVF 2.809 = LS 53W) says: "They [the Stoics] say that the soul is subject to generation and destruction. When separated from the body, however, it does not perish at once but survives on its own for certain times, the soul of the virtuous up to the dissolution of everything into fire, that of fools only for certain definite times. By the survival of souls they mean that we ourselves survive as souls separated from bodies and changed into the lesser substance of the soul, while the souls of non-rational animals perish along with their bodies." Even so it could be claimed that the individual soul is indestructible in two ways. First, although it may lose its individuality at its reabsorption, it is still part of the cosmic soul; secondly, the individual soul is reborn each time in the infinite series of worlds, and so in a way has an eternal existence.*

Lines 1–11

Plotinus summarizes the Stoic position and makes his reply.

12, 1 *every soul*: The Greek phrase is *pasa psukhê* (used by Plato at *Phaedrus* 245c), which as we have seen is ambiguous, and can mean either "every soul" or "soul as a whole." In both cases, since soul is that which gives life to bodies, its destruction must result in the destruction of all else, both at a cosmic and an individual level. But universal destruction is a concept alien to ancient thought.

12, 4 *each soul is a principle of motion*: As outlined at 9, 6–13.

12, 5 *grasps the same things by the same activity*: All souls, both those of the gods and those of humans, share the same experience as described at *Phaedrus* 246dff.; as they are carried around the circuit of the heavens they see both what is within and what is beyond the heavens. *The same activity* is intellection.

12, 6 *of what is in the heavens and of what is beyond the heavens*: In *Republic* 514aff. the philosopher-king ascends from the cave into the upper world, where, after a period of habituation to the brightness, he is able to see first "the heavenly phenomena, the heavens themselves more easily in the darkness of night, and the stars and moon . . . finally the sun itself." This image reflects the analogy made earlier between the sun, which gives light and generation to the contents of the sensible world, and the Good, which gives truth and being to the contents of the intelligible world. (Slightly confusingly the sun in the cave analogy stands for the Good in the former analogy.) The Good is said at 509b to be "beyond being"; the Greek word for "beyond" is *epekeina*, used here by Plotinus and there by Plato; it is sometimes translated as "transcending." See note on 13, 16 for its opposite, *epitade*, lit. "on this side of."

12, 7 *the first principle*: This echoes what Socrates says at *Republic* 533c: "Dialectic is the only method that proceeds in this way, doing away with suppositions, up to the first principle."

12, 8 *its internal intellection*: As described in Chapter 10.

12, 9 *recollection*: Plotinus generally has little to say about the Platonic doctrine of Recollection, since his own doctrine of the noetic soul's continuing existence in the intelligible world supersedes it. Plato presents it at *Phaedo* 72eff., and *Meno* 79eff. See Gerson (1994, 179–180), who cites V.3.2, 9–14 as an important passage.

12, 10 *prior to body*: Prior in both the ontological and the temporal sense.

Lines 4–11 encapsulate succinctly Plotinus' conception of the human soul, drawing on much of what he has said earlier in the treatise. He weaves together into a composite whole different strands of Platonism: soul as a principle of motion, soul as having life essentially, soul enjoying intellection of its own contents—the eternal contemplation of real being.

Lines 12–20

Plotinus now turns away to a denial that soul can have the properties of body. Soul is not a material entity that can be divided into parts in the way that a magnitude can. These lines take the form of a dialogue between an objector and Plotinus himself, perhaps reflecting a debate in one of the seminars.

12, 12 *Everything that can be broken up*: This typification of a compound can apply either to a composite material body, where the parts are of the same order of being, and which can be reduced ultimately to its basic constituents, typically the four elements; or to the compound of form and matter, where the parts are of different orders. Plotinus follows Aristotle in calling the living creature "the composite" (*to suntheton*). The living creature has its being *qua* living creature through being a compound of soul and body. Of these body is further reducible to its material elements; but that is not at issue here—Plotinus discusses it at length in III.6.7–19. Soul is not further reducible, being "a simple nature, a simplex."

12, 15 *But after all*: The soul is a thing of parts in that, according to Plato, it is divided into rational, appetitive, and spirited—a division familiar to all Platonists from especially *Republic* and *Phaedrus*. So the objector's complaint is that the soul has acquired its being through being a composite of parts, so that when it is broken up at death, then it ceases to have being. That is true to an extent—the soul as the soul of the particular individual ceases to be just that at death. Plotinus' answer is that the way that the parts are present in the body is not as a mass or magnitude. Certain soul parts have an appropriate place in the body according to *Timaeus* 69cff., but as Archer-Hind (*ad loc.*) says: "It seems that these three *eidê* are but names for one and the same vital force manifesting itself in different relations." So the soul, being a single nature, is not truly divided in this way into "parts," but retains its single nature.

12, 16 *as has been demonstrated*: At 5, 24–51.

12, 17 *by being qualitatively changed*: Plotinus denies that the soul can be affected, i.e., qualitatively changed, and at III.6.2, 47 he suggests that an apparent affection in the soul is "an alteration of a different sort," a change from potentiality to actuality, which is not like the destructive qualitative change occurring in material bodies.

Chapter 13

At IV.8.1, 23 Plotinus says: "We are left with the divine Plato, who has said in many places in his works many noble things about the soul and its arrival here, so that we can hope for some clarity from him. So what does this philosopher say? It is clear that he does not always speak with sufficient consistency for us to make out his intentions with any ease. But he always holds the sensible world in low esteem, and censures the association of the soul with the body." The question which is given brief consideration here in IV.7 is given more extensive treatment in IV.8, a later but near contemporary treatise. See translation and commentary in this series (Fleet 2012).

In IV.8 it is not always clear when Plotinus is dealing with the soul of the cosmos, when he is dealing with the individual soul and when he is dealing with "soul as a whole." That ambiguity is less apparent in this chapter (IV.7.13), where Plotinus is talking in the main about the individual human soul, at least from line 4 onward, and in lines 9–10 he talks of the soul acting "together with the entire soul of the cosmos." Even so, what he says in lines 1–11 applies equally to individual and to cosmic soul. In the intelligible world individual noetic soul, having achieved "assimilation to the divine," is effectively indistinguishable from Intellect and Soul. Nor does he here address the fundamental issue—to what extent the descent of the soul is voluntary and to what extent it is involuntary—an issue on which Plotinus is in general equivocal. But in this treatise we are not concerned with the descent of the soul into bodies, but focus our attention on the individual soul in its noetic phase in the intelligible world, where its activity will be akin to that of Intellect. That is a token of its immortality. Plotinus' discussion here draws on his own interpretation of Platonic psychology, whereby "there is always some part of our soul in the intelligible world" (IV.8.8, 3).

Lines 1–4

The noetic soul remains entirely and eternally unaffected in the intelligible world.

13, 2 *The element which is pure intellect*: This is the part which is "always . . . in the intelligible world." See Fleet (2012, 183–186).

13, 3 *cannot suffer affection*: See note on 12, 17. The noetic soul cannot suffer any sort of affection, whereas the lower, irrational part, "the so-called affective element" is rather the cause of affection in other things (III.6.1, 14). Although the arguments in III.6.1–5 attempt to show that the soul is in no way subject to affection, Plotinus is hard put to it to show that emotions such as anger are not affections of the soul.

13, 3 *urge or desire*: Blumenthal (1971, 33) sees the two words as "more or less equivalent," but a better analysis is given by Leroux in Gerson (ed., 1996, 301): "The Plotinian psychology is extraordinarily rich as concerns the analysis of desire and of inclination . . . and directly intersects with what we might call the lexicon of freedom, mostly inherited from Aristotle and the Stoics . . . : the boundary is often indistinct between simple inclination and a voluntary surge of fully willing spontaneity. But . . . this vocabulary does not clearly develop into a neat conceptual vocabulary of willingness and freedom as an autonomous power distinct from inclination." Plotinus' position as explicated here and in the rest of the chapter is that although the soul can match Intellect in its noetic phase and be without "urge or desire,"[37] as it re-orients itself away from pure intellection it does have desire "added to it"; but as Bréhier (209n1) remarks: "Desire (*orexis*) here is not desire as an affection, but desire as a propensity to

37 Gerson (1994, 62) notes passages where Plotinus states that both Intellect and Soul display desire (*ephesis*) and says: "But whereas intellects are directly and eternally related to the Good, everything else seeks the good in something other than the One itself." A later treatise, VI.8, is titled "On free will and the will of the One." where "will" (*thelêma*) must certainly fall into the category of non-affective activities.

act." In Plato's view neither the demiurge nor the soul of the cosmos has an irrational element, although the latter does have a rational concern for the cosmos and so a desire to organize it, which leads to "sure and true judgments and beliefs" about the contents of the sensible world, and "rational understanding and knowledge" of the intelligible (*Timaeus* 37bc). But these are not affections.

Lines 4–11

Soul turns away from its purely noetic activity and gains a desire to organize Nature. This is an activity shared by individual and cosmic soul.

13, 4 *receives in addition desire*: Desire is adventitious, not belonging to the soul in its noetic phase. But there is no mention here of the soul receiving its irrational parts, the spirited (*to thumoeides*) and the appetitive (*to epithumêtikon*), and Plotinus avoids the term *thumos* here, which would have suggested the element of irrationality which accompanies the soul in its descent into body. We keep our eyes on the noetic soul.

13, 5 *it proceeds*: The Greek verb is *proerkhesthai*, one of Plotinus' terms for the procession from the unity of the One to the increasing plurality which follows.

13, 6 *further afield*: The Greek word is *epipleon*, which Plotinus uses on other occasions in this sense, sometimes in contrast to *epi elatton* ("to a lesser extent"). It is possible, but unlikely, that it could bear the sense either (a) "into plurality," or even (b) as the participle of the verb *epiplein*, "overflowing"; both would be appropriate.

13, 6 *what it has seen in its intellective phase*: Just as the Ideal Living Creature in *Timaeus* stands as the model for the demiurge, through the medium of the soul of the cosmos, to bring the cosmos itself into being, so the Forms as contemplated by individual souls in their noetic phase stand as models for the coming into being of individual sensibles. At IV.8.1, 41–50 Plotinus, in a strongly teleological announcement, tells us: "In *Timaeus*, when he is speaking of this All, he praises the cosmos and calls it a blessed god; and he says that its soul was bestowed by the demiurge in his goodness so that this All might be intelligent, since it had to be intelligent and could not be so without soul. So that was the reason why the soul of the All was sent by the god; and the soul of each one of us was sent so that the All might be perfected. For it was necessary that all the same kinds of living creatures should exist in the sensible world as exist in the intelligible."

13, 6 *as if this had made it pregnant*: The imagery of pregnancy is found in two passages in Plato. First, *Symposium* 202eff., where the words of the priestess Diotima describe the birth of Love, "a great spirit . . . between divine and mortal," at the feast of the gods celebrating the birth of Aphrodite. "Provision" went into the garden of Zeus to sleep off the intoxication caused by the nectar he had drunk. "Poverty," who had come begging at the door, took advantage of his state, lay with him, and so became pregnant and gave birth to Love. Plotinus discusses this story in III.6.14, 10ff. and V.9.9, 20ff. Secondly, *Theaetetus* 148e–151d, where Socrates claims that although he himself is barren, he acts as the midwife in allowing young men who are pregnant with ideas to give birth to them. See Sedley (2004, 28–37).

13, 8 *it becomes a craftsman*: The verb used is *dêmiourgein,* a term which, with its cognate noun *dêmiourgos*, usually, but not exclusively, echoes Plato's demiurge of *Timaeus*. Here the noetic soul assumes the role.

13, 9 *it stretches out*: The verb used, *teinein*, can signify either (a) a physical stretching out, as when god "set soul in the center [of the cosmos] and stretched it through the whole and enfolded its body from outside with this soul" at *Timaeus* 34b; similarly at 36e; or (b) a figurative stretching out towards, a yearning for (*orexis*).

13, 11 *shares in caring for the cosmos*: At *Phaedrus* 246b we are told that "all soul cares for what is lacking in soul."

Lines 11–19

The individual soul, unlike the soul of the cosmos, is subject to pluralization; but it nevertheless does not entirely lose its integrity.

Bréhier (209n2) remarks: "We must make a careful distinction between the propensity by which the soul controls the body—a propensity common to all souls, even to that of the cosmos—and the wish to isolate itself, which amounts to the descent of the soul." The latter becomes the subject of IV.8 and is merely touched on here in IV.7.13, where Plotinus goes on to reiterate its immortal noetic nature.

13, 11 *it wishes*: The turning of the soul to what is below it is initially an act of its own will. At IV.8.2, 5 he asks whether the soul inhabits the cosmos "willingly, or under compulsion, or in some other way." Generally speaking Plotinus is equivocal on the nature of the descent of human souls. At times he suggests that it is voluntary, at others involuntary. O'Brien (1977) suggests that the two terms need not be mutually exclusive, and refers to IV.3.13, 17: "Souls go down neither voluntarily nor because they are sent; at least such volition is not like a choice, but like a natural jump such as the urge for sexual intercourse or for noble action."

13, 11 *a part of it becomes isolated*: Soul becomes embroiled in the pluralized sensible world and becomes isolated in that phase of itself from the intelligible. But we are not concerned with that part of the soul in this treatise, so Plotinus quickly reminds us that there is another ("divine and immortal") part which remains outside the body.

13, 15 *the primary real beings*: Intellect and the Forms.

13, 16 *the third realities*: This is a puzzling phrase; BP point to *Epistle* 2 312e1–4: "All things concern the king of all things and are for his sake, and he is the cause of all that is good. Concerning the second things are the second things, and concerning the third are the third." It is generally agreed nowadays that this *Epistle* was not written by Plato, although Plotinus may have considered it genuine and may be alluding to it here. If so "the king" must be the One, "the second things" the world known to rational thought, and "the third things" the world known by the senses. See further Loeb Plato IX, 400. The explanatory phrase *in this world below Intellect* would support this interpretation. The Greek phrase *ta epitade nou* (lit: "on this side of Intellect") is the opposite of the phrase noted above (12, 6) *epekeina*, lit. "on the other side of."

13, 16 *proceeds*: See note above on line 5.

13, 17 *being the activity*: HS print this word in the nominative case in apposition to *it* (the individual soul). Others emend to the dative case = "by the activity." I follow HS. Plotinus is alluding to his doctrine of double activity. Intellect has two "activities" (*energeiai*), the first contained entirely in itself and the second emerging as individual intellects to be housed in souls, as the only faculty in the case of the soul of the cosmos and the souls of the stars and planets, and as the rational faculty in the case of individual souls. The first or internal activity of anything is equated to its essence and called by Plotinus at V.4.2, 21 "the activity of its essence" (*energeia tês ousias*) and the second or external activity "the activity coming from its essence" (*energeia ek tês ousias*). Here the noetic soul, as it proceeds, is the second activity of Intellect.

13,18 *the immortal through the immortal*: Intellect, which is immortal, is the well–spring of creation through soul, which is immortal—its first activity is translated into its second activity, soul. Plotinus reminds us again of their immortality.

13, 19 *it will everlastingly be itself*: Intellect, whose "ceaseless activity" is its first activity, its contemplation of its own contents.

Chapter 14

In this chapter Plotinus widens the scope to include souls of all living beings, including those of plants. He makes two points. First, that the soul of every living creature, in so far as it is alive, is immortal. Secondly, that even the lower part of the soul does not perish. In the background is the belief in the transmigration of souls.

Lines 1–8

Animal souls are immortal, just as are any other souls, particularly those of plants. All are soul, and derive from a living (and thereby immortal) source.

14, 1 *other living creatures . . . the bodies of animals*: Plotinus is alluding to the doctrine of reincarnation (otherwise known as metempsychosis or metensomatosis: Plotinus makes a distinction between the two terms at IV.3.9, 6 and 14). The doctrine had a long history in Greek philosophical and religious thought, and probably originated in Egyptian beliefs: Herodotus *Histories* 2.123 (= KRS 261) tells us: "The Egyptians were the first to have given this account, saying that the human soul is immortal, and that on the death of the body it enters another living creature which is being born at the time.

When it has passed through all the creatures of earth, sea and air it returns to the body of a man. This cycle lasts for three thousand years." Cf. Diogenes Laertius *Lives of the Philosophers* 8.4–5, which traces the journey of a soul through successive human lives until eventually being born as Pythagoras. These beliefs were linked in the popular imagination to Pythagoras, an important influence on Plato. Empedocles too (Diogenes Laertius *Lives of the Philosophers* 8.77 = DK 117) "says that the soul takes on differing forms of animals and plants" and adds that "he himself has been a boy, a girl, a bush, a bird and a . . . fish." The reason for this descent (DK 127 = KRS 408) is sin, such as violence and bloodshed, but (DK 126 and 147 = KRS 209) it is possible to ascend back up the scale as far as "the greatest gods." These earlier beliefs are very much bound up with inhibitions about bloodshed and the consequent pollution, and with the hope of salvation. The cycle of descent and ascent embraces all living creatures.

Plato talks in many of his works about reincarnation.[38] Many of the details are inherited from the above tradition, but he added three features of his own. First, the reasons for the demotion of a soul to a lower form of animal body were more broadly moral—being a bad citizen, not devoting oneself to philosophy (*Phaedo* 63e), in short being

38 E.g. *Phaedo* 63e–64a, 70d–72e, 107c–108a; *Meno* 81b; *Republic* 612a–621d; *Gorgias* 493a, 523a–527e; *Phaedrus* 246a–257b; *Timaeus* 41e–42e, 44c, 76e–77b, 89e–92c; and *Laws* 872e.

nearer to the bottom of the scale of human lives given at *Phaedrus* 248cd, which descends from philosopher through king, politician, gymnast, prophet, poet, craftsman/farmer, sophist, to tyrant. Secondly, the individual has a degree of choice over the next life, as portrayed in the Myth of Er at *Republic* 617dff. Thirdly, the doctrine of Recollection plays an important part in Plato's account.

On more than one occasion, for example in *Republic* and *Gorgias*, he uses myth to convey his ideas, although he does warn us of the shortcomings of such a method, for instance at *Phaedo* 114d. Furthermore there are many inconsistencies in his account, which led Plotinus at III.6.12, 9 to complain that Plato "raised many problems in his eagerness to achieve his aim." Among these problems we can identify: (a) To what extent do we retain our individuality between lives? (b) Do animals have a rational faculty? (c) Which parts, if any, of the soul are mortal? (d) Why does the soul not forget all of the knowledge gained in prior lives and between lives? (e) What are the relative roles of chance, destiny, and free choice? (f) What role does our *daimôn* play? (g) How many "parts" does our soul have? Plotinus engages with a range of these questions, for example in III.2.13, III.4.5–6, and IV.3.13 and 24; in fact Porphyry grouped a number of treatises concerning the soul within *Ennead* IV, of which three (including two lengthy ones, 3 and 4, and one shorter one, 5) are titled "Problems of the Soul."

Plotinus' clearest statement on reincarnation comes at III.4.2, 16–30: "All those that have cherished the human in them become men again. Those that have lived solely by their senses become animals. If their senses have become combined with anger (*thumos*), then they become wild animals; differences among men of this kind account for the different species of beast they become. Those who have lived with appetite (*epithumia*) and the pleasures of appetite become intemperate and greedy animals. If they have lived not by their senses with passions, but by a sluggishness of sense with passions they even become plants; for such, or mainly such, is the behavior of plants, and these men have made it their concern to become like trees—root and branch! Those that have been obsessed by music but have been otherwise pure become songbirds. Kings whose only vice has been irrationality become eagles. Those who speculate about the heavens, forever building castles in the air, become birds that soar aloft. Those who practice civic virtues become men again, while those whose participation in civic virtues is inferior become social creatures such as bees."

Here in IV.7 these issues are laid to one side, and he makes some brief comments which assume in the reader some knowledge and acceptance of the doctrine.

14, 3 *And if there is any other sort of soul*: This somewhat vague, apparently catch-all, clause seems to refer especially to the souls of plants, where the particles *kai dê kai* in line 6 are used to narrow the general to the particular (Denniston 255–257). But the description could include, for example, semen, of which Aristotle at *Generation of Animals* 735a10 says: "It is clear that it (semen) has soul and that it is soul potentially"; and we have seen in the passage from III.4.2 quoted above that Plotinus considers that insects such as bees have souls.

14, 4 *it too must derive from a living nature*: All souls, as we have seen in Chapter 9, derive and gain their life in the first place from Intellect.

14, 6 *This is particularly true of the souls of plants*: Plato at *Timaeus* 77ab differentiates between cultivated and wild plants, but says that "everything whatsoever that has life can be termed a living creature"; seeds are included in the count.

Lines 8–13

The fact that the human soul is composite does not mean that all or any of its parts suffer dissolution.

14, 8 *If it is claimed:*[39] The suggestion is made at *Republic* 611b, where Socrates says: "It is not easy for anything that

39 There is a difficulty with the text here. See HS_1 and HS_2 *apparatus criticus* and Blumenthal (1971, 23).

is a composite of many parts and not constituted in the best manner to be everlasting (*aidion*, which translators tend to render as 'immortal')." Plato expresses his uncertainty about the question of the "parts" of the soul on more than one occasion, for example *Republic* 612a and *Timaeus* 72d, where he confesses that his account is only "probable," awaiting divine confirmation. In *Phaedo*, where the tripartite division is not made, Socrates says that "the immortal part of a man (viz. his soul) retires as death approaches, while the mortal part (viz. his body) dies" (106e), and there is no suggestion that there are any lower parts of the soul. Similarly in *Phaedrus* the charioteer at no point disengages the two horses, which represent the lower part of the soul. By contrast, at *Timaeus* 69c Plato (through the mouth of Timaeus) makes a clear distinction between the immortal and the mortal parts of the soul. The former (the rational "divine" part), once it enters the body, is located in the head, while the latter (the irrational parts) are located in the lower parts of the body; there are clear physical divisions between the different locations. So despite the disclaimer at 72d mentioned above, Plato is unequivocal here. It is only the rational part of the soul that is immortal. Cf. Bostock (1986, 40); Adam (1963, vol. 2, 427) seeks a compromise: "Now that he has proved the soul to be immortal, Plato takes the opportunity to suggest a revision of the psychology of *Republic* IV, in which the soul was treated as a composite; for nothing that is composite can be immortal. According to the theory which is rather suggested (612a) than fully worked out in this chapter, the so-called lower 'parts' are not of the essence of soul at all, but only incidental to its association with the body and consequently perishable . . . Plato expresses himself with great reserve (612a), but apparently intends us to believe that the soul in its truest nature is rational (*logistikon*), and that the rational alone is immortal." It is not obvious either just what Plotinus' position is. At IV.8.8 he states his own conviction that the rational part of the soul remains for ever in the intelligible world, and it is tempting to assume that on the death of the body the lower parts of the soul go into a sort of suspended animation until the next incarnation. Here, in line 12, he offers a different solution.

14, 10 *when souls are released in a pure state*: The purification of the soul by philosophy was a recurrent and important feature of Platonism, for example *Phaedo* 114bc, Diotima's speech in *Symposium*, and *Republic* 614d, where we are told that souls that have become pure can escape the cycle of birth and death altogether.

14, 10 *what has been added to them at birth like a molding*: At *Timaeus* 69c souls are given a body "as a vehicle" (*okhêma*); see Fleet (2012, 135–136) for the development of this idea among Neoplatonists; the "astral" body in which the nascent soul is enveloped gradually becomes a body consisting in a mixture of the four elements. Plato offers a different image at *Republic* 611d, where the soul is likened to the sea-god Glaucus encrusted with shells, seaweed, and rock. This is how we see the soul at the mercy of countless evils.

14, 11 *for a very long period*: For example the long period of punishment and the lengthy cycle of lives recounted by Er in *Republic*.

14, 12 *But even the inferior part . . . as long as its source endures*: Plotinus leaves us with a puzzling statement, especially since it is not clear what is meant by "its source" (*arkhê*). But we have been told in Chapter 9 that Intellect is the well-spring of the soul, and so it is reasonable to accept Rist's interpretation (1967, 87): "We are presumably to understand that they (the inferior parts) will be put to other purposes in the cosmos. The point is therefore that immortality of some kind is the mark not only of Intellect (*Nous*) but of the products of Intellect"; he cites VI.4.16 as evidence for this. See also Blumenthal (1971, 94n21).

Chapter 15

Plotinus adds a brief postscript addressed to non-philosophers, alluding to "oracles of the gods" and the power of the souls of the dead to affect human life through the medium of oracles. For Plotinus such a departure from philosophical discourse is unique, and has led some to believe that this chapter is a spurious addition to the treatise.[40] *Bréhier (188) suggests that if it is genuine it shows Plotinus presenting a brief summary of "crass superstitions" as a sop to the many adherents of the spiritualism of his day, for whom he had a deep-rooted contempt. In this treatise he does not consider such beliefs and practices, which were undoubtedly widespread in the ancient world. Perhaps the most vivid account of such an incident is in Lucan* Pharsalia *VI 450–830, which recounts the attempt of the witch Erichtho to invoke the spirits of the Underworld through the corpse of a recently killed youth, in order to predict the outcome of the civil war to Sextus Pompeius. Another fanciful story is told by Thelyphron in Apuleius* Metamorphoses *3. (See Dickie 2001, 237–239.) Cicero dismisses this sort of necromancy at* On Divination *1.132 and at* Tusculan Disputations

40 Bréhier (210n1) cites a parallel example from Aristotle's lost work *Eudemus*, fragment 44, preserved in Plutarch *Consolatio ad Apollonium.*

1.37. Porphyry Life of Plotinus *10 tells us of an encounter in Rome between Plotinus and the magician Olympius, whose attempts at sorcery directed against Plotinus failed because Plotinus "had a soul whose power was so great that it was able to throw assaults made on him back onto his attackers." Plotinus himself must have been familiar with a wide range of religious non-philosophical teachings about some form of life after death. In his early years in Egypt he would have come across the worship of Isis and a growing Christian community, while after his arrival in Rome he would have encountered the popular religion of Mithras. Porphyry* Life of Plotinus *3 tells how he joined the emperor Gordian III's ill-starred expedition to Persia in order "to investigate Persian and Indian doctrines";* Life of Plotinus *10 talks of an encounter between Plotinus and an Egyptian priest in the temple of Isis in Rome, and* Life of Plotinus *22 recounts an anecdote about an oracle delivered by Apollo concerning Plotinus' soul. O'Meara (1993, 3–4) suggests that Porphyry is editing the facts to suit his own purposes; Armstrong, however, explored Plotinus' interest in the East in a series of articles in the* Downside Review.

Rather Plotinus is concerned with the more respectable aspects of prophecy through the medium of oracles, particularly those which demonstrate the survival of the individual soul after death. Oracles had been established at a very early date, notably at Delphi and Dodona in Greece, and their popularity and influence had continued until Plotinus' day, often with imperial support, notably from the emperor Hadrian, although demographic forces had moved their main centers from Greece to Asia Minor, especially at Claros (near Colophon) and Didyma (near Miletus). (See Parke 1967, chapter 12, 3.) Of these Plotinus singles out (a) oracles demanding the appeasement of the dead, and (b) oracles established by dead humans for the benefit of posterity. In each case the survival of the souls of the dead is implied.

15, 1 *proof . . . belief based on the evidence of the senses*: Plotinus is making a distinction between philosophers, who require proof, and those non-philosophers who look for *belief based on the evidence of the senses*. The vocabulary is unequivocal; the Greek word for proof here is *apodeixis*, by which Plato denotes "demonstration by argument" (as at *Theaetetus* 162e where the criticism of Theaetetus and his circle is that they do not utter any "proof of a necessary argument whatsoever"), while in Aristotle it has an even more technical meaning, "deductive proof" as opposed to "inductive proof" (*epagôgê*). By contrast non-philosophers rely on their senses (*aisthêseis*) to gain belief (*pistis*), both words used by Plato extensively in *Republic* to signify the status of psychic engagement with the sensible world, as opposed to the knowledge of the intelligible world gained by rational thought, which is the goal of the philosopher. Such non-philosophers are the materialists we have already met at *Sophist* 246aff.

15, 3 *the extensive body of findings on this topic*: Perhaps this is a veiled reference to Porphyry's work entitled *Philosophy to be Gleaned from Oracles*, probably written before he came to Rome and joined Plotinus' circle. Another writer whose works Plotinus was familiar with and whom he may well have in mind here is Plutarch, two of whose treatises deal specifically with oracles: *On the Decline of Oracles* and *On the Pythian Oracles.* Others who had written on peripheral topics include Publius Nigidius Figulus (first century BCE), Oenomaus of Gadara, and Julianus "the theurge" (both second century CE). Julianus had published a review of the Chaldaean Oracles and other works on theurgy (see Parke 1967, 141–144).

15, 4 *the oracles of the gods*: Plotinus perhaps has in mind *Laws* 865d, where Plato is prescribing the action to be taken concerning homicide; the vocabulary is very similar to that used by Plotinus here (see on 15, 6 below). Plato appeals to "the oracular pronouncement of the god" as couched in "ancient and venerable myth," which ordains that the anger of a man slain unjustly, who is intensely aware of the wrong done to him, must be appeased.

15, 6 *on the grounds that they are aware of them*: It was commonly accepted that the souls of the dead were aware of events among the living. Offerings to the dead in the expectation that the dead were aware of them was a commonplace of Roman belief; see Hopkins (1983, chapter 4, sections 5 and 6). This belief could find a more homely expression in domestic practices, or a grander one, as in epic poetry, such as in the instructions given by the prophetess to Aeneas in *Aeneid* 6 concerning the burial of Misenus.

15, 6 *to benefit mankind*: It was a long-standing tradition in ancient Greece that great men and heroes continued to benefit the community after their death; for example the plot of Sophocles' *Oedipus Coloneus* revolves round the competing claims of Athens and Thebes to house the body of Oedipus, and Cimon won great prestige from returning the bones of Theseus from Scyros to Attica. At *Laws* 926e Plato, referring back to the words noted above at 865d, says: "We clearly made an apposite statement in our earlier words, that the souls of the deceased have some power after death by which they take care of human affairs." He goes on to comment on the lengthy tradition of such beliefs, and adds of the dead that "it is in their nature to take especial care of their descendants, to be benevolent to those who honor them and malevolent to those who dishonor them."

15, 9 *by establishing prophetic oracles*: *Nekyomanteia* or *nekromanteia*, which purported to put the living in touch with the dead, had been established in Greece from an early date. Among the best known were (a) the oracle of Amphiaraus at Oropus in Boeotia, which Plutarch (CE

50–120), in his work *On the Decline of Oracles* tells us was defunct in his day. See Parke (1967, 134f.); (b) the *nekyomanteion* of Thesprotia in Epirus, mentioned by Herodotus 5.92 as having been consulted by Periander, tyrant of Corinth (c. 627–587 BCE), and which was destroyed by the Romans in 167 BCE; and (c) the *nekyomanteion* of Trophonius at Lebedaea in Boeotia; this was certainly still functioning in Roman times at least as late as the 2nd century CE, when it was described in some detail by Pausanias, who had himself consulted the oracle in his *Guide to Greece* IX.39. Temple (2005) quotes this passage and a range of other authors of the Roman period, notably Cicero, Lucian, and Plutarch. See Parke (1967, 126–127). So it is possible that this oracle was still there in Plotinus' day. More controversial is the oracle consulted by Aeneas in Vergil *Aeneid* VI. Temple confidently identifies this with the tunnel complex partially excavated at Baiae, near Naples (Temple 2005, chapters 1 and 2); he claims that it was destroyed by Agrippa in a fit of unexplained pique during the reign of Augustus. Parke (1967, 49–55) takes a more skeptical view.

Also Diogenes Laertius at *Lives of the Philosophers* 7 32 quotes Pythagoras as claiming that "the whole of the air is full of souls, which are called *daimones* and heroes, by whom dreams and signs of health and sickness are sent to men." See further Beard, North, and Price (1998), and Flint and de Blecourt (1999).

So by the end of the treatise the reader is entitled to ask whether Plotinus has given satisfactory answers to the questions he poses at the outset: "Is each one of us immortal? Or do we perish entirely? Or do some parts of us perish through dispersal and decay, while others—the true self—survive for ever?" The brief conclusion must be that each one of us is immortal and we certainly do not perish entirely. Nor does any part of the true self perish through dispersal or decay, which is the hallmark of the material soul. The true self is the noetic soul, which transcends the other parts of the soul and outlives the body, which houses the other parts during our lifetime. Any suggestion that the soul is a material or supervenient entity has been entirely ruled out.

Select Bibliography

I. Ancient Authors

ALCINOUS: *The Handbook of Platonism*, ed. J. Dillon. Oxford, 1993.

ALEXANDER OF APHRODISIAS: *On the Soul*. ed. A. Fotinis. University Press of America, 1979.

ALEXANDER OF APHRODISIAS: *Supplement to On the Soul*, trans. R. Sharples. Ithaca: Cornell, 2004.

ALEXANDER OF APHRODISIAS: *Supplement to On the Soul*, ed. R. Sharples. Berlin & New York, 2008.

ARISTOTLE: *Metaphysics*, 2 vols, ed. D. Ross. Oxford, 1924.

ARISTOTLE: *On the Soul*, ed. R. Hicks. Cambridge, 1907.

PLATO: *Phaedo*, ed. D. Bostock. Oxford, 1986.

PLATO: *Phaedo*, ed. J. Burnet. Oxford, 1911.

PLATO: *Phaedrus*, ed. R. Hackforth. Cambridge, 1952.

PLATO: *Symposium*, ed. C. Rowe. Aris & Phillips, 1998.

PLATO: *The Timaeus of Plato*, ed. R. Archer-Hind. Cambridge, 1888.

PLOTINUS: *Ennead* III.6, ed. B. Fleet. Oxford 1995.

PLOTINUS: *Ennead* IV.8, ed. B. Fleet. Las Vegas, 2012.

PLOTINUS: *Ennead* V.1, ed. M. Atkinson. Oxford, 1985.

SIMPLICIUS: *On Aristotle Categories* 7 & 8, ed. B. Fleet. Duckworth/Cornell 2002.

SIMPLICIUS: *On Aristotle Physics 2*, ed. B. Fleet. Duckworth/Cornell 1997.

II. Editions and Translations of the *Enneads*

Arabic Commentary: Lewis, G. *English translation of sections of the medieval Arabic commentary on the* Enneads *(Theologia Aristotelis ["The Theology of Aristotle"],* 8th cent. CE.

Armstrong, H. (ed. and trans.). *Plotinus.* 7 vols. Cambridge (Mass.) & London, 1966–1988.

Bréhier, E. *Plotin Ennéades.* Vol. IV. Budé: Paris, 1956.

Brisson, L. and Pradeau J.-F. *Plotin.* Traités, vol. 1. Paris, 2002.

Henry, P. & Schwyzer, H-R. *Plotini Opera.* Paris & Brussels, 1959 (editio major) (HS_1).

Henry, P. & Schwyzer, H-R. *Plotini Opera.* Oxford, 1977 (editio minor) = OCT (HS_2).

MacKenna, Stephen. *Plotinus: The Enneads*. English Translation Revised by B. S. Page. London: Faber & Faber, 1962[3].

MacKenna, Stephen. *Plotinus. The Enneads*. Selected Treatises Revised with Notes by John Dillon. London: Penguin, 1991.

III. Select Publications

Adamson P., Baltussen H., Stone M., eds. *Philosophy, Science and Exegesis*, vol. 1. London, 2004.

Algra K., Barnes J., Mansfeld J. and Schofield M., eds. *The Cambridge History of Hellenistic Philosophy*. Cambridge, 1999.

Alt, K. *Weltflucht und Weltbejahung. Zur Frage des Leib-Seele Dualismus bei Plutarch, Numenius, Plotin*. Stuttgart: Franz Steiner Verlag, 1993.

Armstrong A., ed. *The Cambridge History of Later Greek and Early Medieval Philosophy*. Cambridge, 1970.

Armstrong, A. H. *The Architecture of the Intelligible Universe in the Philosophy of Plotinus*. Cambridge: Cambridge University Press, 1940.

Armstrong, A. H., ed. 1967. The Cambridge History of Later Greek and Early Medieval Philosophy. Cambridge: Cambridge University Press.

Arnou, R. *Le Désir de Dieu dans la philosophie de Plotin.* 2nd ed. Rome: Presses de l'Université Grégorienne, 1968.

Barnes J., Schofield M. and Sorabji R. *Articles on Aristotle,* vol. 4. London: Duckworth, 1979.

Beard M., North J., and Price S. *Religions of Rome.* Cambridge, 1998.

Benson H., ed. *A Companion to Plato.* Blackwell, 2006.

Blumenthal H. "Soul, World Soul and Individual Soul in Plotinus," in *Le Néoplatonisme; colloques internationaux.* Paris, 1971.

Blumenthal H. *Plotinus' Psychology.* The Hague, 1971.

Bobzien S. *Determinism and Freedom in Stoic Philosophy.* Oxford, 1998.

Bostock D. "The Soul and Immortality in Plato's *Phaedo,*" in Fine G., ed. 1999.

Boys-Stones, G. *Post-Hellenistic Philosophy.* Oxford, 2001.

Bréhier E. *The Philosophy of Plotinus* (tr. J. Thomas). Chicago, 1958.

Burnyeat M. *Aristotle's Divine Intellect, the Aquinas Lecture.* Marquette University Press, 2008.

Cornford F. *Plato's Cosmology.* Routledge, 1937. Reprinted by Hackett, 1997.

Cornford F. *Plato's Theory of Knowledge*. London: Routledge, 1935.

Curd P. and Graham D. *The Oxford Handbook of Presocratic Philosophy*. Oxford, 2008.

Denniston J. *The Greek Particles*. 2nd ed. Oxford, 1954.

Dickie M. *Magic and Magicians in the Greco-Roman World*. London: Routledge, 2001.

Dillon, J. 1977/1996. *The Middle Platonists: A Study of Platonism, 80 B.C.–A.D. 220*. London: Duckworth, 1977, 19962.

Dodds E., ed. *Les Sources de Plotin*. Geneva, 1960 (English translation).

Dodds E. *The Greeks and the Irrational*. Berkeley/Los Angeles, 1951.

Dodds, E. *Pagan and Christian in an Age of Anxiety: Some Aspects of Religious Experience from Marcus Aurelius to Constantine*. Cambridge: Cambridge University Press, 1965.

Emilsson, E. K. *Plotinus on Sense-Perception*. Cambridge: Cambridge University Press, 1988.

Emilsson, E. K. *Plotinus on Intellect*. Oxford: The Clarendon Press, 2007.

Ferrari G. *Listening to the Cicadas*. Cambridge, 1987.

Ferrari, G., ed. *The Cambridge Companion to Plato's Republic*. Cambridge, 2007.

Fine, G., ed. *The Oxford Handbook to Plato*. Oxford, 2008.

Fine, G., ed. *Plato 1: Metaphysics and Epistemology*. Oxford, 1999.

Fine, G., ed. *Plato 2: Ethics, Politics, Religion and the Soul*. Oxford, 1999.

Flint, V. and de Blecourt W. *Witchcraft and Magic in Europe*, vol. 2. London: Athlone, 1999.

Frede, D. in Wagner E., ed. 2001.

Frede, M. *Essays in Ancient Philosophy*. Oxford, 1987.

Gatti, M. L. *Plotino e la metafisica della contemplazione*. Milan: Vita e Pensiero, 1996.

Gerson, L. P. *Plotinus*. London & New York: Routledge, 1994.

Gerson, L. P., ed. *The Cambridge Companion to Plotinus*. Cambridge: Cambridge University Press, 1996.

Gerson, L. P., ed. *The Cambridge History of Philosophy in Late Antiquity*. 2 vols. Cambridge: Cambridge University Press, 2010.

Gottschalk, H. B. "Soul as Harmonia," in *Phronesis* 16 (1971).

Gottschalk, H. B. *Heraclides of Pontus*. Oxford: Oxford University Press, 1980.

Gould, J. *The Philosophy of Chrysippus*, in *Philosophia Antiqua* XXVII. Leiden, 1970.

Graeser, A. *Plotinus and the Stoics*. Leiden, 1972.

Graham, D. *Explaining the Cosmos*. Princeton, 2006.

Griffin, M. and Barnes, J., eds. *Philosophia Togata*. Oxford, 1989.

Guthrie, W. K. C. *A History of Greek Philosophy*, 5 vols., Cambridge: Cambridge University Press, 1967–1978.

Hadot, Pierre. *Plotinus on the Simplicity of Vision*. Translated by M. Chase. Chicago: Chicago University Press, 1993.

Henry, P. *Les Etats du Texte du Plotin*, Etudes Plotiniennes 1. Paris: Louvain, 1961.

Hopkins, K. *Death and Renewal*. Cambridge, 1983.

Inge, W. R. *The Philosophy of Plotinus*. 3rd ed. London: Longmans, Green, 1948.

Inwood, B., ed. *The Cambridge Companion to the Stoics*. Cambridge, 2003.

Inwood, B. *Ethics and Human Action in Early Stoicism*. Oxford, 1985.

Keyt, D. "The Fallacies in Phaedo 102a–107b," in *Phronesis* 8 (1963).

Kraut, R., ed. *The Cambridge Companion to Plato*. Cambridge, 1992.

Kupreeva, I. in Adamson P., Baltussen H. and Stone M., eds. *Philosophy, Science and Exegesis*, vol. 1. London, 2004.

Les Sources de Plotin. Entretiens Fondation Hardt V. Vandoeuvres-Genève, 1960.

Lloyd, G. *Aristotle: the Growth and Structure of his Thought*. Cambridge, 1968.

Lloyd, Anthony C. *The Anatomy of Neoplatonism*. Oxford: Clarendon Press, 1990.

Long, A. *Problems in Stoicism*. London, 1971.

Long, A. *Hellenistic Philosophy*. 2nd ed. London: Duckworth, 1986.

Long, A. *Stoic Studies*. Cambridge, 1996.

Long, A., ed. *The Cambridge Companion to Early Greek Philosophy*. Cambridge, 1999.

MacCulloch, D. *A History of Christianity*. London: Allen Lane, 2009.

Meijer, P. A. *Plotinus on the Good or the One (Enneads VI, 9): An Analytical Commentary*. Amsterdam: J. C. Gieben, 1992.

Miller, F. Jr. "The Platonic Soul," in Benson, ed. 2009.

Noble, D. *The Music of Life*. Oxford, 2006.

O'Daly, G. *Plotinus' Philosophy of the Self*. Irish University Press: Shannon, 1973

O'Meara, Dominic J., *Plotinus: an Introduction to the Enneads*. Oxford: Oxford University Press, 1993.

O'Brien, D. "Le Volontaire et la Nécessité" in *Revue Philosophique* 167 (1977): 401–422.

Parke, H. *Greek Oracles*. London, 1967.

Pépin, J. *Mythe et allégorie: les origins grecques et les contestations judéo-chrétiennes*. Paris: Aubier, 1958.

Remes, Pauliina. *Plotinus on Self: The Philosophy of the 'We.'* Cambridge: Cambridge University Press, 2007.

Remes, Pauliina. *Neoplatonism*. Berkeley: University of California Press, 2008.

Rist, John M. *Plotinus: The Road to Reality*. Cambridge: Cambridge University Press, 1967.

Rist, John M. *Stoic Philosophy*. Cambridge, 1969.

Ross, D. *Aristotle*. 5th ed. London: Methuen, 1949.

Sambursky, S. *Physics of the Stoics*. London: RKP, 1959.

Sandbach, F. *Aristotle and the Stoics*. Proceedings of the Cambridge Philological Society, Supplementary vol. 10, 1985.

Sandbach, F. *The Stoics*. 2nd ed. Bristol, 1988.

Schniewind, Alexandrine. *L'Éthique du Sage chez Plotin*. Paris: J. Vrin, 2003.

Sedley, D. *Creationism and its Critics in Antiquity*. Berkeley: University of California Press, 2004.

Sedley, D. *The Midwife of Platonism*. Oxford, 2004.

Smith, A. *Porphyry's Place in the Neoplatonic Tradition: A Study in Post-Plotinian Neoplatonism*. The Hague: Nijhoff, 1974.

Smith, A. "Potentiality and the Problem of Plurality in the Intelligible," in *Neoplatonism and Early Christian Thought*, eds. H. J. Blumenthal and R. A. Markus. London: Variorum, 1981, 99–107.

Smith, A. *Philosophy in Late Antiquity*. London: Routledge, 2004.

Sorabji, R. and Sharples, R., eds. *Greek and Roman Philosophy 100 BC–200 AD*. 2 vols. London, 2007.

Sorabji R., ed. *The Philosophy of the Commentators*. Vol. 1. Duckworth, 2004.

Temple, R. *Oracles of the Dead*. Rochester/Vermont, 2005.

Theiler, W. "Plotin zwischen Platon und Stoa," in *Les Sources de Plotin*, Entretiens Fondation Hardt V, Vandoeuvres-Genève: Fondation Hardt, 1960, 63–103.

Thesleff, H. *The Pythagorean Texts of the Hellenistic Period*. Åbo, 1965.

Todd, R. *Alexander of Aphrodisias on Stoic Physics*. Leiden: Brill, 1976.

Wagner, E., ed. *Essays in Plato's Psychology*. Lexington, 2001.

Wallis, R. T. *Neoplatonism*. 2nd ed. London: Duckworth, 1995.

Warren, J., ed. *The Cambridge Companion to Epicureanism*. Cambridge, 2009.

Waterlow, S. *Nature, Change and Agency in Aristotle's Physics*. Oxford, 1982.

Weller, C. in Wagner, ed. 2001.

West, M. L. *Hesiod Theogony*. Edited with Prolegomena and Commentary. Oxford: Clarendon Press, 1966.

Index of Ancient Authors

PLOTINUS

Enneads

Index of Names and Subjects

PRE-SOCRATICS

By Being, It Is: *The Thesis of Parmenides* by Néstor-Luis Cordero

The Fragments of Parmenides: *A Critical Text with Introduction and Translation, the Ancient Testimonia and a Commentary* by A. H. Coxon. Revised and Expanded Edition edited with new Translations by Richard McKirahan and a new Preface by Malcolm Schofield

The Legacy of Parmenides: *Eleatic Monism and Later Presocratic Thought* by Patricia Curd

Parmenides and the History of Dialectic: *Three Essays* by Scott Austin

Parmenides, Venerable and Awesome: *Proceedings of the International Symposium* edited by Néstor-Luis Cordero

Presocratics and Plato: *A Festschrift in Honor of Charles Kahn* edited by Richard Patterson, Vassilis Karasmanis, and Arnold Hermann

The Route of Parmenides: *Revised and Expanded Edition, With a New Introduction, Three Supplemental Essays, and an Essay by Gregory Vlastos* by Alexander P. D. Mourelatos

To Think Like God: *Pythagoras and Parmenides. The Origins of Philosophy.* Scholarly and fully annotated edition by Arnold Hermann

The Illustrated To Think Like God: *Pythagoras and Parmenides. The Origins of Philosophy by* Arnold Hermann (with over 200 full color illustrations)

PLATO

***A Stranger's Knowledge: Statesmanship, Philosophy, and Law in Plato's* Statesman** by Xavier Márquez

God and Forms in Plato by Richard D. Mohr

***Image and Paradigm in Plato's* Sophist** by David Ambuel

Interpreting Plato's Dialogues by J. Angelo Corlett

One Book, the Whole Universe: *Plato's* Timaeus *Today* edited by Richard D. Mohr and Barbara M. Sattler

Platonic Patterns: *A Collection of Studies* by Holger Thesleff

Plato's Late Ontology: *A Riddle Resolved* by Kenneth M. Sayre

***Plato's* Parmenides:** *Text, Translation & Introductory Essay* by Arnold Hermann. Translation in collaboration with Sylvana Chrysakopoulou with a Foreword by Douglas Hedley

Plato's Universe by Gregory Vlastos

***The Philosopher in Plato's* Statesman** by Mitchell Miller

ARISTOTLE

Aristotle's Empiricism: Experience and Mechanics in the Fourth Century B.C. by Jean De Groot

***One and Many in Aristotle's* Metaphysics**—*Volume I: Books Alpha-Delta* by Edward C. Halper

***One and Many in Aristotle's* Metaphysics**—*Volume 2: The Central Books* by Edward C. Halper

Reading Aristotle:* Physics VII.3 *"What is Alteration?" *Proceedings of the International ESAP-HYELE Conference* edited by Stefano Maso, Carlo Natali, and Gerhard Seel

HELLENISTIC PHILOSOPHY

A Life Worthy of the Gods: *The Materialist Psychology of Epicurus* by David Konstan

THE *ENNEADS* OF PLOTINUS

Translations with Introductions & Philosophical Commentaries
Series edited by John M. Dillon and Andrew Smith

Ennead* I.6: *On Beauty by Andrew Smith

Ennead* II.5: *On What Is Potentially and What Actually by Cinzia Arruzza

Ennead* IV.3–IV.4.29: *Problems concerning the Soul by John M. Dillon and H. J. Blumenthal

Ennead* IV.4.30–45 & IV.5: *Problems concerning the Soul by Gary M. Gurtler

Ennead* IV.8: *On the Descent of the Soul into Bodies by Barrie Fleet

Ennead* V.1: *On the Three Primary Levels of Reality by Eric D. Perl

Ennead* V.5: *That the Intelligibles are not External to the Intellect, and on the Good by Lloyd P. Gerson

Ennead* VI.4 & VI.5: *On the Presence of Being, One and the Same, Everywhere as a Whole by Eyjólfur Emilsson and Steven Strange

ETHICS

Sentience and Sensibility: *A Conversation about Moral Philosophy* by Matthew R. Silliman

PHILOSOPHICAL FICTION

Pythagorean Crimes by Tefcros Michaelides

The Aristotle Quest: A Dana McCarter Trilogy. Book 1: Black Market Truth by Sharon M. Kaye

AUDIOBOOKS

The Iliad (unabridged) by Stanley Lombardo

The Odyssey (unabridged) by Stanley Lombardo

The Essential Homer by Stanley Lombardo

The Essential Iliad by Stanley Lombardo

FORTHCOMING

Plato in the Empire: Albinus, Maximus, Apuleius. Text, Translation, and Commentary by Ryan C. Fowler

Ennead **I.1: *What Is the Living Being, and What Is Man?*** by Gerard O'Daly

Ennead **I.2: *On Virtues*** by Suzanne Stern-Gillet

Ennead **I.3: *On Dialectic*** by Pauliina Remes

Ennead **I.4: *On Well-Being*** by Kieran McGroarty

Ennead **II.4: *On Matter*** by Anthony A. Long

Ennead **II.9: *Against the Gnostics*** by Sebastian Ramon Philipp Gertz

Ennead **III.4: *On Our Allotted Guardian Spirit*** by Wiebke-Marie Stock

Ennead **III.5: *On Love*** by Sara Magrin

Ennead **III.7: *On Eternity and Time*** by László Bene

Ennead **III.8: *On Nature and Contemplation*** by George Karamanolis

Ennead **V.3: *On the Knowing Hypostases*** by Marie-Élise Zovko

Ennead **V.8: *On Intelligible Beauty*** by Andrew Smith

Ennead **V.9: *On Intellect, Ideas, and Being*** by Matthias Vorwerk

Ennead **VI.7: *The Forms and the Good*** by Nicholas Banner

Ennead **VI.8: *On Free Will and the Will of the One*** by Kevin Corrigan and John D. Turner

Ennead **VI.9: *On the Good or the One*** by Stephen R. L. Clark